# DISMANTLING THE PUBLIC SPHERE

# DISMANTLING THE PUBLIC SPHERE

Situating and Sustaining Librarianship in the Age of the New Public Philosophy

JOHN E. BUSCHMAN

A Member of the Greenwood Publishing Group

Westport, Connecticut • London

**Library of Congress Cataloging-in-Publication Data**

Buschman, John

    Dismantling the public sphere : situating and sustaining librarianship in the age of the new public philosophy / John E. Buschman.

    p. cm.

    Includes bibliographical references.

    ISBN 0–313–32199–X (alk. paper)

    1. Libraries and society.   2. Library science—Philosophy.   3. Public interest.   I. Title.

Z716.4.B87 2003

020′.1—dc21      2003053882

British Library Cataloguing in Publication Data is available.

Library of Congress Catalog Card Number: 2003053882

ISBN: 0–313–32199–X

First published in 2003

Libraries Unlimited, Inc. 88 Post Road West, Westport, CT 06881
A Member of the Greenwood Publishing Group, Inc.
www.lu.com

Printed in the United States of America

The paper used in this book complies with the
Permanent Paper Standard issued by the National
Information Standards Organization (Z39.48–1984).

10  9  8  7  6  5  4  3  2  1

# CONTENTS

# PREFACE

It is almost a cliché to say that librarianship does not exist in a vacuum. Nevertheless, it is a cliché we in the field seem to forget—and often. This book is an extended analysis of librarianship in light of huge economic, technological, and intellectual trends that have shaped—and are shaping—the circumstances under which we do our work and try and carry through on our values. I have chosen to rely in part on critical educational scholarship as a basis of analysis for two reasons: there is a clear affinity between the two fields and there is no need to reinvent the critical wheel for librarianship. These works form a coherent and critical view of our society and economy, providing a workable frame of analysis for librarianship. Along with these sources, my earlier studies of the Frankfurt School led me to the work of Jürgen Habermas, whose work on the public sphere provides a brilliant and fundamentally important metaframework for librarianship. I have chosen a path through these literatures, adapting the analyses to librarianship in productive ways. I have undoubtedly simplified it—sometimes too much—and if I have erred, the fault is entirely my own and should not reflect on those thinkers.

If librarianship does not exist in a vacuum, then this book represents an extended discussion of the circumstances in which librarians and our institutions are operating. In order to shape a reasonable and straightforward narrative about librarianship, I have had to avoid some of the more interesting side roads and arguments made in much of this literature. A sampling of some of those issues is included in the content of the notes, sometimes significantly fleshing out the argument made in the body of the text. I urge the reader to browse the chapter notes, if for no other reason than to get the flavor of the intellectual ferment that is taking place (and has taken place) in the discussion of public purposes and issues for our cultural institutions.

This book had its genesis in many classrooms, but in particular those of Michael Carbone, Richard Brosio, and Victor Lidz. Two colleagues at Rider University—Jeff Halpern and the late John Long—have also taught me much over the years. Mark Tyler Day was generous enough to provide me with prepublication copies of his most recent work and to share ideas that helped deepen my analysis, and he did so during a very difficult personal time. Everyone who undertakes a task such as this relies on two very important things: good libraries and thoughtful help in getting at what one needs. In this I must thank Darlena Dyton for her help in acquiring items quickly and, in particular, Diane Hunter for her almost insane responsiveness in getting me things from Rider's collections that I did not have the full time to acquire for myself. I must also thank the Research and Development Committee for department chairs at Rider University and the provost for the leave time to write this. It would not have been possible without contiguous, extended time away. Finally, I want to thank Dorothy Warner for her questions and observations while reading the manuscript; her unflagging support, courier service, and patience while I talked out and through much of this; and for "lessons" more valuable than she knows.

I

# THE FRAMEWORK OF CRITICAL ANALYSIS: THE NEW PUBLIC PHILOSOPHY AND THE PUBLIC SPHERE

# 1

# INTRODUCTION: CRISIS CULTURE AND THE NEED FOR A DEFENSE OF LIBRARIANSHIP IN THE PUBLIC SPHERE

## CRISIS CULTURE

This book begins by asking a question suggested by the title of this chapter: what is our crisis culture and why do we need a defense of librarianship?[1] The simplest answer to the first part of that question is that librarianship *is* in a crisis, but not the crisis-du-jour fashionable in the literature or among managers at any given moment. Rather, the crisis stems from the simple fact that we have been declaring crises in the field for more than thirty years. Further, we seem unable to clearly identify what we mean or effectively address the problems we identify. For instance, in declaring in 1973 that "it is no longer controversial to affirm that . . . there exists a library crisis and that some changes are in order," Gerald Salton quotes a 1971 study of university libraries that concluded that *they* were "largely in a state of quiet crisis." Salton's analysis noted a "breakdown of the established operations, an intellectual crisis among . . . library management, and a deepening space and budget problem." His solution was to automate—a very early version of the crises being declared now.[2]

Michael Harris and Stan Hannah have reviewed the crisis-ridden, postindustrial "paperless society" library literature emanating from F. W. Lancaster's work from the mid-1970s into the early 1990s. They argue persuasively that this was the dominant metaphor adopted in the writing in the field and characterize it as "impoverished and incestuous" and written "without benefit of knowledge or understanding of the critical debate" over Daniel Bell's thesis (also a dominant metaphor). They contend that Lancaster himself misunderstood Bell's analysis, was out of touch with the larger critical debate over the postindustrial metaphor, and was deeply one-dimensional in making his predictions for libraries in the year 2001—which he only belatedly revised.[3] Within the library literature in Lancaster's wake, Harris and Hannah compiled a list of professional attributes that librarians *must* abandon in order to survive the crisis posed to the profession by the impending information paradigm. Among the attributes were an orientation to the humanities, information as a public good, the book, and a female-dominated workforce. They concluded that the profession's response was based as much in fear as in analysis.[4]

There are countless other examples of continual calls of a crisis of one sort or another in librarianship (presented in approximate chronological order):

- The Information Age has swept around the world like a poorly forecast winter storm [and] has been as bewildering as it has been challenging. This is the nature of the Information Age, but unlike the snows of February, it is here to stay. The necessity is for all of us to become acclimatized to it. (1984)[5]

- Because library schools are usually small and unable to bring in much money . . . they are vulnerable. . . . Whether a school will continue or be eliminated, however, depends on circumstances [but] precisely because we are in a period of transition and experimentation, we must attempt to supply a satisfactory definition of who we are and what we are about. (1988)[6]

- The disappearance of the profession is not happening directly and blatantly, but through a process called marginalization. (1992)[7]

- It is widely recognized that the research library is in serious difficulty [but] a long-term solution to the library's crisis is beginning to emerge, as the research/higher education community takes advantage of the new information technology. (1993)[8]

- Are we the last generation of a profession being swept away by the rising tide of technology [and] will we be relegated to dealing with the great mass of print-on-paper [in] a gigantic mausoleum of old information? Or do we have the courage to enter into a deliberate metamorphosis and forever transform ourselves and librarianship? (1993)[9]

- Higher education and librarianship are in the midst of dramatic transformation [in their responses to] calls for innovation and accountability, and efforts to improve quality and contain costs. [T]he basic tenants of higher education and librarianship are being questioned. (1996)[10]

- I [am] calling for a radical expansion of librarian's recognition of information literacy as the new foundation for . . . our critical role in imparting these concepts. (1998)[11]

- [C]hange is relentless and remorseless; . . . we have libraries on the frontiers of knowledge and libraries on the verge of extinction. (1998)[12]

- What's going to happen is pretty straightforward: as a device for supporting un-dergraduate students in their coursework [the library] will fade away. (2000)[13]

- [W]e must reorganize to educate in a new environment, for a future filled with unsettling possibilities and unprecedented potential [and] the possible necessity for a complete reformation of familiar physical institutions brought about by globali-zation. (2001)[14]

- We live in an age . . . in which more people have more and faster access to more information than ever before [and] we can barely keep up with the information flow about the information flow. . . . The public library, which used to be a major pur-veyor and "keeper" of information, is now just one of the crowd [and is] barely considered as part of the information revolution. (2002)[15]

- The year is 2020. Libraries are flourishing. But it wasn't always this way. At the turn of the 21st century, their future was uncertain[:] in the late 1990s . . . others, including machines, seemed able to take the place of librarians and libraries [and] observing that the numbers of questions asked at library reference desks were stead-ily declining, library administrators questioned the need for professionally staffed reference desks. (2002)[16]

The authors quoted here do not represent the fringes of librarianship. On the contrary, they represent the pinnacle of the profession: a blue-ribbon U.S. Department of Education panel, successful corporate information profes-sionals, a former president of a major state university, the former president and chief executive of OCLC, deans of major research libraries, and a head librarian at a major public library.

One leader in the profession—a former director at New York Public Library who held high administrative posts at Harvard and the University of Penn-sylvania libraries and was part of the leadership of the Research Libraries Group and the Association of Research Libraries—typifies the confusion. He wrote in 1983 that the predicted "end to all but the most popular books, journals, and libraries by the year 2000" was flatly "simplistic" and "imprac-tical" as a guide for the work of librarianship. But that same year he hedged on that analysis, writing that it was an open question "*whether or when* tech-nology will make books and libraries obsolete." His 1984 address to a library technology conference skeptically notes the "vast gap between promise and reality" when the "wonders of the new information processing technology" are described and librarians urged to "embrace [them] or be left behind on the ash heap of the technological revolution." But only three years later he described "vast retrospective collections" as "*both* an asset *and a liability* in the electronic future." In the same essay it was noted that "revolution is one of those strong words that has lost its impact [through] overuse," but he goes on to assert that the primary "effect of technology on libraries over these four decades has been to bring about a revolution in access to library resources" as the resources of a library are made available "beyond its walls, and the resources beyond its walls available within the library." These pronouncements themselves came *only* a short time after his sternly writing that "dramatic predictions about the future of books, libraries, and information technology tend to be made by men of thought rather than men of action [who] do not have to implement [them] and take personal responsibility for the results." Our prominent library administrator then goes on to describe some poor library building decisions based on such predictions and cites *defenses* of books and critiques of forecasts, concluding with another admonition about the "intellectual sport of speculating" and asserting that "only those with authority and responsibility can decide how and when" such analyses should be implemented in libraries.[17]

This author was certainly *not* the worst in these matters—those quoted earlier made more extreme and sillier statements, some much more recently. Rather, his case is emblematic and instructive for three reasons: the length of time he served in prestigious and influential library positions; his writing was from a position of authority (he clearly makes pronouncements in print as such) during a crucial period of thinking about *how* the profession would respond to and adapt information technologies; the seeming air of caution, responsibility, and soberness with which he approached these potential changes in librarianship did not prevent him from to-and-fro pronouncements on the future of librarianship in the span of about five years that these quotes cover. My contention is that this confusion represents a fundamentally shallow analysis of the nature of events buffeting the profession, and the continual naming of and responding to crisis has come to represent our professional culture. When the "leading lights" of the field (like those quoted at the beginning of the chapter) almost continually engage in contradictory and unbridled hyperbole and "futuring" in the literature over such a long period of time, then it is little wonder that librarians have felt almost perpetually under siege. The future need for their institutions and their expertise seems always in doubt. Further, by focusing on the epiphenomena of the moment, authors in the field and the leadership of the profession will never adequately address the issues that are at the core of what is happening to librarianship. The call-and-response of crisis, quick and shallow adaptation (and the resultant perpetual status anxiety of librarians), will go on indefinitely. I am not alone in a critique of the literature of librarianship. There are a wide variety of scholars who have questioned librarianship's ability or willingness to assimilate relevant interdisciplinary research findings into our own research and professional practice. The literature for many years has been described as relentlessly practical, featuring faddish and quick adoption of popularized management trends. Information science research and paradigms are inadequate, and the epistemology of library science research has been thoroughly attacked as positivistic.[18] The core issue of what lies behind librarianship's intellectual, ethical, and fiscal indeterminacy is at the heart of this book.

## THE NEED FOR A DEFENSE OF LIBRARIANSHIP

The second half of the question that began this chapter and the book now comes more into focus. In the crisis culture of librarianship just described, the field is almost always in a defensive mode. Librarianship *is* defended quite routinely, and those defenses tend to come in two basic forms. First, libraries and librarians—and the ensuing professional ethics we espouse—are routinely described as essential to a democracy. Access to and preservation of information for an informed citizenry is a cornerstone of this argument, and frequently the library-provided riches of the Web are touted as dramatically expanding democratic information access and the ability to organize for action.[19] The second defense reasons that librarianship "will continue to be a critical link in the chain [of] knowledge that has created and sustains our information society." Or, put another way, we'll simply be there to collect, preserve, and disseminate whatever information is produced "when people choose to embrace this or that format."[20]

I take the bases of both of these defenses seriously, but their current form (and frankly, their effectiveness) is grossly inadequate. For instance, the connections between libraries and democracies are more a matter of rhetoric and faith than substance. Clear back in 1934 J. Periam Danton asked if we could assume libraries were essential in a democracy. Even if the answer was yes, he concluded we could not further assume that they were "essential government functions" (e.g., for funding purposes) or among "democracy's principle agencies," and he noted that proving so would be difficult.[21] Perhaps worse, the democratic argument is discredited by prominent glosses like the American Library Association's "12 Ways Libraries are Good for the Country." Two whole sentences are devoted to the number one reason, "libraries inform citizens," but we also find that libraries "return high dividends," "make families friendlier," and "offer sanctuary."[22] Scholarly glosses are similarly shallow whether about the past or the present in that they merely catalog events in a happy consensus of information-equals-democracy narrative.[23] Even serious attempts to examine the issue get lost in theories of the "autopoietic state" and chaos, and the profession has yet to come up with real theoretical answers to the cogent questions posed by Neil Postman in 1983 about freedom of information in an electronic age.[24] It is little wonder that Harris and Hannah found a lack of intellectual consensus in the profession's response to the 1980s onslaught of privatization of public information and the democratic defense of public information as a rehearsed litany that constituted "little more than the ritual deployment of slogans."[25]

The inadequacy of the second defense is well-illustrated by the quotes at the beginning of this chapter. If librarianship is merely reactive, we will continue to see the same rapid cycles of crisis-naming and professional and institutional responses to the issues of the moment. On the ultimate unimportance of formats, the thinking in the profession continues to be amazingly shallow. There is a vast body of literature examining and questioning the facile assumption that one format is as good as another in terms of learning, thinking, and preservation.[26] Nicholson Baker has justifiably embarrassed the profession in a number of high-profile ways (and on our own turf) for this cavalier attitude.[27] Lastly, the continual consternation in library literature over funding, journal inflation, and the cost of new resources and the ability to afford to house, offer, and preserve them puts the lie to the bland assertion that we'll just slide over and do whatever needs doing in whatever format that happens to be the flavor of the decade. The simple act of just holding on to those electronic resources that have already been bought and paid for by a library promises to be daunting and extraordinarily expensive.[28] Librarianship needs a meaningful, consistent, and sustainable intellectual basis for its defense, and that project is also at the heart of this book.

## STRUCTURE OF THE BOOK

If, as I have argued, we have a crisis culture in the profession and in turn have weakly defended librarianship in response to those ever-declared and poorly analyzed crises, then our framework of analysis and defending librarianship must change and that change must begin in critique. Michael Walzer writes that the power of criticism is to "elucidate the values that underlie [common] complaints. [I]t is founded in hope; it cannot be carried on without some sense of historical possibility [and] human agency [and the belief that] institutions can be more justly organized than they now are."[29] I stated previously in this chapter that I would define the core of librarianship's challenges. That core issue is the critique embodied in what has been called the "new public philosophy." Essentially this thesis identifies a radically reconceptualized relationship between the public and private good—and the means and boundaries of analyzing those competing visions. Chapter 2 will summarize the new public philosophy thesis and its origins and explore its application in critical educational scholarship. I will conclude with an argument for the efficacy of this critical framework for other public cultural institutions.

Central to the new public philosophy critique is the concept of the public sphere—and its importance and diminution. Chapter 3 will briefly examine and explain the public sphere based in particular on the ideas of Jürgen Habermas and those who have extended and refined his work. The critique embedded in the public sphere analyses—its extension of the work of the Frankfurt School and response to postmodern challenges—will be summarized with the critical educational scholarship used as a touchstone. The chapter will conclude by placing librarianship within the public sphere analysis.

The next five chapters of the book will explore my thesis that librarianship is a classic case study of the dismantling of the public sphere in an era of radically market-oriented public philosophy toward public cultural institutions (like schools and libraries). Chapter 4 will focus on funding patterns in librarianship. Chapter 5 will examine the leadership of the profession and the nature of its response in light of the new public philosophy. Chapter 6 will focus on the customer rhetoric and emphasis within libraries, chapter 7 will review ALA and its move toward a business model of operation, and chapter 8 will examine technology and technocratic trends in the field. Chapter 9 will conclude the book by adapting a democratic theory of public institutions and further exploring Habermas's notion of the critical public sphere—and his philosophical attempt to rescue democratic possibility. I will suggest that this represents a powerful framework and argument for librarianship in a democracy. These ideas form a solid and coherent intellectual basis to defend librarianship. They connect it to the project of democracy and cultural vitality, and they place libraries back in the "contested terrain" of the critical and democratic public sphere. In the spirit of social criticism described by Walzer, this book seeks to cogently complain and place democratic principles and possibility back at the core of our work and our institutions. In so doing, the critique of the field and the essential case for viewing librarianship as part of the democratic public sphere will be incrementally advanced and built through each successive chapter.

## PUBLIC CULTURAL INSTITUTIONS: A NOTE ON THE CONNECTIONS BETWEEN EDUCATION AND LIBRARIANSHIP

I can find no elegant segue to introduce the historical and professional connections between the education and library fields. It fits logically at the conclusion of this introduction as well as any place in the book, and since I have already frequently mentioned the touchstone of critical educational scholarship as one of the keys to my framework of analysis in this book, it should come sooner rather than later. I have previously explored and written at some length on those connections and argued that they are salient, productive, and legitimate.[30] I will not repeat the full thesis here, but briefly note that both professions and institutions were founded in the nineteenth-century era of public institution building and both workforces face very similar professional status, pay, and control issues. Both teaching and librarianship are gendered professions and have historically drawn similar demographic profiles recruited to work in the field. Both institutions and professions also have been fundamentally challenged by the introduction of technology. Libraries are typically appended to schools and universities (and their missions). Public libraries are expected to fill an important role in support of further learning and inquiry beyond the school curriculum. Like librarianship, education has been in a perpetual state of declared crises for some time. Lastly, as Amy Gutmann points out, libraries and schools frequently face the exact same issues of censorship (often from the same local constituencies).[31]

In this sense then, the educational analyses and critiques I rely upon form a larger context into which librarianship fits—albeit not in a crude mechanical way. This connection also firmly places libraries in the arena of public cultural institutions in league with museums, schools, and higher education. Most such institutions are publicly funded, but for those that are in part or primarily privately funded there is a strong argument to be made that all fit the bill of "public" institutions: they hold nonprofit, tax-exempt status; state and local laws protect them from vandalism and theft; municipalities, governing boards, and the courts recognize the need to protect minority expressions on their shelves, walls, classrooms, and services; those same bodies have extended privileges to the professionals of those institutions (intellectual and academic freedom, for instance) in order to push forward the boundaries of human understanding and knowledge and the preservation of cultural output. Even well-endowed private university libraries (like those in the Ivy League) implicitly acknowledge their public status by describing their missions and collections in national terms, participating in interlibrary lending, sharing cataloging records, and making access to their collections available to scholars worldwide—even if only reluctantly at times.

In sum, there are strong arguments, well grounded in historical fact and scholarly analysis, that place libraries among the public cultural institutions, sharing in the educative mission of schools and colleges. It is on this basis that I rely on and adapt the work of critical education scholars who have been involved in critique and reclaiming education in the public sphere.

## NOTES

1. The terms "librarianship" or the "library field" are used throughout this book and are inclusive of the people and institutions of the three traditional areas of the field: public, academic, and school libraries and the professionals who work in those contexts.

2. Gerald Salton, "Proposals for a Dynamic Library," in *Libraries in Post-Industrial Society,* ed. Leigh Estabrook (Phoenix: Oryx Press, 1977), 273.

3. Michael Harris and Stan Hannah, *Into the Future: the Foundations of Library and Information Services in the Post-Industrial Era* (Norwood, N.J.: Ablex, 1993), vii. See pp. 33–45 on F. W. Lancaster and the debate over Daniel Bell's postindustrial metaphor and his influence on librarianship.

4. Harris and Hannah, 56, 106–7.

5. U.S. Department of Education, Center for Libraries and Education Improvement, *Alliance for Excellence: Librarians Respond to A Nation at Risk,* (Washington, D.C.: U.S. Government Printing Office, 1984), 1.

6. Pauline Wilson, "Mission and Information: What Business Are We In?" *Journal of Academic Librarianship* 14, no. 2 (1988): 82–83.

7. Bruce Park, "Libraries Without Walls; Or, Librarians Without a Profession," *American Libraries,* October 1992, 746.

8. Eldred Smith and Peggy Johnson, "How to Survive the Present While Preparing for the Future: A Research Library Strategy," *College and Research Libraries,* September 1993, 389.

9. Jerry Campbell, "Choosing to Have a Future," *American Libraries,* June 1993, 560.

10. Terrence Mech, "Leadership and the Evolution of Academic Librarianship," *Journal of Academic Librarianship* 22, no. 5 (1996): 345.

11. Carla Stoffle, "Literacy 101 for the Digital Age," *American Libraries,* December 1998, 48.

12. K. Wayne Smith, "The OCLC Connection," interview with Ron Chepesiuk, *American Libraries,* August 1998, 64.

13. John Lombardi, "The Fate of the Undergraduate Library," interview, *Library Journal,* 1 November 2000, 40.

14. Dees Stallings, "The Virtual University: Organizing to Survive in the 21st Century," *Journal of Academic Librarianship* 27, no. 1 (2001): 4.

15. Susan Kent, "The Public Library Director in the Dot (.) World," *New Library World* 103, no. 1/2 (2002): 48.

16. Anne Grodzins Lipow, "Point-of-Need Reference Service: No Longer an Afterthought" (Future of Reference Panel, American Library Association Annual Conference, Atlanta, 2002).

17. Richard De Gennaro, *Libraries, Technology, and the Information Marketplace: Selected Papers* (Boston: G. K. Hall, 1987) 4, 10–11, 49–50, 139–40, 229–230 (emphasis added).

18. An excellent summary—noting that significant critiques of the library science research and literature go back to 1967—can be found in Michael Harris, "State, Class, and Cultural Reproduction: Toward A Theory of Library Service in the United States," *Advances in Librarianship* 14 (1986): 211–53. Other important reviews include Harris and Hannah; Michael Harris, "The Dialectic of Defeat: Antimonies in Research in Library and Information Science," *Library Trends* 34, no. 3 (1986): 515–31; Michael Harris and Masaru Itoga, "Becoming Critical: For a Theory of Purpose and Necessity in American Librarianship," in *Library and Information Science Research: Perspectives and Strategies for Improvement,* Information Management, Policy, and Services Series (Norwood, N.J.: Ablex, 1991), 347–57; Wayne Weigand, "The Structure of Librarianship: Essay on an Information Profession," *Canadian Journal of Information and Library Science,* 24, no. 1 (1997): 17–37; Wayne Weigand, "Tunnel Vision and Blind Spots: What the Past Tells Us About the Present: Reflections on the Twentieth-Century History of American Librarianship," *Library Quarterly* 69, no. 1 (1999): 1–32; Wayne Weigand, "MisReading LIS Education," *American Libraries,* 15 June 1997: 36–38; Roma Harris, *Librarianship: The Erosion of a Woman's Profession* (Norwood, N.J.: Ablex, 1992); Bernd Frohmann, "The Ethics of Information Science Theory" (Information Democracy session, 55th Annual American Society for Information Science Meeting, Pittsburgh, 27 October 1992); Thomas Mann, "The Importance of Books, Free Access, and Libraries as Places—and the Dangerous Inadequacy of the Information Science Paradigm," *Journal of Academic Librarianship* 27, no. 4 (2001): 268–81; and John Buschman, ed., *Critical Approaches to Information Technology in Librarianship: Foundations and Applications* (Westport, Conn.: Greenwood, 1993). For a not-unthoughtful critique from the Right, see Gertrude Himmelfarb, "Revolution in the Library," *American Scholar* (Spring 1997): 197–204. For examples of less-thoughtful critiques from the Right, see Blaise Cronin, "Shibboleth and Substance in North American Library and Information Science Education," *Libri* 45 (1995): 45–63; and Cronin's regular column in *Library Journal.*

19. See Kathleen de la Pena McCook, "Poverty, Democracy and Public Libraries," in *Libraries & Democracy: The Cornerstones of Liberty,* ed. Nancy Kranich (Chicago: American Library Association, 2001), 28–46; Michael Harris, "Public Libraries and the Decline of the Democratic Dogma," *Library Journal,* 1 November 1976: 2225–2230; Carolyn Gray, "The Civic Role of Libraries," in *Critical Approaches,* ed. Buschman, 151–71; Ronald Heckart, "The Library as a Marketplace of Ideas," *College & Research Libraries,* November 1991, 491–505; Harris and Hannah; Martin Fricke, Kay Matheisen, and Don Fallis, "The Ethical Presuppositions Behind the Library Bill of Rights," *Library Quarterly* 70, no. 4 (2000): 468–91; and Jean Key Gates, *Introduction to Librarianship,* 2d ed. (New York: McGraw-Hill), 1976.

20. Quotes respectively from De Gennaro, 69; and Michael Harris, "The Fall of the Grand Hotel: Class, Canon, and the Coming Crisis of Western Librarianship," *Libri* 45 (1995): 231.

21. J. Periam Danton, "Plea for a Philosophy of Librarianship," in *American Library Philosophy: An Anthology,* ed. Barbara McCrimmon (Hamden, Conn.: Shoe String Press, 1975), 82–83.

22. American Library Association, "12 Ways Libraries Are Good for the Country." *American Libraries* online edition. 2000 revision of a list that was published in 1995. 26 August 2002, <http://www.ala.org/alonline/news/12wayshtml>.

23. See, for example, Scott Bennett, "The Golden Age of Libraries," *Journal of Academic Librarianship* 27, no. 4 (2001): 256–59; and Elizabeth Smith, "Equal Information Access and the Evolution of American Democracy," *Journal of Educational Media & Library Sciences* 33, no. 2 (1995): 158–71. Note: I am *not* including in this assessment those authors previously cited in note 19.

24. See, respectively, Leah Lievrouw, "Information Resources and Democracy: Understanding the Paradox," *Journal of the American Society for Information Science* 45, no. 6 (1994): 350–57; Brenda Dervin, "Information—Democracy: An Examination of Underlying Assumptions," *Journal of the American Society for Information Science* 45, no. 6 (1994): 369–85; and Neil Postman, "The Contradictions of Freedom of Information," *WLA Journal,* June 1985, 4–19.

25. Harris and Hannah, 78–79.

26. The following represent good *summaries* of the issues and/or the literature and only scratch the surface: Buschman, *Critical Approaches;* Neil Postman, *Technopoly: The Surrender of Culture to Technology* (New York: Vintage, 1993); Neil Postman, *Teaching as a Conserving Activity* (New York: Delta, 1979); Albert Teich, ed., *Technology and Man's Future* (New York: St. Martin's Press, 1981); Douglas Sloan, ed., *The Computer in Education: A Critical Perspective* (New York: Teachers College Press, 1984); C. A. Bowers, *The Cultural Dimensions of Educational Computing* (New York: Teachers College Press, 1988); Dorothy Warner, "'Why Do We Need to Keep This in Print? It's on the Web . . . ': A Review of Electronic Archiving Issues and Problems," *Progressive Librarian* 19/20 (Spring 2002): 47–64; and Alexander Stille, *The Future of the Past* (New York: Farrar, Straus and Giroux, 2002).

27. Nicholson Baker, *Double Fold: Libraries and the Assault on Paper* (New York: Random House, 2001); Nicholson Baker, "Discards," *New Yorker,* 4 April 1994, 64–86; Nicholson Baker, "The Author vs. the Library," *New Yorker,* 14 October 1996, 50–62; Nicholson Baker, "A Couple of Codicils About San Francisco," *American Libraries,* March 1999, 35; and Nicholson Baker, "The Collector," interview with Dwight Garner, *New York Times Book Review,* 15 April 2001, 9.

28. See Warner, "Why"; Alexander Stille, "Overload," *New Yorker,* 8 March 1999, 38–44; and Clifford Stoll, *Silicon Snake Oil: Second Thoughts on the Information Highway* (New York: Doubleday, 1995), 180–81.

29. Michael Walzer, *The Company of Critics: Social Criticism and Political Commitment in the Twentieth Century* (New York: Basic Books, 1988), 16–19.

30. John Buschman and Michael Carbone, "A Critical Inquiry into Librarianship: Applications of the 'New Sociology of Education,'" *Library Quarterly* 61, no. 1 (1991): 15–40; and John Buschman, "Conclusion: Contexts, Analogies, and Entrepreneurial Directions in Librarianship," in *Critical Approaches,* ed. Buschman, 211–19.

31. Amy Gutmann, *Democratic Education* (Princeton, N.J.: Princeton University Press, 1987), 235–38. For other good reviews of the points noted, see also Harris, "State, Class"; Gates; Harris, "Democratic Dogma"; Wayne Wiegand, "Research Libraries, the Ideology of Reading, and Scholarly Communication, 1876–1900," in *Libraries and Scholarly Communication in the United States: The Historical Dimension,* Beta Phi Mu monograph series (New York: Greenwood Press, 1990), 71–87; and Wayne Wiegand, "The Development of Librarianship in the United States," *Libraries and Culture* 24, no. 1 (1989): 99–109.

# 2

## THE NEW PUBLIC PHILOSOPHY AND CRITICAL EDUCATIONAL ANALYSIS: THE CONTEXT OF PUBLIC CULTURAL INSTITUTIONS

### THE NEW PUBLIC PHILOSOPHY THESIS

"New," as Richard Sennett notes, "is a suspect word, the favored adjective of advertisers,"[1] and in a sense his description is the correct one for the new public philosophy. There is nothing "new" in that it was named more than twenty years ago by the political theorist Sheldon Wolin in response to the then-new policies of the Reagan administration. In a relatively brief paper, Wolin outlined both the nature and the extent of those changes and argued that they were "effecting a species of radical change" on American public philosophy.[2] He pointed out that historically, the political culture of the country was grounded in a "stock of notions": Protestantism, English common law, and Enlightenment political ideas. This enabled a "language of public discourse for discussing and arguing about [people's] common condition and its problems. It gave Americans their basic ideas of 'power,' 'justice,' 'right and wrong,' 'equality,' 'freedom,' and 'authority.'" There was, he argues, a "bias toward treating political questions in moral/religious or legal terms [and] in a sense, Americans had no notion of economic policy independent of politics and morality. [O]ne is struck by the moral and religious fervor [in the eighteenth and nineteenth century] debates over fiscal and monetary policy." As long as this synthesis held sway, "economic modes of thought remained marginal and Americans retained their historical skepticism about the motives of businessmen."[3]

The ideas and changes of the 1980s were not themselves new, as Wolin noted: "the importance of economics in public councils is not a Reagan innovation [but] the prominence of economics is both the herald and the agent of a profound transformation in American political culture."[4] There was "Reaganism before Reagan,"[5] in other words, but Wolin argues that the era represented a sudden acceleration and significant extension of those policies and ideas. In order to justify and enact radical and painful changes—"a far-reaching program of spending cuts, tax changes, deregulation, and reduced social services"—a new and different "public language" would have to be found. Economics would serve as the public philosophy for a "society being evolved through the collaborating powers of capitalism, science, and the state."[6] This is what he identifies as the key—and lasting—change beyond the mere policies of a new administration: "economics now dominates public discourse. [It] becomes the paradigm of what public reason should be [and] prescribes the form that 'problems' have to be given before they can be acted upon, the kinds of 'choices' that exist, and the meaning of 'rationality.'" Economics as a new public philosophy now "frame[s] the alternatives in virtually every sphere of public activity, from health care, social welfare, and education to weapons systems, environmental protection, and scientific research."[7] If, as Wolin suggests, language expresses our limits, then the

change in public discourse implies that some of the things that the old language was suited to express and emphasize are being lost or downgraded by a new public vocabulary. [R]elegated to secondary importance are the main notions through which the society once understood its identity . . . such as "democracy," "republic," "the Constitution," and "the nation" whose meaning was essentially political. . . . The state of the nation becomes meaningful [now] only when we are able to talk about it as "rates" of various kinds.[8]

Under such a public philosophy and language regime, "that all public questions can be converted into economic terms has no doubt." Wolin critiques the academic and media treatment of public issues in this way as a masking of "power by presenting what are essentially political and moral questions in the form of economic choices," obscured by the claim that economics as a "technique is neutral, and that whatever use is made of the results of a technical analyst is not the responsibility of the analyst."[9] Wolin and many others have noted that this change has been coming for some time and that it had a significant contemporary companion in Thatcherisim,[10] but he was among the first to identify and name its sudden acceleration and radical depth as a new public philosophy and the displacement of an older language of civic values as a framework of public and political choice. As I will show later in this chapter, the ideas and language Wolin identified continue to characterize the situation and context of public cultural institutions and form the foundation of an important vein of critical educational scholarship.

In putting forward this sketch of Wolin's thesis, he does not (and I do not) ignore the significant shortcomings of the American experience and the democratic public discourse that have been displaced. There have simply been too many histories written that reveal the absence or suppression of Indians and slaves—then Freedmen and then African American citizens, women, the propertyless, and later, immigrants, gays, and lesbians. Gary Nash characterized the mythology as the "greatest success story of human history, the epic tale of how a proud, brave offshoot of the English-speaking people tried to reverse the laws of history by demonstrating what the human spirit, liberated from the shackles of tradition, myth, and oppressive authority could do in a newly discovered corner of the earth."[11] The initial attempts to "include" those originally left out of the story—and by implication, its benefits— amounted only to "plug[ing] a few feathers, woolly heads, and sombreros into the famous events of American history."[12] This still left the measure of the past defined in terms of the dominant, white, male, and propertied class, and we are struggling with and arguing over when and where and how to revise this vision and its aftermath—and it is high time.[13] It is an unmitigated good that the histories and voices of women have been rediscovered and the assumption that the "matter of American experience is inherently male" has been deeply and fundamentally challenged.[14] It is an unmitigated good that the history and experiences of gay men and lesbians have been excavated and documented and current lives and histories recorded.[15] The study of the African American historical experience—and its consequent emphasis on the multiculturalism of American history—have been around long enough and have become at least prominent enough to be questioned by educational conservatives as a "frill" in the curriculum, pulling students away from "real" or more central academic content.[16] Nor is Wolin among those who interpret the history of American political culture as a bland process of consensus, stable and without serious ideological conflict. I am reminded of Richard Hofstadter's reply to a scholar's contention that the Civil War did "not represent a real failure of the American consensus." He replied that, if this were so then "we can only conclude that Americans do not *need* ideological conflict to shed blood on a large scale."[17]

Rather than the denying the historical facts of those excluded from democratic public discourse, Wolin sees in the new public philosophy the danger of diminution of democratic possibility and of the ability to further *extend* inclusion and political participation. He writes that, in the changeover of language and values, we no longer have a "principle for transcending conflict to find common ground [and] no basis for common action. . . . When the economy becomes the polity, *citizen* and *community* become subversive words."[18] Implicit in his argument is the idea that the replaced language and values of American political culture helped *expand*—however slowly, haphazardly, and with struggle—democratic participation and possibility over time. The nature of that jagged expansion was summarized by Carl Boggs:

The . . . aftermath of the French and American revolutions produced universal norms of consent, citizenship, participation, rights and national identity. [R]ational discourse

[was] made possible by the spread of scientific and technological values, diffusion of education and knowledge, and increasing levels of material abundance. . . . The ascendancy of the public over the private was made possible by [these developments] and popular demands for wider citizen participation. [C]lear definitions of rights, procedures, and obligations could be established. Even while class, racial, patriarchal, and (later) bureaucratic forms of domination permeated the social order, [there was] the glimpse of a "great transformation" where market and participatory values could coexist. [T]hough unevenly manifested, [there was] a plethora of quasi-democratic structures: parties, labor unions, interest groups, political machines, social movements, ad hoc popular initiatives. Of course [the ideal] was never close to the reality [but] there was a gradual broadening of the public [and] barriers to participation were pushed back or overturned and new groups became mobilized. By 1945, with the defeat of fascism and the eclipse of other authoritarian regimes, this historical trend was further consolidated [and] reached its peak in the 1960s and 1970s with the appearance of strong left-wing parties, the new left, and a mélange of progressive forces including the new social movements.[19]

The language that has been replaced—as Wolin noted—was centered around religious morality, an English concept of rights, and especially eighteenth-century political ideas like those in the Declaration of Independence and in Paine's *Common Sense:* "For all men being originally equals, no *one* by *birth* could have a right to set up his family in perpetual preference to all others forever." "For as in absolute governments the king is law, so in free countries the law ought to be king; and there ought to be no other." "A government of our own is our natural right." "Let the name of whig and tory be extinct; and let none other be heard among us, than those of a *good citizen; an open and resolute friend; and a virtuous supporter of the* RIGHTS OF MANKIND, *and of the* FREE AND INDEPENDENT STATES OF AMERICA."[20] Paine's words were—and still are—radical arguments that "broke through the categories and conventions . . . and set forth far wider democratic claims."[21] They were important components of the extension of freedoms and rights in spite of the elitist beginnings of America because they were "potentially applicable universally because of their abstract (not rooted directly in custom) character."[22] Nor did this public rhetoric—and its extensions—end with the eighteenth century. Frederick Douglass asked in 1852, "what to the slave is the Fourth of July?" and answered to his "Fellow citizens!" In situating himself as a citizen speaking to his equals, he declared invalid the argument for "the pro-slavery character of the Constitution. In *that* instrument I hold there is neither warrant, license, nor sanction of the hateful thing; but, interpreted as it *ought* to be interpreted, the Constitution is a GLORIOUS LIBERTY DOCUMENT."[23]

After confessing that he could not consider blacks "politically and socially our equals" in 1854, Lincoln goes on in the same speech to formulate his own principles that would lead him to seek the destruction of slavery and form the basis of equal civil rights for blacks: "no man is good enough to govern another man, *without that other's consent,*" calling it "the leading principle—the sheet anchor of American republicanism." In linking this principle to the Declaration of Independence, he concludes that the "relation of masters and slaves is . . . a total violation of this principle. The master not only governs the slave without his consent; but he governs him by a set of rules altogether different from those which he prescribes for himself. Allow ALL the governed an equal voice in the government, and that, and that only is self government."[24] When Wolin writes of a democratic language and discourse, this powerful and longstanding legacy is what he means, and it did not end with the nineteenth century either. Accused of extremism in the fight against segregation in Birmingham, Alabama, Martin Luther King, Jr. asked if the Old Testament's Amos was an extremist in his call for justice to "roll down like waters," or if Jesus, Jefferson, or Lincoln were extremists in their clarion calls for justice and equality. "So the question is not whether we will be extremists but what kind of extremists we will be. . . . Will we be extremists for the preservation of injustice or for the extension of justice? Perhaps the south, the nation and the world are in dire need of creative extremists."[25] Though most certainly meant to be more limited when originally written, the ideas King used carried forward within themselves the seeds of their extension. As a basis of common political discussion and thought, they defined public issues in political and moral terms and choices. Their replacement by the falsely neutral economic rhetoric and choices now constitutes our new public philosophy and is the fundamental essence of Wolin's critique.

## EDUCATIONAL CRITIQUES AND THE NEW
## PUBLIC PHILOSOPHY

There has been an important vein of educational scholarship that has used, and extended in some very important ways, Wolin's critique. I will focus primarily on the work of two important and prolific scholars: Henry Giroux and Michael Apple. These two thinkers have been at the center of much of the critical educational scholarship written over the past twenty-five years. Their work did not begin with Wolin, and his thesis does not define the limits of their work, let alone the entire field. There has in fact been a long tradition of critical and radical educational scholarship. Their scholarship continued, and in some ways deepened, Wolin's initial analysis by focusing on the *specific* (and often contentious) public issue of education, the subject of much local and national policy discussion. By linking that work to Wolin's thesis, the explanatory efficacy of both was enhanced, and the analyses continue to this day. Finally, like Wolin, critical educational scholars do not gloss the injustices done in American educational history but rather seek to identify the democratic nature of schooling in that history and thoroughly critique the new public philosophy that is undermining the potential for its extension.

## Henry Giroux and Education for Democracy

The connection of critical educational scholarship to Wolin's thesis began with an article by Henry Giroux in the *Harvard Educational Review* in 1984.[26] In it, he identifies the various reports on education (à la *A Nation at Risk,* etc.) produced in the early Reagan era, noting "hints of the magnitude of the crisis in the[ir] language" and that they reveal a "'new' public philosophy [that] is as problematic as the crisis that it attempts to define and resolve." Giroux goes on to observe that "what is most striking in the current debate is the relationship that is being drawn between the state of the U.S. economy . . . and the failure of the schools to educate students to meet the economic needs of the dominant society. [This debate is] a discourse that defines economic rationality as the model of public reason. . . . The important issue here is that economic rationality becomes both the referent and the ideal for change."[27]

So far, Giroux seems to be making an apt but straightforward application of Wolin's ideas. However, his analysis takes a much more specific turn that deepens the meaning of the new public philosophy for education by identifying issues that logically will be neglected if educational policy is enacted under such a public philosophy: failure and dropout rates, the differential performance of minorities, and absenteeism, for example. "[S]chools become important only to the degree that they can provide the forms of knowledge, skills, and social practices necessary to produce the labor force for an increasingly complex, technological economy."[28] He further identifies a key issue at stake: funding. The new public philosophy "does not contain an adequate rationale for defending schools [and] in fact lends support to programs aimed at severely reducing funding, [like] tuition tax credits, educational vouchers, [and] the reduction of federal funding for education." The core issue is that, if this new economic public language now defines the relationship between the purpose of schooling and society, then the basic historical *reasons* for originally funding education become a contradiction. The new public philosophy assumes that "schools [are] means to increasing individual achievement and promoting [economic] needs. Such a view makes it difficult to defend public education in political and ethical terms."[29]

In a series of later writings, Giroux goes on to further elaborate and expand this linkage, though he does not always explicitly cite Wolin or use the new public philosophy phrase.[30] He identifies a "conservative attack" on schools through reforms and policies that include accountability programs, testing, accreditation processes, and an emphasis on credentials,[31] "competency-based testing for teachers, a lockstep sequencing of materials, mastery learning techniques, systematized evaluation schemes, standardized curricula, and the implementation of mandated 'basics.'" He has critiqued the primary developments of the last twenty years—privatization, increasing corporate information in the classrooms, and the continuing conservative nature of reform

efforts—characterizing all of those as promoting cultural uniformity and linking schools to an economic agenda at a cost to citizenship and democracy in
the schools.[32] He has extended this analysis to higher education, although
again, he is not alone in that.[33] What has distinguished Giroux's work is his
consistency in critiquing the new public philosophy in light of the democratic
project of education. He writes that when

schools simply mimic the free market, with the assumption that its regulatory and
competitive spirit will allow the most motivated and gifted students to succeed [then]
there is a shameful element of racism and a retrograde Social Darwinism that permeates
this discourse, one that relinquishes the responsibility . . . to provide all young people
with the cultural resources, economic opportunities, and social services necessary to
learn without having to bear the crushing burdens of poverty, racism, and other forms
of oppression. . . . There also is the issue of how individual achievement is weighed
against issues of equity and the social good, how teaching and learning get defined,
and what sorts of identities are produced when the histories, experiences, values, and
desires of students are defined through corporate, rather than democratic, ideals.[34]

Under such prevailing circumstances, the "language of democracy seem[s]
to lose its vitality and purpose as an organizing principle for society," making
it crucial to defend the democratic public space and arena of the classroom:
they are "indispensable to the life of the nation because they are one of the
few public spaces left where students can learn the power of and engage in
the experience of democracy."[35] Again and again, Giroux's critique returns
to the idea of schools and universities as democratic—not economic—spaces,
"centers of critical literacy and civic [education] rather than merely training
sites."[36] Giroux's work is central to the purposes of this book for three reasons. First, he made the express link between education and the new public
philosophy critique. Second, he extended that critique through a specific
identification of trends and problems in schooling and higher education.
Third, Giroux successfully situated funding as a key issue at stake within the
new public language and policy framework.

## Michael Apple and the Extension to Content and the
## Competitive Market

Michael Apple has been engaged in what I would call an analysis of the
concrete specifics inherent in the new public philosophy critique. This is not
to say that Apple lacks a coherent and extensive set of explanatory ideas concerning education. Rather, important parts of his work can be viewed as a
specific critical explication of the new public philosophy at work in schools,
and he has extended its ideas and terms up to the present moment. To be
accurate, Apple has not written specifically on Wolin's thesis and like Giroux,
his critical scholarship began much earlier. For instance, he had previously

explored the commodification of education and democratic schooling.[37] Like Giroux—and in parallel to Wolin's analysis—he saw a significant change in the language of education policy beginning in the Reagan era, and his analyses of the governmental and blue-ribbon reports on education formed part of the basis for Giroux's extension of the critique of the new public philosophy to education.[38] It is a good place to begin in examining Apple's fundamental contribution.

His analysis of the reports—there have been about twelve of them starting from 1983[39]—concludes that they represent a conservative ideological shift in the language of the debate over education.[40] "The reports are as much political as they are educational documents [and] the specific content of each of these proposals is less consequential than the overall tendencies they represent. [They] are calls for action, calls to use scarce resources and political power for specific ends."[41] The nature of those ends is decidedly economic: he notes that *A Nation at Risk* calls for educational "rearmament" to successfully meet the crisis of international economic competition, and Apple very specifically outlines the nature of the inequalities that will go unaddressed or even exacerbated under the regime and logic of the reports.[42] At base, the reports represent a reassertion of authority: "the vision of the economy . . . may be unequal and wrong, but there is little doubt that they have had considerable success in moving the debate onto capital's terrain" in that they represent a merging of old and new values essential to the economy and "disarticulating the . . . themes of social democratic accord."[43] In sum, Apple's analyses of the reports firmly established their conservative and economic agendas and their framing of educational issues under such rubrics as "at risk" and "excellence." In other words, they represent the point at which the new public philosophy was installed at the center of the debate over educational policy.

Like Giroux, Apple has identified a "conservative alliance" influencing schools and policy. Examining the nature of that conservatism and alliance—which came to dominate educational policy—is a further contribution Apple makes to the critique of the new public philosophy in education. He pulls apart the specific components of that alliance and has explicated its direct impact on the *subject matter and content* of schooling. He notes that the conservatism is not merely economic in nature and that the alliance elected Reagan (and successive administrations have furthered the redefinition of public issues in economic terms). But as Apple notes, "the successes of the policies of the Reagan administration, like that of Thatcherism in Britain, should not be evaluated simply in electoral terms. These policies need to be judged by their success . . . in shifting the terms of political, economic, and *cultural* debate onto the terrain favored by capital *and the Right*."[44] He identifies the electoral alliance of the 1980s as comprised of the "authoritarian populism" embodied in the New and Christian Right—which is focused primarily on conservative social issues like prayer in the schools, abortion, and antigay agendas—and the business interests of corporations. The two camps are fundamentally a bundle of contradictions: business interests relentlessly modernize and secularize while the conservative Right culturally fights those same trends.[45]

In spite of this internal contradiction, the results have been and continue to be an effective coalition that dominates and defines educational policy in economic and culturally conservative terms. In addition, the conservative alliance has been quite effective in influencing content in schools and universities through "a 'return' to higher standards, a revivification of the 'Western tradition,' and patriotism," in combination with the agenda of the far Right, which seeks to base public educational practices in, among other things, Biblical precept and likewise expunge historical explorations of racism, to name one instance. The radical Right positions make the authoritarian educational views of conservatives like William Bennett or Lynn Cheney appear more "moderate."[46] At the same time, Apple notes that this hybrid conservative political stew also skews content in favor of corporate capitalism. The political economy of textbooks drives curriculum content in the schools and is one of the prime sources of legitimation of the economic order.[47] Whittle Communications' *Channel One,* which is "donated" to schools as a news program in exchange for two minutes of ads, represents another venue of the domination of this public philosophy. Apple has reviewed the contents of *Channel One* and finds in it "a new version of the [school] 'text' [and] the officially sponsored opening up of the school content to commercial sponsorship and organization [, which] is a sea change," the primary purpose of which is to "create a captive audience."[48] He notes that all of these challenges to and influence on content—both overt and covert—are discussed in the public policy framework of the conservative alliance. For instance, in the combination of a conservative business atmosphere and the conservative Right's mistrust of anything secular and public, tax support for schools has dwindled. *Channel One* is therefore "necessary" and represents a "reform"—and it is gladly accepted because schools are starved for money, current materials, and content.[49] Apple repeatedly notes the difficulty in forming alternatives—specifically democratic ones—within this environment. In so doing, he has again made specific the workings of the new public philosophy in classrooms and schools and connected them thoroughly to "the daily realities of and struggles over the actual policies and practices of curriculum, teaching, and evaluation."[50] He has also made the important explicit connection between this new public language and content and *format* as well[51] (which will be important concepts in extending this critique to librarianship).

Finally, Apple has most recently again extended this analysis in a concrete way. In some of his most recent work, Apple links current reform efforts to this earlier conservative alliance and characterizes it as neoliberal. Far from being at odds with the conservative public philosophy that has dominated educational policy and provided its framework, "neo-liberals are the most powerful element within the conservative restoration. They are guided by a vision of the weak state. Thus, what is private is necessarily good, and what is public is necessarily bad. Public institutions such as schools are 'black holes' into which money is poured [without] anywhere near adequate results."[52] The answer posited by the most recent educational reform efforts: "only by turning our schools, teachers, and children over to the competitive market will we find a solution. [N]othing can be accomplished . . . without setting the market loose on schools so as to ensure that only 'good' ones survive."[53] Market reforms of education are often couched in the language of the best way to serve those students whose schools are failing them (most often minorities). The current President Bush's slogan of "leave no child behind" and the resultant educational policies are a perfect example. Neoliberalism's market metaphor also assumes in public education outcomes a responsiveness to diversity by equating market choice to the diversity of goods available in the supermarket or the mall. While Giroux has characterized market reforms and privatization schemes, Apple brings the new public philosophy analysis right up to the specifics of the present. Neoliberal arguments in their current form have again "redefined the terrain of the debate of all things educational" and again reconstructed common sense, this time around the needs of economic globalization.[54] He traces the current public philosophy transformation of educational policy beginnings back to the Reagan era and finds a further redefinition in emphasis "from student needs to student performance and from what the school does for the student to what the student does for the school."[55] In such a vision of education, students are "human capital," schools should respond to their "customers," and "'consumer choice' is the guarantor of democracy. [N]eo-liberalism is willing to spend more state and/ or private money on schools only if schools meet the needs expressed by capital. Thus, resources are made available for 'reforms' and policies that further connect the educational system to the project of [the] economy."[56]

Apple goes on to summarize some of the studies of actual market "reforms" of education[57]—and brings the new public philosophy analysis to the concrete specifics of how schools operate for students and society. Through an examination of those reforms and their rhetorical justifications he finds that, despite neoliberal claims to the contrary, "the market did *not* encourage diversity in curriculum, pedagogy, organization, clientele" and in fact was an incentive to underserve those students most in need.[58] Market-based reforms of education further homogenize school content and serve primarily to promote commercial and individualistic values. The moral "principles of the common good are the ethical basis for adjudicating policies and practices, [but] markets are grounded in [different] principles. They are constituted out of the sum of individual goods and choices [and] hierarchy and division based on competitive individualism."[59] Apple has brought us up to the neo-liberal present and clearly connected it to the origins of the new public philosophy. He has further linked those "reforms" to issues of content and in the process thoroughly dissected the ideas behind and language of the privatized market in public institutions. The market as a metaphor and model for public institutions is the most current form of this new public language and philosophy concerning education (and again, this critique has particular relevance for librarianship).

## The Historically Rooted Vision of Education

The critical educational extension of the new public philosophy thesis does not deny the historical realities of American education (and thus parallels the original thesis). In the work that has been covered, both Giroux and Apple write extensively of the historical injustices that have been embedded in current school structures, funding, practices, and content. They both insist that education can not be understood apart from larger social and economic trends—and that any truly successful reform of education must be linked to wider social and economic reform. They have fully absorbed the historical conditions of American education that scholars like Joel Spring[60] and Michael Katz[61] have identified and they have both noted the need to work through the theoretical dead end of economic determinism and resultant pessimism.[62] But they have also thoroughly absorbed the notion that the curriculum has in historical terms been a "contested terrain" in American educational history, and the results represent a compromise of differing values and ideologies.[63] In that history they find current possibilities.

Giroux's argument for preserving, recapturing, and extending the civic, democratic, and open and fair education has been summarized already. Apple as usual makes the theoretical more concrete. His work extensively explores the nature of a democratic education at work in actual schools.[64] The argument for a democratic vision of schools does not make the "history of education into a celebration of the glorious evolution of the public school and its triumph over reactionary foes,"[65] but it *is* rooted in American educational history. Yes, the beginnings and growth of the common school movement *were* rooted in fears about immigrants and the need to enculturate and discipline them for the American workforce. Yes, there was an imposition of "the one best system." Yes, the quality of schooling often went up and down with the state of local tax laws. Yes, racial and religious minorities were mostly excluded from—some few actually had the choice to opt out of—the system. And yet, and yet . . . there *were* democratic ideals built into the system and they are there to be recaptured. Apple and Giroux put such emphasis in their work on the *masking* of educational and historical conflicts in the new public philosophy because it does not serve the interests of the powerful to acknowledge that alternatives in the past (recent or otherwise) were—and by extension still are—available. This represents another important and logical extension of the original new public philosophy thesis.

Horace Mann's reforms in the founding of the common school were *both* conservative (educating the urban immigrant for the social stability of the nation) and democratic (schools should be for educating the general population, they should be free and universal, and they should educate a moral and critical citizen). His study of phrenology resulted in the introduction of music and art into the curriculum, and he saw the class and wealth divisions of England in the light of the denial of access to free public education. Henry Barnard's work gave us the notion of the "sacred space" of the school and the classroom[66] (an idea we still utilize). Many of those ideas were themselves rooted in the country's founding ideas (not myths) about education—like Jefferson's.[67] New immigrants sometimes avidly sought an education *not* to be trained as workers or to pull them away from their ethnic groups to make them "better" Americans but to improve themselves economically, intellectually, as citizens, and to help their communities.[68] The *denial* of an equal, integrated, and fairly funded education to free blacks in the North was one of the keys to keeping them from the full benefits of and participation in the economy and the potential of citizenship before the Civil War.[69]

The critique of the new public philosophy in education does not deny the incomplete realization of democratic ideals but rather seeks to revive and extend them. Maxine Greene has written that the common schools were the response to the "ancestral promise [to] provide a common experience and a common heritage for the diverse children of the nation, they would also equip the young for the responsibilities of freedom [and] insure individual equality." She reminds us that it is "difficult today to feel the ardor and the urgency" of that struggle to establish the common school (and that any attempt to recapture its democratic character must abandon its original Christian religious foundations and motivations). It is a difficult task. Then as now, the "validity of the claim that a community of common [people] could be created in an open world—and that it could survive" was a contentious and open question, and education was at its center. The ideals of American education can be recaptured, but preservation of a false innocence and historical purity cannot be the basis, she argues.[70] Rather, critical educational scholars seek out the "traditional utopian mission," in the words of Barbara Finkelstein, "to nurture a critical and committed citizenry that would stimulate the processes of political and cultural transformation and refine and extend the workings of political democracy."[71] As Apple writes, a good many of the historical conflicts and compromises that formed our educational system "signify victories, not losses, for the majority of people,"[72] and any new process will begin in critique.

Giroux and Apple have accomplished two important things in the work reviewed: they demonstrated the continuing efficacy of the critical framework of the new public philosophy to explain an important and ongoing area of public policy and policy debate; in extending the analysis to the field of education, they have provided a relevant framework for the critical analysis of librarianship. In sum, they enable us to put librarianship in a context in order to understand what has happened—and is happening—in the field apart from the epiphenomena of our crisis culture. Wolin's thesis was a powerful one, and Apple and Giroux have deepened it in specific ways that are significant to the library field.

## PUBLIC CULTURAL INSTITUTIONS AND THE NEW PUBLIC PHILOSOPHY

I have already argued in the previous chapter that the education field comprises an important context in which to view librarianship. By extension, I am arguing that the critical framework of the new public philosophy analysis of education is a significant context and lens with which to view our field. Part 2 of the book will apply this framework of critique through case studies, but I would like to briefly explore this idea in a couple of related areas in order to further establish this relationship. I stated at the end of the previous chapter that librarianship was in a league with other public cultural institutions and mentioned a number of similarities of situation (legal, fiscal, etc.). A brief review of the fate of information policy in the Reagan era (an explicit connection to the new public philosophy framework) and some trends in museums will make a strong argument for the saliency of this context and critique for librarianship.

### Information Policy and Librarianship in the Reagan Era

As ought to be well known in the field by now, the policies of the Reagan era were a major shift—an ideological shift—in federal information policy. Essentially, through a series of Office of Management and Budget (OMB) regulations, executive orders, and the Paperwork Reduction Act of 1980, government information became the object of control and redirection to private hands. Donna Demac notes that such powers were "interpreted according to the values of the Reagan Administration." For example, between 1982 and 1985, about four thousand government documents were eliminated—among them titles like *Statistical Reporter* and *Health Care Financing Trends*. The infamous Circular A-130 was issued in 1985 and mandated that "the expected public and private benefits derived from government information . . . should exceed the public and private costs of the information" and further instructed agencies to explore commercial distribution and storage of public information.[73] A 1984 entry in the *Congressional Record* notes that these commercial agreements require agencies to "deny Freedom of Information Act requests for the records in automated form." At the same time costs for publications went up and the Federal Depository Library Program was seriously curtailed.[74] (Demac called the OMB in those years "the closest thing the country has ever had to a Ministry of Information."[75])

The entire emphasis was a shift in public information over to electronic formats—to then be provided to the commercial sector for repackaging and selling. This was the ideological touchstone of the Reagan administration: a rhetoric of "frontal assault on the welfare state" followed by budget cuts and austerities and a consequent "reformist" reliance on the private sector—all well coordinated with the information industry.[76] Herbert and Anita Schiller write that the 1982 report of the National Commission on Libraries and Information Science ("The Public/Private Sector Report") signaled a "turning point." The former emphasis in White House Conferences on Library and Information Services had been increasingly on access, freedom of information, and information as a public good in a democracy. With the 1982 "Public/Private Sector Report," "it was clear that the balance had moved decisively toward the commercial information industry and away from the principle of information as a social good. [T]he position that emerges in the report is the private industry's challenge to the right of the public sector (government, libraries, universities, etc.) to engage in *any* informational activities the industry regards as its own province." There was stiff resistance to the changes and some protest, but they note that the playing field was never equal.[77]

Even this brief review shows clear applications of the new public philosophy context and framework to understanding an important turning point for librarianship. The essentials are all there: a radical ideological shift in information policy, a blue-ribbon government panel providing the rhetorical justification, the denigration of the public good, a bias toward the private and the market, and last but not least—technology and funding were key issues. Leaving aside the public language aspects of this example for librarianship, the effects of these changes over the last twenty years continue to reverberate in and shape the agendas of libraries in the form of equity, access, preservation, and cost issues surrounding government information. It is not that there have been no critiques of these policies in our field—there have been a number of cogent and important ones. Rather, the new public philosophy provides a context and framework to pull together a coordinated whole—a picture—of what was happening to librarianship via the 1980s shift in government information policy. This context supplies some of what is missing in our analyses and our crisis culture.

## Museum Developments

It would not be appropriate in the scope of this book to thoroughly review the issues museums have faced over the last twenty or more years. Rather, through a few vignettes I would like to suggest the efficacy of the new public philosophy context to frame some trends and issues in museums since I have argued that it should help us understand the situation of public cultural institutions. A number of the trends that faced museums in the 1980s have been described by the art critic Robert Hughes. For instance, the blockbuster show reached its apogee during that time. Hughes called it "cultural Reaganism: private opulence, public squalor" with the private receptions for the wealthy for shows like the 1984 "Van Gogh in Arles" exhibit at the Metropolitan Museum. In contrast, the public would "struggle for a peek through a milling scrum of backs [and] be swept at full contemplation speed (about thirty seconds per image) through the galleries" once the show was opened.[78] The shows were the museums' response to the need for audiences and their money, and those needs were rooted in three related trends: cuts in funding from governmental sources, art inflation, and the rewriting of tax laws that ended many incentives for the wealthy to donate art (presumably the private shows were to attract donations). At the same time art became exceedingly expensive for museums to acquire (prices were fueled by the redistribution of wealth upward in those years) and the commodity value of the art became itself a draw with the fetish of looking at something worth $30 million. In this environment the production and marketing of art began to warp museum collections and programs. "Although art has always been a commodity, it loses its inherent value and its social use when it is treated only as such," Hughes notes.[79] Without laboring the point, the trends he identifies fit well in the context I have summarized.

Relatively recent events at the Smithsonian Institution's museums and other general developments provide interesting cases in point:

- The Smithsonian does blockbuster shows like "The Information Age: People, Information, and Technology" for much the same reasons as Hughes noted.[80]

- The controversy over the *proposed* exhibit on the Enola Gay and the fiftieth anniversary of the end of World War II resulted in the cancellation of the show. Objections from the Right to the possible content—particularly references to the effects of the atomic bomb on the ground in Japan and on the decidedly mixed reasoning of President Truman to drop it—were key in its demise.[81]

- Noting severe budget restraints, the Smithsonian accepted a gift that represented "an unusual abdication of power" over content and presentation: ten of the fifteen nominees to a "Hall of Fame of Achievers" will be made by the donor. The *New York Times* observed that the exhibit was "too trivial to warrant mounting with its own funds," and while "the whims of wealthy people have long shaped museum exhibitions, [this] project underscores the extent to which private money can dictate the structure and content . . . at an institution like the Smithsonian" in such a funding environment.[82]

- Museums are no longer "sacred spaces" to enable people to absorb art but are now "vehicles for entertainment . . . just one of many cultural attractions" like Disneyland competing for "customers." It is both logical and necessary to incorporate "shopping, eating, performances, [and] fund-raising" into the mandates that museums must meet and when new buildings are designed.[83]

## CONCLUSION

This chapter has been an attempt to outline and trace Sheldon Wolin's thesis of the new public philosophy and its extension and updating via critical educational scholarship and to argue for its saliency as a context for librarianship and public cultural institutions. I have argued that librarianship has a crisis culture and needs a more vigorous and coherent defense. That project must begin in critique, but the context and framework of critique is not yet complete. Central to the ideas contained in the new public philosophy thesis is the idea of the public sphere. Prior to applying my critical framework to librarianship in five chapters in part 2 of the book, I will first briefly present the public sphere concept as it has been formulated primarily by Jürgen Habermas and will relate the concept to the new public philosophy application in education. The public sphere—and its dismantling—is an important critical concept, and it is vital to the concluding project of the book: providing a coherent intellectual defense of librarianship.

## NOTES

1. Richard Sennett, "The New Capitalism," *Social Research* 64, no. 2 (1997): 161.
2. Sheldon Wolin, "The New Public Philosophy," *Democracy* 1, no. 4 (1981): 23.
3. Wolin, 25, 33.
4. Wolin, 27.
5. Retrospective accounts of the Reagan era confirm Wolin's initial point. The phrase is from Dan Clawson and Mary Ann Clawson, "Reagan or Business? Foundations of the New Conservatism," in *The Structure of Power in America: The Corporate Elite as a Ruling Class,* ed. Michael Schwarz (New York: Holmes & Meier, 1987), 201–17. See also Daniel Yergin and Joseph Stanislaw, *The Commanding Heights: The Battle Between Government and the Marketplace That Is Remaking the Modern World* (New York: Simon & Schuster, 1999) 331–38; and Don Slater and Fran Tonkiss, *Market Society: Markets and Modern Social Theory* (Malden, Mass.: Blackwell, 2001), 137–41.
6. Wolin, 24, 26.
7. Wolin, 28.
8. Wolin, 27–28.
9. Wolin, 28, 34–35.
10. For two very different views see Yergin and Stanislaw, 105–24; and Michael Apple, *Official Knowledge: Democratic Education in a Conservative Age* (New York: Routledge, 1993), 15–43.
11. Gary Nash, *Red, White, and Black: The Peoples of Early America* (Englewood Cliffs, N.J.: Prentice Hall, 1974), 1.
12. Vine Deloria, Jr., in Nash, 2.
13. It is beyond the scope of this book to thoroughly review all of these arguments. Suffice it to say that we are just now recognizing that American history and our intellectual history are characteristic of a fractious "family" arguing about "what disagreements are primary [and] how should the tradition be structured to ensure its

THE NEW PUBLIC PHILOSOPHY

continuation and critical revision." In David Hollinger and Charles Capper, preface to *The American Intellectual Tradition: Volume II 1865 to the Present,* 2nd ed., ed. David Hollinger and Charles Capper (New York: Oxford University Press, 1993), vii.

14. Nina Baym quoted in Joyce Warren, introduction to *Ruth Hall and Other Writings,* by Fanny Fern (New Brunswick, N.J.: Rutgers University Press, 1986), xxxvi.

15. See, for example, Jonathon Katz, ed., *Gay American History* (1976; New York: Harper, 1985); Martin Duberman, "Reclaiming the Gay Past," *Reviews in American History,* 16, no. 4 (1988): 515–25; Martin Duberman, *Stonewall* (New York: Plume, 1994); and Neil Miller, *In Search of Gay America: Women and Men in a Time of Change* (New York: Atlantic Monthly Press, 1989).

16. Stanley Aronowitz and Henry Giroux, *Education Still Under Siege,* 2nd ed. (Westport, Conn.: Bergin & Garvey, 1993), 162–63, 167–68, 195–212.

17. Richard Hofstadter, *The American Political Tradition* (1948; New York: Knopf, 1986), xvi–xvii. Consensus history was seriously questioned in such early works as Barton Bernstein, ed., *Towards a New Past: Dissenting Essays in American History* (New York: Vintage, 1967); and Howard Zinn, *A People's History of the United States* (New York: Harper & Row, 1980).

18. Wolin, 35–36.

19. Carl Boggs, "The Great Retreat: Decline of the Public Sphere in Late Twentieth-Century America," *Theory and Society* 26 (1997): 741–44.

20. Thomas Paine, "Selection from *Common Sense,*" in *The American Intellectual Tradition: Volume I 1630–1865,* 2nd ed., ed. David Hollinger and Charles Capper (New York: Oxford University Press, 1993), 126, 128; and Paine in Robert Downs, *Books That Changed the World* (New York: New American Library, 1956), 37 (emphasis in original).

21. Harvey Kaye in Richard Brosio, *A Radical Democratic Critique of Capitalist Education* (New York: Peter Lang, 1994), 337. The effects of Paine's writings are made clear in Downs, 28–40; and preface, *American Intellectual Tradition: Volume I,* ed. Hollinger and Capper, 121.

22. Brosio, *Radical Democratic,* 345.

23. Frederick Douglass, "What to the Slave Is the Fourth of July?" in *American Intellectual Tradition: Volume I,* ed. Hollinger and Capper, 412 (emphasis in original).

24. Abraham Lincoln, "Speech at Peoria, Illinois," in *American Intellectual Tradition: Volume I,* ed. Hollinger and Capper, 420.

25. Martin Luther King, Jr., "Selection from 'Letter from the Birmingham Jail,'" in *American Intellectual Tradition: Volume II,* ed. Hollinger and Capper, 330.

26. Henry Giroux, "Public Philosophy and the Crisis in Education," *Harvard Educational Review* 54, no. 2 (1984): 186–94. Note: Giroux's radical critique of education did not begin with this publication; see, for example, "Schooling and the Culture of Positivism: Notes on the Death of History," *Educational Theory* 29, no. 4 (1979): 263–84. He cites in this 1984 article an earlier conference paper on "Education and Democratic Citizenship: Toward a New Public Philosophy," by James Giarelli. However, Giarelli did not publish extensively (or influentially) on the topic after that. Giroux's paper on the topic has been extensively cited and he has utilized the public philosophy and democratic/civic public sphere concepts since in many publications. I think that, without a terribly close reading, one can argue that Giroux found a con-

sistent language in the public philosophy and democratic/civic public sphere concepts that he has utilized frequently—even repetitively—up to the present.

27. Giroux, "Public Philosophy," 186–88; see also the single most important of the blue-ribbon and corporate reports, U.S. Department of Education, National Commission on Excellence in Education, *A Nation At Risk: The Imperative for Educational Reform* (Washington, D.C.: U.S. Government Printing Office, 1983).

28. Giroux, "Public Philosophy," 188–89, 191.

29. Giroux, "Public Philosophy," 191.

30. See, for example, Aronowitz and Giroux; Henry Giroux, "Citizenship, Public Philosophy, and the Struggle for Democracy," *Educational Theory* 37, no. 2 (1987): 103–20; Henry Giroux, "Liberal Arts Education and the Struggle for Public Life: Dreaming About Democracy," *South Atlantic Quarterly* 89, no. 1 (1990): 113–38; and Henry Giroux and Peter McLaren, "Teacher Education and the Politics of Engagement: The Case for Democratic Schooling," *Harvard Educational Review* 56, no. 6 (1986): 213–38.

31. Giroux, "Citizenship, Public Philosophy," 112.

32. Giroux and McLaren, 219; see also Henry Giroux, "Education Incorporated?" *Educational Leadership,* October 1998, 12–17; and Henry Giroux, "Schools for Sale: Public Education, Corporate Culture, and the Citizen-Consumer," *Educational Forum* 63 (Winter 1999): 140–49.

33. See Giroux, "Liberal Arts"; Aronowitz and Giroux; Henry Giroux, "Vocationalizing Higher Education: Schooling and the Politics of Corporate Culture," *College Literature* 26, no. 3 (1999): 147–61; Henry Giroux, *Corporate Culture and the Attack on Higher Education and Public Schooling* (Bloomington, Ind.: Phi Delta Kappa, 1999); see also the David Noble series, "Digital Diploma Mills," Part I, 1998, Part II, 1998, Part III, November 1998—all available at <http://www.ucsd.edu/dl.htm>, Part IV, November 1999 distributed on e-mail by pagre@alpha.oac.ucla.edu on 26 November 1999, Part V, June 2001 at <http://www.ucsd.edu/dl/ddm5.htm>; and John Palatella, "Ivory Towers in the Marketplace," *Dissent,* Summer 2001, 70–73.

34. Giroux, *Corporate Culture and the Attack,* 31, 33.

35. Giroux, "Vocationalizing," 148, 158.

36. Giroux, "Public Philosophy," 194.

37. Michael Apple, *Education and Power* (Boston: Routledge & Kegan Paul, 1982). I think a case can be made that (like Giroux) Apple used a more consistent language after the issues were framed in the new public philosophy analysis. In addition to the work that will be summarized in this section, his later work on democratic schools can be characterized within this framework. He has acknowledged the relationship between his work and Giroux's, while noting—as I will—that he seeks to avoid "over-abstractions" and to directly connect to what actually happens in schools. Finally, Apple cites the importance of Giroux's work in keeping "a language of possibility" alive (see the interview with Apple in which he traces the relationships and influences on his work, printed in the appendix of: Apple, *Official Knowledge,* 163–81). He notes many other influences along these lines—especially Gramsci and Friere. The remainder of this section of the chapter will outline his work in some of the specifics of trends Giroux has identified in the new public philosophy framework.

38. Giroux's "Public Philosophy" lists a number of the current reports and then cites three initial critiques—including a parallel one on the new public philosophy in England—on pp. 186–87. He later summarizes the language change in the reports,

noting that they have been "convincingly refuted and need not be argued" again in Giroux and McLaren, p. 217, where he cites Michael Apple, "National Reports and the Construction of Inequality," *British Journal of Sociology of Education* 7, no. 2 (1986): 171–90 (in press at the time).

39. In addition to the list in Giroux's "Public Philosophy," see a similar update in Frank Margonis, "The Cooptation of 'At Risk': Paradoxes of Policy Criticism," *Teachers College Record* 94, no. 2 (1992): 343–64; and Apple, "National Reports."

40. Apple, "National Reports," 174.

41. Michael Apple, "Producing Inequality: Ideology and Economy in the National Reports on Education (AESA R. Freeman Butts Lecture—1986)," *Educational Studies* 18, no. 2 (1987): 201–2; see also Michael Apple, *Teachers and Texts: A Political Economy of Class & Gender Relations in Education* (New York: Routledge, 1986) 128–49.

42. Apple, "Producing Inequality," 203–12.

43. Apple, "Producing Inequality," 216–17. See also Ira Shor, *Culture Wars: School and Society in the Conservative Restoration* (New York: Routledge & Kegan Paul, 1986) on this point. Shor traces the beginnings of this back to the business reaction to the social gains of the 1960s, but he also noted that the "restoration" trends accelerated in with the election of Reagan in 1980. For updated examples, see former Assistant Secretary of Education Chester Finn, "A Nation Still At Risk," in *The State of U.S. Education,* ed. Robert Long (New York: H. W. Wilson, 1991), 44–59; and Myron Lieberman, *Public Education: An Autopsy* (Cambridge, Mass.: Harvard University Press, 1993).

44. Michael Apple, "Redefining Equality: Authoritarian Populism and the Conservative Restoration," *Teachers College Record* 90, no. 2 (1988): 171 (emphasis added).

45. See Apple, "Redefining Equality"; Michael Apple, "Conservative Agendas and Progressive Possibilities: Understanding the Wider Politics of Curriculum and Teaching," *Education and Urban Society* 23, no. 3 (1991): 279–91; and Michael Apple, "Knowledge, Pedagogy, and the Conservative Alliance," *Studies in the Literary Imagination* 31, no. 1 (1998): 5–23.

46. Apple, "Knowledge, Pedagogy," 12, 18–19 (he recounts the case of successful Right-wing pressure to excise all references to racism in the school textbook version of King's "I Have A Dream" speech); see also Michael Apple, "Standards, Subject Matter, and a Romantic Past," *Educational Policy* 15, no. 2 (2001): 323–34; the conservative agenda is summarized succinctly in Michael Apple, *Cultural Politics & Education* (New York: Teachers College Press, 1996), 98–99.

47. Apple, *Teachers and Texts,* 81–105.

48. Apple, *Official Knowledge,* 94; see generally 93–117.

49. Apple, *Official Knowledge,* 94–101; Apple, "Knowledge, Pedagogy," 8–9.

50. Apple, *Official Knowledge,* 93.

51. Beyond the analysis of Whittle's cable television station, Apple has analyzed the role and effects of computers in the classroom and on the framing of information. See *Official Knowledge,* 93–117, 118–42; and *Teachers and Texts,* 150–74.

52. Apple, "Knowledge, Pedagogy," 6.

53. Michael Apple, "Comparing Neo-Liberal Projects and Inequality in Education," *Comparative Education* 37, no. 4 (2001): 409, 412; see also Michael Apple, "Markets, Standards, Teaching, and Teacher Education," *Journal of Teacher Education* 52, no. 3 (2001): 182–96. Both Giroux and Apple have analyzed these trends. The

market as a model for the public schools took real root in the Reagan era calls for "privatization," which continue today. See, for example, Myron Lieberman, *Privatization and Educational Choice* (New York: St. Martin's, 1989) and the reprinted articles on "Restructuring the Schools: Equitable Financing and Choice" in *The State of U.S. Education,* ed. Long, 123–42.

54. Apple, "Comparing Neo-Liberal," 412.

55. Apple, "Comparing Neo-Liberal," 413.

56. Apple, "Knowledge, Pedagogy," 6–7.

57. Apple extensively cites the work of Geoff Whitty on this point. See, for example, Geoff Whitty and Tony Edwards, "School Choice Policies in England and the United States: An Exploration of their Origins and Significance," *Comparative Education* 34, no. 2 (1998): 211–27; Sally Power and Geoff Whitty, "Teaching New Subjects? The Hidden Curriculum of Marketized Education Systems" (American Educational Research Association Annual Meeting, Chicago, March 1997; distributed as ERIC document ED 406 757); Sally Powers, David Halpin, and Geoff Whitty, "Managing the State and the Market: 'New' Education Management in Five Countries," *British Journal of Educational Studies* 45, no. 4 (1997): 342–62.

58. Apple, "Comparing Neo-Liberal." 417, 413–18 generally.

59. Apple, "Comparing Neo-Liberal," 420.

60. Joel Spring, *The American School: 1642–1985* (New York: Longman, 1986).

61. Michael Katz, ed., *Education in American History: Readings on the Social Issues* (New York: Praeger, 1973).

62. See Apple, *Education and Power;* Michael Apple, "Review Article—Bringing the Economy Back into Educational Theory," *Educational Theory* 36, no. 4 (1986): 403–15; and Henry Giroux, *Theory & Resistance in Education: A Pedagogy for the Opposition* (South Hadley, Mass.: Bergin & Garvey, 1983). The leanings toward pessimism and determinism can be found in Clarence Karier, "Liberalism and the Quest for Orderly Change," *Education in American History,* ed. Katz, 303–18; David Cohen and Marvin Lazerson, "Education and the Corporate Order," *Education in American History,* ed. Katz, 318–33; and Colin Greer, "Immigrants, Negroes, and the Public Schools," *Education in American History,* ed. Katz, 284–90.

63. Herbert Kliebard is widely acknowledged as the essential source on this. See his *The Struggle for the American Curriculum* (Boston: Routledge & Kegan Paul, 1986) and his summary in "The Effort to Reconstruct the Modern American Curriculum," in *The Curriculum: Problems, Politics, and Possibilities,* ed. Landon Beyer and Michael Apple (Albany: State University of New York Press, 1988), 19–31. See also Kenneth Teitelbaum, "Contestation and Curriculum: The Efforts of American Socialists," in *The Curriculum,* ed. Beyer and Apple, 32–55; and Apple, "Bringing the Economy Back." This point is made very clearly in the interview in the appendix of Apple, *Official Knowledge,* 163–81. Apple notes that historical conflict *and* historical possibility are a modus operandi of his work.

64. See Michael Apple and James Beane, eds., *Democratic Schools* (Alexandria, Va.: Association for Supervision and Curriculum Development, 1995); Apple, *Teachers and Texts,* 177–205; and Apple, "Conservative Agendas and Progressive Possibilities," 284–90.

65. Katz, vii.

66. Summary from H. W. Button and Eugene Provenzo, *History of Education and Culture in America*, 2d ed. (Englewood Cliffs, N.J.: Prentice Hall, 1989), 93–148.

67. Jefferson called for legislation "to begin a public library and gallery, by laying out a certain sum annually in books, paintings, and statues," in Thomas Jefferson, "Selection from *Notes on the State of Virginia*" in *American Intellectual Tradition: Volume I*, ed. Hollinger and Capper, 171. He also clearly defended taxing for such purposes: "by far the most important bill in our whole code, is that for the diffusion of knowledge among the people," going on to argue that "the tax which will be paid for this purpose, is not more than the thousandth part of what will be paid to kings, priests, and nobles, who will rise up among us if we leave the people in ignorance." In a letter to George Wythe, 13 August 1786, *The Life and Selected Writings of Thomas Jefferson*, ed. Adrienne Koch and William Peden (New York: Modern Library, 1944), 394–95.

68. Timothy Smith, "Immigrant Social Aspirations and American Education, 1880–1930," in *Education in American History*, ed. Katz, 236–50.

69. Leon Litwack, "Education: Separate and Unequal," in *Education in American History*, ed. Katz, 253–66.

70. Maxine Greene, *The Public School & the Private Vision: A Search for America in Education and Literature* (New York: Random House, 1965), 3–4, 166.

71. Barbara Finkelstein quoted in Giroux and McLaren, 217.

72. Apple, "Bringing the Economy Back," 413.

73. Donna Demac, "Hearts and Minds Revisited: The Information Policies of the Reagan Administration," in *The Political Economy of Information*, ed. Vincent Mosco and Janet Wasko (Madison: University of Wisconsin Press, 1988), 141, 137–43 generally; "OMB Circ. A-130 Revision," *Coalition on Government Information Newsletter* 6, no. 2 (April 1992): 1–2; see also Michael Harris, Stan Hannah, and Pamela Harris, *Into the Future: The Foundation of Library and Information Services in the Post-Industrial Era*, 2nd ed. (Greenwich, Conn.: Ablex, 1998), 69–71; and Reprints of speeches given by Wayne Kelly, the Superintendent of Documents, and Robert Oakley, "Documents," *Progressive Librarian* 12/13 (1997): 49–59.

74. Quoted in Carolyn Gray, "The Civic Role of Libraries," in *Critical Approaches to Information Technology in Librarianship: Foundations and Applications*, ed. John Buschman (Westport, Conn.: Greenwood, 1993), 156–57. See also John Buschman and Michael Carbone, "A Critical Inquiry into Librarianship: Applications of the 'New Sociology of Education,'" *Library Quarterly* 61, no. 1 (1991): 15–40.

75. Demac, "Hearts and Minds," 138.

76. Demac, "Hearts and Minds," 142–43.

77. Herbert Schiller and Anita Schiller, "Libraries, Public Access to Information, and Commerce," in *The Political Economy of Information*, ed. Mosco and Wasko, 159–60.

78. Robert Hughes, *Nothing if Not Critical: Selected Essays on Art and Artists* (New York: Penguin, 1992), 22–23, 142.

79. Hughes, 20, generally 3–28, 387–404.

80. Edward Tenner, "'Information Age' at the National Museum of American History," *Technology and Culture* 33, no. 4 (1992): 780–87.

81. Elaine Harger, "The 'Enola Gay' Controversy as a Library Issue," *Progressive Librarian* 10/11 (Winter 1995/96): 60–78.

82. "Gifts That Can Warp a Museum," *New York Times,* 31 May 2001, A26; and Elaine Sciolino, "Smithsonian Is Promised $38 Million, with Strings," *New York Times,* 10 May 2001, A16.

83. Victoria Newhouse, *Towards a New Museum* (New York: Monacelli Press, 1998), 11, 190–92.

# 3

---•••---

# THE PUBLIC SPHERE: ROUNDING OUT THE CONTEXT OF LIBRARIANSHIP

## INTRODUCTION

If public institutions (schools, universities, libraries, museums) are to play a role in recapturing and extending democratic processes and potential, then the idea at the base of that role is the public sphere. Put at its most basic, if these institutions should *not* be thought of primarily in economic terms (in the sphere of the economy), then they must be situated in the public sphere. Henry Giroux clearly utilizes the concept in his critique of the framing of education policy in the new public philosophy. He called for schools not only to be reformed and structured to serve democratic ends but also to be redefined as

public spheres . . . designed to awaken the moral, political, and civic responsibilities of its youth. . . . Such a philosophy would take as its starting point . . . the relationship of schools to the demands of active forms of community life [and] by recognizing the relationship between the public sphere and the state, on the one hand, and the notion of learning and citizenship on the other. The public sphere . . . refers to those arenas of social life . . . where dialogue and critique provide for the cultivation of democratic sentiments and habits.[1]

With his consistent calls for extending democratic possibilities in and through schools, Giroux has equally consistently linked that concept to the public sphere. He has done so in his analyses of higher education and teacher education and in his explorations of citizen and civic education right up to the present:

In the absence of a strong civil society and the imperatives of a strong democratic public sphere, the power of corporate culture . . . appears to respect few boundaries based on self-restraint and those non-commodified, broader human values that are central to a democratic civic culture . . . [E]ducation must be treated as a public good and not merely as a site for commercial investment or for affirming a notion of the private good based exclusively on the fulfillment of individual needs. Reducing higher and public education to the status of a handmaiden of corporate culture works against the critical social imperative of educating citizens who can sustain and develop inclusive democratic public spheres.[2]

Michael Apple has framed the issues similarly. As will be seen in the coming review of this concept, defining curricula in political terms and the consequent discussion of power questions fits the public sphere framework: "from whose perspective are we seeing or reading or hearing?"[3] Apple's emphasis on grassroots activism, community coalitions, and making conscious connections between schools and the actual lives of those in the community and democratic change also fits this framework well. Like Giroux, schools as a democratic public sphere stand in contrast: "political and institutional life are [not] shaped by equitable, active, widespread and fully informed participation [but rather] democracy is increasingly defined as unregulated business maneuvers in a free market economy. Applied to schools, this redefinition has . . . abandon[ed] the broader ideals of public education."[4] Again, Michael Apple has fruitfully explored the specific meanings and structure of schools in the public sphere.

There are two points worth noting here. First, unlike Sheldon Wolin's new public philosophy thesis, Apple and (especially) Giroux are not particularly extending and deepening the public sphere concept but rather usefully applying it to education. Second, in this context, the outline of the public sphere concept in relation to librarianship begins to come into view: the potential of democracy realized through independent institutions—widespread and equitably funded and accessibly organized—connected in a meaningful way to their communities, able to meet the needs of fully informed participants, and acting as a space apart from the commodification that characterizes so much of the culture. Just as I have argued that the new public philosophy critique forms a compelling context in which to view librarianship, I will also argue in parallel that there is an equivalence between the idea of classrooms, schools, and colleges as democratic public spheres and libraries in the public sphere. This concept rounds out the context and critique of librarianship (dismantling the public sphere) and *also* forms the basis of a fundamental and sound intellectual defense of the library field.

## HABERMAS AND THE PUBLIC SPHERE: A SUMMARY

Did Giroux and Apple pull the public sphere concept out of the ether? No. Giroux has most thoroughly applied the concept to education. In seeking to escape the philosophical problems of idealism critiqued thoroughly by the Frankfurt School ("The existence of objective truth that can be known [and there is] a common core of essential knowledge that must be transmitted" in schools[5]) and the pessimism and deterministic views of structuralism (Marxism and the totalized analysis of the Frankfurt School that left no room for some of the *actual* democratic gains made in the history of schooling), Giroux turned to the work of Jürgen Habermas. The connection goes beyond mere similarities in language. Habermas's concept of the public sphere "represents a theoretical grounding [and] both a rallying point and a . . . referent for understanding the nature of the existing society."[6] The historical alternative inherent in the idea of the public sphere represented a valuable "mediating space between the state and private existence . . . rooted in collective self-reflection and discourse [and] under conditions free from domination. As a referent for critique, it calls into question the gap between the promise and the reality of the existing liberal public spheres."[7] From this point Giroux goes on to call for "alternative" or "counter" public spheres—schools and universities among them—and launch his new public philosophy critique, linking the two concepts. (We are quite familiar with this language by now.) Habermas's work is worth reviewing, even if only in truncated form, because it represents a wellspring of ideas and critiques that go beyond the new public philosophy and the educational context in explaining some of the issues at stake when librarianship is reconceptualized in economic terms. I will argue that, in some ways, the public sphere represents an even more compelling concept for librarianship.

Habermas's work is by no means limited to the public sphere, and it is ongoing and evolving: a veritable cottage industry of analysis and conceptual refinement. In this brief and, it must be noted, by definition inadequate review of the concept, I can not represent the full detail and sophistication of the analysis and its refinement. Like the ideas of John Dewey, Habermas's work is often usefully presented in secondary sources and in digested form since the writing and analyses are similarly dense (and in Dewey's case, impenetrable). Also like Dewey, Habermas has spawned a wide variety of interest, investigation, commentary, criticism, and refinement of his ideas—and he continues to absorb that work and refine his own thinking and work in the process. Lastly, Habermas is widely considered to be the heir of the Frankfurt School (or Critical Theory, if you will), but his work is concerned with the philosophical search for an epistemology and a means of analysis that provides for democratic possibilities without Critical Theory's pessimism of total domination of people and societies by capitalism.[8] In so doing, Habermas absorbs *both* radical critique *and* he forms a basis for fundamental democratic possibility. This summary represents the "middle cut" (to use a phrase from whisky making in Scotland) of the public sphere and related concepts, some of its critics and the adjustments Habermas has made along the way.

Habermas roots the idea of the public sphere in an ancient distinction between public and private: it is not the equivalent of the state or of a crowd but rather it is the historically developed "sphere of non-governmental opinion making."[9] He notes that "it is no coincidence that . . . the public sphere and public opinion arose for the first time only in the eighteenth century. . . . Public discussions about the exercise of political power which are both critical in intent and institutionally guaranteed have not always existed—they grew out of a specific phase of bourgeois society and [came about] only as a result of a particular constellation of interests."[10] Previously there had been unity in feudal authority in the unity of public and private, the divine and secular. All were linked ("represented") in the person of the king, but the eighteenth century saw them "broken apart into private elements on the one hand, and into the public on the other."[11] Why and how did this historical change come about?

Society had become a concern of public interest . . . in the wake of the developing market economy [that] had grown beyond the bounds of private domestic authority. The *bourgeois public sphere* could be understood as the sphere of private individuals assembled into a public body, which almost immediately laid claim to the officially regulated "intellectual newspapers" for use against the public authority itself.[12]

It was the development and growth of the market economy—and a bourgeoisie whose interests did not lie with the unregulated powers of feudal authority (tradition)—that led to an altered concept of public authority (that is, based on reason). Power was not to merely be shared with kings through a system of rights but instead "their ideas infiltrated the very principle of the existing power[:] supervision—that very principle which demands the proceedings be made public [and] thus a means of transforming the nature of power, not merely one basis of legitimation exchanged for another."[13] Eighteenth-century constitutions and catalogs of rights "were a perfect image of the liberal model of the public sphere" in that they outlined private autonomy and the limits of state power and were based on the "presuppositions of free commodity exchange."[14] The public sphere was thus constituted, Habermas argued, through communication. "The press [was] an institution of the public itself, effective in the manner of a mediator and intensifier of public discussion, no longer a mere organ for the spreading of news but not yet the medium of a consumer culture."[15] In short, communication (in the press) was the basis of debate, critique, and supervision of state authority through gradually less-fettered information and making the exercise of authority and state decisions more transparent—all principles of democracy. Peter Hohendahl has summarized the ideas well:

The public sphere grew up between the absolutistic state and bourgeois society [and] consists of discoursing private persons who critically negate political norms of the state and its monopoly on interpretation. . . . Public opinion institutionalizes itself with the goal of replacing . . . secret politics with a form . . . that is legitimated by means of rational consensus among participating citizens. This model of the public sphere recognizes neither social differences nor privileges. Equality of the members and general accessibility are assumed, even if they cannot be realized in specific functions.[16]

And further, "in order to secure this position, rational legal principles were instituted which were binding for all."[17] This concept of the new basis of limiting, mediating, and legitimizing authority has launched a thousand explorations, critiques, and explications in dozens of fields. In the process

Habermas has done a great service by reconstructing a largely forgotten concept that still lies, officially, at the foundation of constitutional government: the idea of a sovereign, reasonable public, nourished by the critical reporting of the press and engaged in the mutually enlightening clash of arguments. Over time . . . the "civic forum" arrives at a rational "public opinion" which then both legitimizes and dictates the actions of the government. The dream of a participatory and reasonable public, however much it seems an eighteenth-century chimera, grounds the constitutional state normatively. The appeal to "the public" . . . is more "than a scrap of liberal ideology" that can be discarded without harm to modern democracies.[18]

## COMMUNICATION AS THE BASIS OF THE PUBLIC SPHERE

The concept of constructing the democratic public sphere through communication is based on Habermas's epistemology. He has (fortunately) summarized this idea himself:

*communicative action* . . . is governed by binding consensual norms, which define reciprocal expectations about behavior and which must be understood and recognized by at least two acting subjects. Social norms are enforced through sanctions. Their meaning is objectified in ordinary language communication [and] is grounded only in the . . . mutual understanding of intentions and secured by the general recognition of obligations.[19]

People can *know* (his epistemology) and construct a society around principles of reason, arrived at through communication. For communication to be successful, it must have at base a rational foundation—"validity claims"—that are in turn recognized. Those claims can be argued for-and-against in the process of reaching an understanding, and (to greatly simplify his ideas) the better—more reasoned—argument forms the rational basis of values/social norms agreed upon through communication. These are taken-for-granted assumptions underpinning everyday speech, without which no communication would be possible.[20] It is these binding consensual norms worked out through the process of language, argumentation, and critique (in short, discourse—whether through conversation or writing) that form the basis of law. This "principle of discourse can assume through the medium of law the shape of a principle of democracy."[21] That writers and speakers have their own interests and may further mask those motivations (or power) through language does not mean the values arrived at through the communication process can not be made universal "through their openness to critique and revision . . . brought about by the 'force' of reason"—or in other words, through communicative action.[22] It is these "universalistic foundations of law and morality [that] have . . . been incorporated (in however distorted and incomplete a fashion) into the institutions of constitutional government, into the forms of democratic will formation."[23]

This is a core idea in Habermas's explanation of the historical construction of the democratic public sphere (how did a system of rights and the transparency of law and constitutions arise out of absolute, divine government?). Universal values of democracy, like the rule of law, equality, and human rights, find their ultimate origin in the rational basis of the speech act (communicative action in the construction of binding, consensual norms). The public sphere arose from the particular (economic) interests of the bourgeoisie and was realized through communication (the construction of a literary public sphere), giving rise to the familiar systems of human rights embedded in laws in order to rationalize state authority and make transparent its deliberations and the information upon which decisions are made. As an ideal type, the public sphere is the space in between the state (and its formal systems of voting and legislation) and private life. It is where unfettered and equally available information is gathered and argumentation and critique (i.e., discourse) takes place among people as the basis of rational public will formation: the genesis of legitimacy in laws, decisions, and ethical norms in a democracy. This is important because, as John Durham Peters writes, "Habermas doesn't want to have to don a powdered wig to take the central ideas of democratic life seriously. . . . The revolutionary moments in the late eighteenth century give birth to the democratic ideas which make constitutional states trustworthy and believable—in other words, legitimate."[24] (I will argue at the end of this chapter that this concept has immediate and clear relevance to libraries, which embody much of Habermas's idea of the democratic public sphere.)

## BEYOND THE IDEAL TYPE: PROBLEMS IN THE PUBLIC SPHERE

Habermas's ideas do not exist in an ideal vacuum. It was noted before that this notion encompasses both democratic possibility and critique, and the critique suggests that all is not well in the public sphere. "The success of deliberative politics depend[s] on the institutionalization of the . . . procedures and conditions of communication"[25] and those procedures and conditions have undergone historical change. The bourgeois basis of the public sphere meant that it was based around two concepts: capitalism *and* democracy, and the first has obviated a great deal of the second. With the establishment of formal rights, the press, "relieved of the pressure of its convictions . . . has been able to abandon its polemical position and take advantage of the earning possibilities of a commercial undertaking,"[26] thus undercutting one basic communicative element of the public sphere. Further, as mass democracy developed in the era of nineteenth-century industrial capitalism, it meant that "the public body expanded beyond the bounds of the bourgeoisie [and lost] coherence . . . and a relatively high standard of education." Consequently the public sphere lost much of the aspect of critical democratic discourse and became an arena for competition and conflict among groups "correspond[ing] in a more or less unconcealed manner to the compromise of conflicting private interests."[27] In other words, the public sphere was corrupted by structural changes in the parallel developments of an industrial economy and mass democracy. Lastly, in response to the economic swings (which were highly pronounced in the capitalism of the nineteenth century), there was a permanent "increase in state intervention to stabilize economic growth . . . and correct the dysfunctional tendencies [in the interests of] the private utilization of capital." The public sphere was disintegrating under such pressures.[28]

Habermas notes that "formally democratic government in systems of state-regulated capitalism is subject to a need for legitimation."[29] Why? The purpose of state intervention is not to more equally distribute social resources through the social welfare system. Rather, these policies essentially represent "government action designed to compensate for the dysfunctions of free exchange [and] a political form of distributing social rewards that guarantees mass loyalty"—the democratic public sphere recast as groups competing for the state's compensatory benefits. Further, "to the extent that practical [political and economic] questions are eliminated, the public realm loses its political function" and must be "depoliticized."[30] The process of depoliticizing the public sphere and legitimating the state and the economy has been primarily accomplished through the media and its "refeudalization" in the form of spectacle, diversion, obfuscation, and misinformation "hollowing out" the public sphere. The media becomes a "court in which prestige is displayed *before* the audience instead of critique developing *in* it" (hence reenacting the traditional feudal display of state authority in the pomp and circumstance surrounding the person of the king).[31] The media thus become part of the process of "administering" the public sphere, concealing contradictions and problems: the "disintegration of the classical public sphere reappear[s] as crises of legitimation and motivation in the realm of the political and sociocultural system [and in] the problem of legitimizing a system primarily interested in stabilizing itself."[32] Because the media have become such a vital core of the economy themselves, like the state they depend on an environment of social and economic stability. Under such circumstances, information is *not* unfettered or uncorrupted or made widely and freely available for the purposes of deliberative democracy. Peters writes that "the spectacle of a stupefied TV audience worries us because it seems a travesty of all the implicit principles of democratic life as we inherit them from the Enlightenment. . . .

Debates about media audiences have such sharp political inflections because we are debating democracy by other means."[33]

Habermas will simply not content himself with a pessimistic, there-is-no-way-out analysis. He is still at base "a believer in the power of conversation." Mass media are ambiguous, contradictory, and "have the Janus face of enlightenment and control," and they contain within them the means for rational and democratic possibility.[34] Communication remains central, and Habermas now more firmly links the private with the public sphere: "the orientation to reaching understanding" in private life provides a basis "for communication among strangers [and in] branches of the public sphere that are quite complex." He sees this now in the work of grassroots interest groups and social movements—former banes of the public sphere—that are rooted in communal and individual experience and response to systemic problems (like the environment and women's and gay rights). Habermas sees them as key in "perceiving and thematising social problems." When these grassroots groups and movements successfully force their way into the chain of communication through protest and highlighting problems and contradictions, they represent democratic communicative success in influencing legislation and public opinion. As such, Habermas notes that the democratic public sphere can still be reconstituted and in the process extended. However, he is always aware that "unrestricted inclusion and equality" does not yet exist, and the mediated nature of entry into the "mass-media dominated public sphere" presents problems to be overcome in realizing and extending democratic possibilities.[35]

## CHALLENGES TO HABERMAS AND THE PUBLIC SPHERE

Needless to say, these ideas have been picked up by not only educational theorists but in media and cultural studies, history, literature, and women's studies among many areas. Needless to say as well, Habermas's concepts have been criticized. To briefly review a few such criticisms, historians seem to have essentially nitpicked at the specificity of time and place that Habermas identified as the emerging point of the public sphere and to note that other public spheres can be identified as well. In the main, they have utilized his concepts and expanded them by examining colonial American print culture, public celebrations, and formal debate over slavery—thereby reinforcing his main thrust. Habermas's response was to concede the points—that there were many public spheres of differing types and that they were not exclusive to the eighteenth-century bourgeoisie—but he maintains his essential point.[36] That is, the problem is typical of historians in that such particulars fail to explain how democratic government came about in the first place—it had to have developed somewhere at some time. Hohendahl noted that a whole host of challenges arose to Habermas's ideas early on from among liberal theorists, Marxists, and systems theory. He summarizes them by concluding that "even when Habermas has been contradicted, it is usually within the framework of his theory" and many such critiques circle back into rhetoric or the problems of pessimism or idealism.[37]

More seriously, feminists have critiqued the patriarchal beginnings of the public sphere founded as it was in the "equation of 'human being' with 'man', 'property-owner' and 'citizen.'"[38] Habermas's response was to again concede the specific points and to argue that from the beginning he claimed that the public sphere was never fully realized nor made fully inclusive (an integral part of his critique, in fact), but that it contains within itself the seeds of its extension. That is its basic power because democratic inclusion *has* historically expanded, and again, Habermas has provided one of the few theoretical explanations of how. In similarity to earlier criticisms, some of the feminist analyses and criticisms ideas tend to adapt and extend his framework, and even his severest critics concede that the idea is still "successful as a normative ideal."[39] Lastly, postmodernism[40] has posed a fundamental and powerful challenge to Habermas's ideas. His "most telling critics draw inspiration from Foucault: the core of the debate is whether modern ideas of publicity and public life . . . are a rational ideal of political participation or a subtly vicious form of control. Habermas is out to prove that democracy and reason are more than a totalizing dream of discipline." In part, the postmodern challenge shares a common notion with the feminist critique: identity. The debate rages around whether or not the universal human (democratic) values posited by Habermas are "an as yet unredeemed claim or a plot against difference and heterogeneity."[41] I agree with the characterization that postmodernism has become

a convenient way of evading political questions altogether. The work . . . cast[s] great doubt upon the classical notions of truth, reality, meaning and knowledge [as] a passing product of words or signifiers, always shifting and unstable, part-present and part-absent. [H]ow could there be . . . any meaning at all? [A]ll of modern life seems uniformly hollow, sterile, flat [and] empty of human possibilities. Anything that looks or feels like freedom or beauty is really only a screen for more profound enslavement and horror.[42]

Frederic Jameson argues that there are in fact many "postmodernisms," but they share a central feature: "a resonant affirmation, when not an outright celebration, of the market as such."[43] As an intellectual movement, postmodernism has been critiqued as the "cultural skin of late capitalism, [with which] it seems to coexist too easily," characterized by a fundamental "absence of sustained cultural criticism of the status quo."[44] The media and market are seen in postmodernism as a domain of cultural expression and identity formation, not one dominated by the imperative of political and economic legitimation (the "hollowing out" or "refeudalization" of the public sphere). Postmodernists assume an ahistorical pretense that "human feeling, expressiveness, play, sexuality and community have . . . just been invented" and its special darling in this is the media's characteristic decontextualized identity formation.[45] Even when resistance is attempted, there is no philosophical foothold to do so. Jean Baudrillard posited consumer culture as a "network of floating signifiers that are inexhaustible in the ability to incite desire." Advertisements "constitute a new language" and the media has constructed a "hyperreality, a world of self-referential signs," ("the code") from which there is no escape: "only death escapes the code."[46] With no basis for knowledge (historical or contemporary) in the airless domination of narrative, and a capitulation to the idea of the media-mediated (or "performative") public and personal identity, postmodernism provides no way out and no means to build democratic community. Nor can it provide any explanations of how democracy, equality before the law, and so forth came to be and have been extended in historical terms. As has been noted, it is "suicidal for embattled minorities to embrace Michel Foucault, let alone Jacques Derrida. The minority view was always that power could be undermined by truth [but] once you read Foucault as saying that truth is simply an effect of power, you've had it."[47] The point, as Habermas and other critics of postmodernism note, is *not* to throw out the postmodern critique of who has been excluded and historically dominated and how, but to retain the epistemological and democratic bases to explain history and extend inclusiveness and justice in the process. Put another way, postmodern epistemology robs not only future possibility but negates the past: "deny that non-context-dependent assertions can be true and you . . . throw out the Nazi gas chambers [and] the American enslavement of Africans. . . . Hobsbawm is right: facts do matter and some facts matter a great deal."[48] One can not transcend historical injustice in a postmodern philosophical context.

## FINALLY, BACK TO LIBRARIES AND THE PUBLIC SPHERE

To come back down from the thin air of the lofty theoretical heights, I think that the public sphere concept has immediate and clear relevance to librarianship. Some of the parallels suggested earlier come further into focus:

- Libraries embody and enact a rational discourse through the organization of collections.

- Librarianship enacts the principle of unfettered information and transparency in concrete ways (collections and services).

- Librarianship enacts the principle of critique and argumentation to rationally arrive at values and conclusions (primarily) through the commitment to balanced collections, preserving them over time, and making a breadth of resources available.

- Librarianship enacts the principle of extending and furthering inclusion in the democratic public sphere through active attempts to make collections and resources reflect historical and current intellectual diversity and in the field's outreach and extension of services to various groups and communities, thus extending the parameters of discourse and affecting the resulting normative conclusions.

- Libraries "act" to verify (or refute) rational validity claims in making current and retrospective organized resources available to check the bases of a thesis, law, book, article, or proposal and thus aiding and continuing the rational communicative process of critique and argumentation.

- Libraries contain within their collections the *potential* for rational critique and individual/community self-realization, thus grounding the communicative process and the possibility to reestablish democratic processes.

I am most certainly not the first to suggest some of the basics of these ideas[49] and will not be the last. I would, however, like to suggest that, in the words of Archibald MacLeish, libraries represent at base an essential "premise of meaning." That is, we (society, the university, the public, the polity) may not be as certain about ends and means as in the past, but libraries remain an "enduring affirmation" that recorded human culture—gathered together and organized to make it accessible—"still speak[s] and still seems to mean."[50] In this sense, librarians are all Habermasians: the mere act of organizing and the purpose of informing are inherent rejections of postmodernist notions and an affirmation of the idea of making rational meaning through communication. Perhaps more than classrooms and schools and universities, libraries *are* the concrete place of the democratic public sphere. To "theorize" the opposite is to end up in a nonsensical and nihilistic dead end (libraries as the embodiment of the Foucauldian "discourse of fear,"[51] for instance). It is interesting to note that two novels in which libraries play central roles confirm these ideas. To keep intellectual inquiry (unfettered information) under control, Umberto Eco's monk/librarian must hide and protect the secret of the library's organization. Without such control, the library becomes a transparent instrument of informing, endangering the security and authority of divinely revealed truths.[52] In James Hynes's parody, the full realization of the culture of postmodernist literary criticism means burning the university's huge research library collections to the ground in an inferno. The preservation of past canons and the systematic organization of text in the library could not be allowed to stand if the ideology of the indeterminacy of truth and texts were to triumph.[53]

To return to the concrete, librarianship *has* historically extended the democratic public sphere within its walls: the flawed democratic bases on which librarianship was founded have been revised, extended, and made more inclusive; the essential purpose of public enlightenment *was* reasonably well-supported by tax and tuition dollars for over 120 years; the Library Bill of Rights has been extended over the years; there have been conscious attempts to reach out to the poor, the disabled, and to better represent the historically underrepresented on our shelves and screens.[54] I agree with Wayne Wiegand's assessment: ours is an incomplete and incompletely realized mission, but for the last fifty years librarianship has supported (sometimes completely alone) a right of access to information and "we want to give [it] away for free [and] insist on serving relatively powerless groups. . . . Librarians have often stood almost alone against the dominant culture in collecting materials [without which] many of the voices of people residing outside the dominant culture would have been lost to posterity." Lastly, our admittedly biased and flawed classification schemes devised over time still "constitute one of the few bridges available to all who use them to help link the separate islands of discourse. . . . Capitalism doesn't necessarily appreciate [all of] this; democracy does."[55]

However, like Habermas's classical formulation of the public sphere, the democratic public sphere of librarianship is in some trouble. The next five chapters will be case studies of some recent and continuing trends, utilizing the contexts just outlined in the first part of the book. Essentially, the coming chapters form a critique of librarianship around the specific analysis that discussion of and decisions about libraries are being made in the context of economic instrumentality (the new public philosophy). Further, the cumulative effect of these decisions has been to dismantle the aspects of the democratic public sphere that have been historically embedded in—and extended through—librarianship. While I have outlined some of those aspects in this concluding section of this chapter, I will highlight more of the specific aspects of the democratic public sphere being dismantled in the next five chapters. This combined context (the new public philosophy and the dismantling of the public sphere) forms a compelling and powerful basis of analysis for librarianship. Like Habermas's ideas, I would argue that it also contains within it the means to overcome our profession's crisis culture and its sense of indeterminacy and form a sound intellectual basis on which to defend librarianship. The concluding chapter will be an initial attempt at this project.

## NOTES

1. Henry Giroux, "Public Philosophy and the Crisis in Education," *Harvard Educational Review* 54, no. 2 (1984): 192.

2. Henry Giroux, *Corporate Culture and the Attack on Higher Education and Public Schooling* (Bloomington, Ind.: Phi Delta Kappa, 1999), 14; see also Henry Giroux and Peter McLaren, "Teacher Education and the Politics of Engagement: The Case for Democratic Schooling," *Harvard Educational Review* 56, no. 6 (1986): 236–37; Henry Giroux, "Citizenship, Public Philosophy, and the Struggle for Democracy," *Educational Theory* 37, no. 2 (1987): 103–20; and Henry Giroux, "Liberal Arts Education and the Struggle for Public Life: Dreaming About Democracy," *South Atlantic Quarterly* 89, no. 1 (1990): 132–34.

3. Michael Apple, "Conservative Agendas and Progressive Possibilities: Understanding the Wider Politics of Curriculum and Teaching," *Education and Urban So-*

*ciety* 23, no. 3 (1991): 288; see also Michael Apple and James Beane, eds., *Democratic Schools* (Alexandria, Va.: Association for Supervision and Curriculum Development, 1995).

4. Apple and Beane, 101. Note: Apple has now eschewed Habermas and Critical Theory, calling them "safe," and notes that he finds in the work of Antonio Gramsci a "better, clearer . . . and more democratic kind of politics." In the interview in the appendix of Michael Apple, *Official Knowledge: Democratic Education in a Conservative Age* (New York: Routledge, 1993), 163–81. However, he acknowledges the value of the public sphere idea in Michael Apple, *Education and Power* (Boston: Routledge & Kegan Paul, 1982), 168, 200, and Gramsci's work has been expressly linked with Habermas's in Paul Lakeland, "Preserving the Lifeworld, Restoring the Public Sphere, Renewing Higher Education," *Cross Currents* 43, no. 4 (1993): 488–502.

5. G. Max Wingo, *Philosophies of Education: An Introduction* (Lexington, Mass.: D. C. Heath, 1974), 136.

6. Henry Giroux, *Theory & Resistance in Education: A Pedagogy for the Opposition* (South Hadley, Mass.: Bergin & Garvey, 1983), 116.

7. Giroux, *Theory & Resistance*, 236.

8. See David Held, *Introduction to Critical Theory: Horkheimer to Habermas* (Berkeley: University of California Press, 1980), 249–59; and Peter Hohendahl, "Critical Theory, Public Sphere and Culture. Jürgen Habermas and His Critics," *New German Critique* 16 (Winter 1979): 89–118.

9. Peter Hohendahl, explanatory footnotes in Jürgen Habermas, "The Public Sphere: An Encyclopedia Article (1964)," *New German Critique* 3 (Fall 1974): 49. Another excellent summary and analysis of Habermas's ideas can be found in Craig Calhoun, "Introduction: Habermas and the Public Sphere," in *Habermas and the Public Sphere,* ed. Craig Calhoun (Cambridge, Mass.: MIT Press, 1992), 1–48.

10. Habermas, "The Public Sphere," 50.

11. Habermas, "The Public Sphere," 51; on the concept ("representative publicity") see John Durham Peters, "Distrust of Representation: Habermas on the Public Sphere," *Media, Culture and Society* 15 (1993): 541–71.

12. Habermas, "The Public Sphere," 52 (emphasis in original).

13. Habermas, "The Public Sphere," 52.

14. Habermas, "The Public Sphere," 52–53.

15. Habermas, "The Public Sphere," 53.

16. Hohendahl, "Critical Theory, Public Sphere," 92–93.

17. Peter Hohendahl, "Jürgen Habermas: 'The Public Sphere' (1964)," *New German Critique* 4 (Fall 1974): 46.

18. Peters, 544.

19. Jürgen Habermas, *Toward a Rational Society: Student Protest, Science, and Politics* (Boston: Beacon Press, 1970), 97 (emphasis in original); for the full theory see Jürgen Habermas, *The Theory of Communicative Action,* 2 vols. (Boston: Beacon Press, 1984, 1987). An excellent summary connecting Habermas's epistemology, the public sphere, and his critique of capitalism can be found in Michael Harrington, *The Politics at God's Funeral: The Spiritual Crisis of Western Civilization* (New York: Holt, Rinehart, and Winston, 1983), 249–52.

20. Held, 332–50.

21. Habermas in Kenneth Baynes, "Democracy and the *Rechtsstaat:* Habermas's

*Faktizitat un Geltung*," in *The Cambridge Companion to Habermas,* ed. Stephen White (Cambridge: Cambridge University Press, 1995), 210.

22. Thomas McCarthy, introduction to *The Philosophical Discourse of Modernity,* by Jürgen Habermas (Cambridge, Mass.: MIT Press, 1987), x.

23. Habermas, *Philosophical Discourse,* 113.

24. Peters, 544.

25. Habermas in Baynes, 215.

26. Habermas, "The Public Sphere," 53.

27. Habermas, "The Public Sphere," 54.

28. Held, 263; see Hohendahl, "Critical Theory, Public Sphere" for an exploration of the "disintegration thesis" generally; for a contemporary analysis see Carl Boggs, "The Great Retreat: Decline of the Public Sphere in Late Twentieth-Century America," *Theory and Society* 26 (1997): 741–80.

29. Habermas, *Toward a Rational Society,* 102.

30. Habermas, *Toward a Rational Society,* 102–4; see also Habermas, "The Public Sphere."

31. Peters, 560; see also Boggs, "Great Retreat," and Carl Boggs, "The Myth of Electronic Populism: Talk Radio and the Decline of the Public Sphere," *Democracy & Nature* 5, no. 1 (1999): 65–94.

32. Hohendahl, "Critical Theory, Public Sphere," 109; see Habermas, *Toward a Rational Society,* 119–20; and John Dryzek, "Critical Theory as a Research Paradigm" in *Cambridge Companion,* ed. White, 104–6.

33. Peters, 559. An excellent review of this idea can be found in Frank Webster and Kevin Robins, "Plan and Control: Towards a Cultural History of the Information Society," *Theory and Society* 18 (1989): 338–44; and Barry Sussman, *What Americans Really Think and Why Our Politicians Pay No Attention* (New York: Pantheon, 1988).

34. Peters, 559, 561.

35. Habermas in Michael Welton, "Civil Society and the Public Sphere: Habermas's Recent Learning Theory," *Studies in the Education of Adults,* 33, no. 1 (2001): 20–34; see also Timothy Luke, *Screens of Power: Ideology, Domination, and Resistance in Informational Society* (Urbana: University of Illinois Press, 1989), 214–17.

36. John Brooke, "Reason and Passion in the Public Sphere: Habermas and the Cultural Historians," *Journal of Interdisciplinary History,* 29, no. 1 (1998): 43–67; and Lisa McLaughlin, "Feminism, the Public Sphere, Media, and Democracy," *Media, Culture and Society* 15 (1993): 617–18. For his responses, see Jürgen Habermas, "Further Reflections on the Public Sphere," in *Habermas and the Public Sphere,* ed. Calhoun, 421–61.

37. Hohendahl, "Critical Theory, Public Sphere," 89; see also Peter Hohendahl, "The Public Sphere: Models and Boundaries," *Habermas and the Public Sphere,* ed. Calhoun, 99–108.

38. McLaughlin, 602; see also Pauline Johnson, "Habermas's Search for the Public Sphere," *European Journal of Social Theory* 4, no. 2 (2001): 315–36; and Mark Poster, *What's the Matter with the Internet?* (Minneapolis: University of Minnesota Press, 2001), 179–82.

39. McLaughlin, 618; and Nancy Fraser Peters, "Rethinking the Public Sphere: A Contribution to the Critique of Actually Existing Democracy," in *Habermas and the Public Sphere,* ed. Calhoun, 109–42. These issues are summarized in Nicholas Garnham, "The Media and the Public Sphere," in *Habermas and the Public Sphere,* ed.

Calhoun, 359–60. For his theoretical accommodations to these critiques, see Habermas, "Further Reflections"; also see the discussion in chapter 9.

40. Generally, I take the field as combined and defined in Madan Sarup, *An Introductory Guide to Post-Structuralism and Postmodernism* (Athens: University of Georgia Press, 1989). I cannot review the whole of this debate, and it has already been summarized well in Madan Sarup and Richard Brosio, *A Radical Democratic Critique of Capitalist Education* (New York: Peter Lang, 1994).

41. Peters, 551, 554.

42. Sarup, 104–5. See Habermas's two chapters on Foucault in *Philosophical Discourse*, 238–93.

43. Frederic Jameson in Richard Brosio, *A Radical Democratic Critique of Capitalist Education* (New York: Peter Lang, 1994), 599; see also Stuart Hall, "On Postmodernism and Articulation," *Journal of Communication Inquiry* 10 (1986): 45–60.

44. Brosio, *Radical Democratic Critique*, 594, 599, generally 552–65; see also Boggs, "Great Retreat," 765–68.

45. Marshall Berman in Brosio, *Radical Democratic Critique*, 597. For example, Mark Poster approvingly quotes a scholar who hoped "to reveal the ways in which the sexed and cyborg body have been linked in both the televised and the critical imagination" and who in turn approvingly cites "television shows like 'Peewee's Playhouse,' 'Max Headroom,' and 'Moonlighting' for their transgressive potential." Another essay in the same volume notes that "because all presences online are textual they are also self-evidently performances, and therefore one can be liberated from the concept of authenticity itself, and enter a different ethics and politics, that of performance; and finally, this ethics and politics, in its most prevalent version, is carried out by 'cyborg' or 'hybrid' identities: they are defined not by a fixed monadic individualization but rather by fluidity and interconnection." The author then shortly concedes that "this programme is incomprehensible if not related to poststructuralist traditions" and goes on to discuss theories of "performativity" in which identities such as gender, race, and sexuality can be (re)presented through new media. In (respectively) Mark Poster, "Introduction: Culture and New Media," in *Handbook of New Media,* ed. Leah Lievrouw and Sonia Livingstone (London: Sage, 2002), 483; and Don Slater, "Social Relationships and Identity Online and Offline," in *Handbook of New Media,* ed. Lievrouw and Livingstone, 536–37. This analysis and language has been wittily parodied in a novel by James Hynes, *The Lecturer's Tale* (New York: Picador, 2001), 211–19. Hynes portrays a lecture by a prominent postmodern scholar who is a candidate for a prestigious position in an English department. The talk is on an Elvis movie called *Viva Vietnam* where Elvis "reifies in his own marginalized ethnicities" as a "half-Cajun, half-Cherokee shrimper working the waters off the Mekong Delta." When the objection is raised (by a more traditional member of the English department) that "the movie doesn't exist and it was never actually made, the candidate responds that "whether the text 'exists' . . . in the extremely narrow sense you mean, does not in any way affect my reading of it." He goes on to assert that, through digitization it could—or will soon—exist anyway, and when it then "'exists,' it will be as if *it had always existed*." He launches an attack on the question because it reveals a "privileging of Elvis's materiality [and] is essentialist in the extreme. Elvis is not his body. Elvis is a bricolage, an infinitely mutable assemblage of signifiers. He is a template, the disintegrating negative from which his image may be struck *in all its infinite diversity*." In the ecstasy of his argument (and through the central device of the novel's parody) he goes on to

wet himself on the stage at the denouement of his talk. (To be fair, the novel does parody *all* the opposing camps as viciously competing over textual dominance.)

46. Mark Poster, introduction to *Jean Baudrillard: Selected Writings,* by Jean Baudrillard (Stanford, Calif.: Stanford University Press, 1988), 3–5.

47. Alan Ryan in Alan Sokal and Jean Bricmont, *Fashionable Nonsense: Postmodern Intellectuals' Abuse of Science* (New York: Picador, 1998), 270; see also Richard Brosio, *Philosophical Scaffolding for the Construction of Critical Democratic Education* (New York: Peter Lang, 2000), 29–31; Tony Smith, "Postmodernism: Theory and Politics," *Against the Current,* July/August 1993, 2–5; and Michael Fischer, "Deconstruction: The Revolt Against Gentility," *Democracy* 1, no. 4 (1981): 77–86. Mark Poster does note the ironies of postmodern/poststructural analysis and their neoconservative nature (as does Habermas), but he does so only in his endnotes. He quotes Nancy Miller, who states flatly that "only those who have it can play with not having it," and he cites Elizabeth Fox-Genovese who makes a telling point: "the Western white male elite proclaimed the death of the subject at precisely the moment [when] women and peoples of other races and classes . . . were beginning to challenge" them. In Poster, *What's the Matter,* 70–71, 191. A West Indian scholar makes a similar point:

> The literature of blacks, women of South America and Africa, and so forth, as overtly "political" literature [is] being preempted by a new Western concept which proclaimed that reality does not exist, that everything is relative, and that every text is silent about something. . . . I do resent the fact that this particular orientation is so privileged, and has diverted so many of us from doing the first readings of the literature being written today as well as of past works about which nothing has been written.

Barbara Christian, "The Race for Theory," *Feminist Studies* 14, no. 1 (1988): 73.

48. Sokal and Bricmont, 274–75. They amusingly invite postmodernists to "transgress" the social and linguistic conventions/construction of physics by stepping out of a twenty-first floor window. The more theoretically sophisticated among them will "concede that empirical statements can be objectively true . . . but claim that the theoretical explanations of those empirical statements are more-or-less arbitrary social constructions." In other words, the fall *will* kill or injure you, but we can't really know how we know that, or know for sure that we know it (269).

49. For a summary, see John Buschman, "History and Theory of Information Poverty," in *Poor People and Library Services,* ed. Karen Venturella (Jefferson, N.C.: McFarland, 1998), 16–28; see also, for example, Miriam Braverman, "From Adam Smith to Ronald Reagan: Public Libraries as a Public Good," *Library Journal,* 15 February 1982, 397–401; John Kenneth Galbraith, "Are Public Libraries Against Liberty?" *American Libraries,* September 1979, 482–85; and Martin Fricke, Kay Matheisen, and Don Fallis, "The Ethical Presuppositions Behind the Library Bill of Rights," *Library Quarterly* 70, no. 4 (2000): 468–91.

50. Archibald MacLeish, "The Premise of Meaning," in *American Library Philosophy: An Anthology,* ed. Barbara McCrimmon (Hamden, Conn.: Shoe String Press, 1975), 235. It must be noted here that Nicholson Baker, *Double Fold: Libraries and the Assault on Paper* (New York: Random House, 2001), 138–39, identifies MacLeish as one of the Librarians of Congress "who became distracted by the idea of using the library for military intelligence and war propaganda," and he hired assistants (Luther Evans and Verner Clapp) who were instrumental for a long time in the microfilm and technology bias (and the lack of willingness to build adequate space for collections) at the Library of Congress. These building issues will be further reviewed in chapter 5.

51. Gary Radford and Marie Radford, "Libraries, Librarians, and the Discourse of Fear," *Library Quarterly* 71, no. 3 (2001): 299–29. They note that "the discourse of fear is a universal and totalizing organizing principle that gives the library its place in modern cultural forms and in institutionalized action. . . . The arguments . . . are indeed sobering [and] they seem to suggest a certain powerlessness in the face of all-powerful discursive forms such as the discourse of fear" (323).

52. Umberto Eco, *The Name of the Rose* (New York: Warner, 1983). This particular interpretation comes from Maxine Greene, "Liberal Learning and Teacher Education," in *Excellence in Teacher Education Through the Liberal Arts: Proceedings of the Conference,* ed. Michael Carbone and Ann Wonsiewicz (Allentown, Penn.: Education Department, Muhlenberg College, 1986), 25–26.

53. Hynes.

54. Buschman, 18–20.

55. Wayne Wiegand, "The Structure of Librarianship: Essay on an Information Profession," *Canadian Journal of Information and Library Science* 24, no. 1 (1999): 17–37.

# II

STUDIES IN LIBRARIANSHIP
AND THE DISMANTLING
OF THE PUBLIC SPHERE

# 4

## FOLLOW THE MONEY: LIBRARY FUNDING AND INFORMATION CAPITALISM

### INTRODUCTION

It is an axiom in our culture: if you want to know what is actually going on, you follow the money. The money—where it is going (or not) and how it is discussed (or not) as a policy issue—reveals the new public philosophy at work in the fiscal heart of librarianship. As a working assumption, one should be able to be reasonably confident that librarianship would prosper and grow significantly in the shift to an information society, information economy, the learning society, the "new" economy, and so forth. Much of the policy rhetoric to be reviewed—and librarianship's rhetoric as well—would point to this conclusion. However, libraries have not prospered because the era in which we are trying to fund libraries is one of information capitalism—a term among many which essentially points to the promised social revolutions of post-industrialism (to be realized through information technologies) that have not materialized. This is so because informational and media resources have been absorbed into the broader purposes and structures of the capitalist economy.[1] To adapt Frank Webster's helpful overview, I would suggest that discussions of funding are characterized by the "foundational tenets" of information capitalism:

- The ability to pay is now a major criterion determining provision of high-quality information.
- Provision is made on the basis of private rather than public supply.
- Market criteria are the primary factors in deciding what is made available.

- Competition for funding (as opposed to a steady tax or tuition basis) is coming to be regarded as the appropriate mechanism for organizing the economics of librarianship.

- Commodification of information is the norm.

- Private information vs. public is favored.[2]

Along with Webster, I am certainly not suggesting such an outline as a lock-step explanation of funding in librarianship, but like Webster, I am suggesting that it "now seems unarguable . . . that these principles have spread round the globe at an accelerated pace in recent decades" and they have come to characterize many assumptions in policy discussions about library funding.[3] Following our new public philosophy analysis, information capitalism is the organizing economic theme (what has come to be called the "new" economy) for funding policy discussion. Private (and privatized) information, networks, and technologies take predominance in that framework. Funding—and where monies are allocated—would follow that general pattern.

In its details the funding picture is a jumble—not unlike the pronouncements noted at the beginning of the first chapter. To take the example of public library funding, the *Library Journal* annual survey reported "fiscal challenges" in 1995 with gains in overall resources of 6%. 1997 saw "solid fiscal gains," and yet the report noted that average total budget increases (4.1%) were well *below* the five-year average of operating income increases by almost .75% (or roughly $40–45 million aggregated nationally in case one felt this was a quibble). 1998 saw the *success* of funding "books *and* bytes" with a 4.4% overall increase (still less than the 1995 increase that posed "challenges"). However, in 2000 *Library Journal* worried about public libraries because their fate and the "relative health of the local economy are inextricably linked" in reporting a 4.6% total increase. That same report noted that "many of those same libraries that were so exultant" over their Gates Foundation technology gifts a few years ago "may find themselves in a technocrisis when the . . . grants end and they are left to their own financial devices to maintain" machinery and services. The report on 2001 noted a "double-whammy" on public library budgets: the September 11th attacks and the recession along with a shift in priorities for public funds to public safety and security issues.[4] Such pop analyses closely follow the to-and-fro pronouncements typical of librarianship's crisis culture outlined in chapter 1.

Nor is the pattern atypical in the field, as we see in the library media all the time. Examples over a recent six months include: "State Library Agency and Collection in Minnesota Gutted."[5] "U[niversity of] N[orth] C[arolina]'s 16 Libraries Face Budget Cuts" and "students from Morgan State University . . . staged a sit-in . . . to protest the decision of the Maryland [legislature] to slash $3.1 million in funding slated for a new university library."[6] The Washington State Library faced a proposal of elimination, the Library of Virginia budget was cut 24%, the State Library of Idaho budget was cut 17% and lost all capital monies, and the South Carolina State Library will cut its entire materials budget and seriously curtail supplies, equipment, and travel.[7] Large public library systems' problems hit the news as well: Cincinnati closed five branches in 2002 due to fiscal problems,[8] and the New York Public Library system faced a 10% budget cut in the continuing economic aftermath of September 11th.[9] Perhaps most pitiful, school librarian positions are cut in the fiscal mess of struggling urban school systems like Philadephia.[10] To focus on whether this library or that (or this university library or that, etc.) is doing well is to focus on the epiphenomena of the moment—and again play into our crisis culture. The gyrating prognoses in the *Library Journal* reports veer, contradict, and double back. In other words, they focus on spinning the "hot" news of the moment and help create the resulting reactive culture in our field. A clearer view of library funding can be had by taking a few steps back and looking at the policy framework in which decisions are made and some of the larger patterns in funding which result. Part of the process of gaining perspective is noting the fact that the U.S. economy was growing rapidly over the last decade: from a gross domestic product (GDP) of about $6.47 trillion in 1992 to about $10.15 trillion in 2001—or an expansion in the value of goods and services of about 57% over those years.[11] As we know (since it was trumpeted so much in the media), a good deal of this growth came in the information sector—and it was again not unreasonable to expect librarianship to grow in funding and importance over this period.

## THE POLICY CONTEXT OF SCHOOL LIBRARY FUNDING

Since I am applying the new public philosophy analysis as adapted through the work of critical educational scholars like Michael Apple and Henry Giroux, it is perhaps appropriate to begin the look at policy and funding in school libraries. As one might expect, in tandem with the ideologically based policy reviews and recommendations on schools, there was a similar document for libraries: *Alliance for Excellence: Librarians Respond to A Nation at Risk*, released in 1984. Though meant to apply to libraries generally, school (and public) libraries occupied a central place in the report. Further, it spawned a follow-up report specifically on school (and again, public) libraries and their role in school reform. It is something of a scandal (to me at least) to note that this follow-up took ten years to be funded and came out fifteen years after *Alliance for Excellence*.[12] The follow-up responds to both *Alliance for Excellence* and *A Nation at Risk*, and subsequent policies (like Goals 2000—which continued Reagan-era "reforms" from the first Bush administration through Clinton's). In tandem these two reports form bookends and a consistent language basis for policy discussion, and that language is revealing. Since they have set the tone for both school and public libraries, they are worth reviewing in some detail here.

Keeping in mind that *Alliance for Excellence* was meant as a follow-up to the ideologically charged *A Nation at Risk* (and the many reports issued in its wake), it is not surprising that it follows in lockstep with that initial policy discussion. The beginning of the report sets the tone immediately, announcing that the Information Age "is here to stay. The necessity is for all of us to become acclimatized to it." In echoing *A Nation at Risk*'s call for creating a "Learning Society," the report notes that "books and periodicals will continue to be vital" but clearly indicates that technology is the future: "no longer are you limited to information resources in your town. Entire networks have been created [and] wherever you are, the information of the nation can be brought to you. Clearly, then, your library can be of real service in [bringing about] the Learning Society that will *have* to be brought about if we are to be competent, knowledgeable citizens in the Information Age."[13] The report again echoes *Risk*'s call for a concentration on the "New Basics" (computer literacy along with more English, math, etc.) in libraries' partnering with school reform, and, it must be remembered, that "reform" was strongly linked to intellectual "rearmament" for the coming information economy and global competitiveness. *Alliance*'s language mirror's it:

"Just check out the book" is no longer an adequate charge to the student. The library . . . is designed to do much more. . . . There is a peremptory need in schools . . . for special, ongoing instruction in information finding and utilization skills. . . . Because of the phenomenal explosion of knowledge, because of the value given increasingly to resources other than books, because of the necessity for students to learn how to find and apply information, the library media center should become a magnet. . . . America's future is being eroded by the educational system of the present [but] there is a force at hand . . . which can and must form the backbone for reform and improvement. The school's library media center can be the place where learning for the twenty-first century occurs.[14]

While the economic biases of library "reform" in this report are quite apparent, given this stirring language *Alliance*'s recommendations are startlingly pallid. Essentially, they boil down to policy recommendations on including teaching effective use of information resources (with the phrase "including libraries" tacked on) in curricula, that schools "have quality library services and resources," professional standards (for librarians and school libraries) should be raised and made measurable, and school libraries should be open long hours. Most of the rest of the recommendations are variations on those themes.[15] What is startling in its absence is the mention of *funding*. One looks in vain for a straightforward statement of the need for money in providing the quantity, quality, long hours, and professional standards called for (including in the specific recommendation for libraries to support the professional information needs of teachers with databases and books). There is a palliative statement about librarians with a graduate degree earning a lot less than engineers (and a recommendation that that shouldn't be so), but the report is at best rife with weasel words. The euphemism "resources" (and the assumption of an open question whether or not more are needed) runs throughout: "libraries *may* need better furnishings, or more highly trained staff, or enhanced resources . . . but the house stands." In the end, the argument in favor of libraries is for a *private* good: if they "had to be shut for lack of support, we could wind up paying a fee . . . which would most likely be much more costly or inconvenient."[16] Needless to say, the cost of higher professional standards and continuing education is implied to be the responsibility of the individual librarian: funding is not mentioned.

The follow-up report, titled "Assessment of the Role of School and Public Libraries in Support of Educational Reform: Final Report on the Study," was issued fifteen years later. That fact alone casts some doubt on the sincerity of the clarion calls for improvement, change, and reform in *Alliance*. The study was conducted under contract by a private firm in cooperation with the American Library Association, and the preliminary report essentially implies that the initial recommendations were left fallow until the National Education Goals were formulated in 1990 and not funded until they were passed in 1994.[17] The final result was not particularly worth the wait. The most valuable results (the statistics) are not as informative as the biennial survey done by *School Library Journal* and they again assiduously avoid collecting data on funding.[18] "Assessment" begins by again recalling *A Nation at Risk* and noting that its purpose was to gauge how well libraries "were responding to the country's urgent demands for school improvement" (which was apparently not so urgent) in providing for some very generally stated "needs" in schools, reviewing information and technology capacities, and identifying "successful" library programs as models. Funding was again underplayed throughout, and the role of technology highlighted. "Needs assessment" was the neutral language in which funding was couched—and the overall combination of technology needs easily ranked highest (above materials or staffing), and again there was no outright discussion of funding of the called-for and wished-for training, resources, and time.[19] Further, the report particularly highlighted the Internet: "as [it] grows in size and the amount of information provided, it is becoming increasingly important to school" libraries.[20] One point that does jump out in contrast to *Alliance* is more of a focus on public libraries in cooperatively meeting some or all of the identified needs, perhaps broadening the responsibility for services and materials provision for school students in light of the minimal talk of financing these initiatives in school libraries. In all, the follow-up was a rather limp walk-through of the assumptions laid out in *Alliance*.

The sum total of these policy discussions fits well into the new public philosophy framework: there is an overarching emphasis on creating the conditions necessary for economic renewal through educational reform (the Learning Society) and an open endorsement of the imperatives of an Information Society. Libraries are generally cast as worth supporting as a private (not a public) good and convenience, and technology is acknowledged as the preeminent "flavor" of resource to be featured (that is, funded by existing monies) in moving to that future. There is significant lack of candor about the funds needed to make the recommendations and goals a reality (certainly no mention of federal funds and local public funding is rarely mentioned). There is a further cost shifting among public institutions (public libraries) to share this burden and an assumption that librarians will personally have to bear the cost of further and continuous training. Lastly, the specific value of Internet resources is highlighted. I would argue that these two bookended reports characterize the policy framework of the discussion of funding school libraries and that the new public philosophy convincingly characterizes its economic biases.

## Funding Trends in School Libraries

In light of this policy framework, it should come as no surprise that school library funding has not soared in the intervening years. These expenditures are a notoriously slippery item to track down in national and aggregated terms, as a coauthor and I found.[21] Remarkably, Microsoft's *Encarta Encyclopedia* reports that "school library expenditures on books dropped from a peak of $478 million in 1974 to $266 million in . . . 1992–93. Much of this reduction . . . is the result of costs associated with providing . . . new technologies."[22] Aggregated data are still not reported routinely, but a regular survey does report average expenditures for school libraries and a review of that data supports the general trend just identified. In 1993–94 total expenditures from all fund sources in school libraries was only $15,499/year, rising to $21,740 in 1999–2000. Some details tell more of the story. When technology, audio-visual, and equipment expenditures are added up, it is fairly apparent that books are no longer the major expenditures of school libraries: "in 2000 median per-pupil spending on books was only $8.09, not even enough to pay for the average trade paperback. Moreover, nearly half the librarians surveyed reported that somewhere between 11 to 30 percent of their books were out of date." The large differences between the average total expenditures in 1999–2000 and the median expenditures (almost $7,700 less per year) points to dramatic inequities and differences among schools, communities and regions: a few schools and systems in wealthy communities can afford to spend *much* more, thus skewing the average.[23] It is instructive to note that data gathered in 1985 indicates that average expenditure per pupil for schools in the seventy-fifth percentile then was about the same as the overall average in 1998, and the number of books per pupil was significantly lower. Staffing—a perennial issue in school libraries—has not increased either from the seventy-fifth percentile group in 1985 to 1999. The 1985 survey found a little over one certified full-time equivalent (FTE) staff in school libraries, but in 1999 only 65% of public school libraries and 87% of private school libraries were staffed by a full-time person. In 1999, somewhat over half of those librarians in public school libraries were certified, while under one-third were certified in private school libraries, and there is still a heavy reliance on volunteers.[24] Because, like public libraries and schools systems, the funding health of school libraries is intimately linked to the wealth of their communities, it is a sure bet to assume that the dramatic resource disparities in schools identified by Jonathon Kozol in 1991 continue in the school libraries (and the public libraries of those communities) today.[25]

The sum total of these patterns is a reorientation toward the economic goals of information capitalism—(logically) very much like the new agendas for education. And, while those goals rhetorically cast the field in a larger role in the information society, funding is noticeably absent as a priority—or even a clear area of discussion. As a result, school libraries have not fared terribly well during a time when they could logically have expected to. Finally, the data show a clear advantage for already well-off libraries in already well-off schools, again replicating the patterns and problems that Giroux and Apple identified in enacting the new public philosophy and its problems for democratic, public purposes.

## THE IDEOLOGICAL CONTEXT OF PUBLIC LIBRARY FUNDING

I have already mentioned that public libraries were included within the bookended policy language just reviewed, so I will not repeat that analysis here. This same framework of policy and discussion characterizes the environment of public library funding and it fits within the new public philosophy. The 1999 follow-up study to *Alliance* is worth looking at briefly since it devotes more attention to the role of public libraries. Essentially, pains are taken to cast public libraries in contrast to the evaluations of the adequacy of resources in school libraries in the report. For instance, the role of public libraries in serving children and in the more extensive holdings (again, particularly in children's books) was highlighted. The extra staffing, hours, and particularly the technology was noted, with the projection that by 2000, 88% of all public libraries would have the Internet. Not surprisingly, outreach programs and analyzing the "barriers" between public and school libraries were the primary subject of the last portion of the report.[26] In light of the supposed "crucial" role of librarianship in moving society toward the "new" economy, the consistent lack of candor about funding as a whole speaks volumes. I think a compelling argument can be made that this represents (as I suggested) a backdoor attempt to cost share in seeing goals for libraries through without actually advocating the spending of public money in either school or public libraries.

There are most certainly other policy statements from the 1980s that bear the ideological hallmarks of the new public philosophy. The outline of changes made to information policies in the Reagan era reviewed at the end of the second chapter most certainly formed a framework for public libraries. As we know, the constitutional principle of public access was turned on its head. The 1982 federal "Public/Private Report" was heavily skewed to favor private (electronic) capturing and distribution of government information, baldly arguing that for-profit distribution did not raise barriers based on the ability to pay. Government was assigned a "leadership role" (that is, it was to pay for the research and generation of the information) but not a "management role": "to encourage development by the private sector of information resources, products, and services that will meet the needs of the public. [T]he government [should] not enter the marketplace unless there are clearly defined, compelling reasons for doing so."[27] It is worth noting that these were operating assumptions, not conclusions. The conclusions were forgone once this new public philosophy foundation was laid. In the words of one analysis of the report, "libraries can provide access, as long as it is not too useful to the user," which is to say, not a potential source of profit for the information industry.[28] This is clearly the new public philosophy assumption inherent in the workings of information capitalism at work in a policy document with tremendous influence in librarianship.

There was one more highly significant policy report for libraries in this era, the 1985 report on "The Role of Fees in Supporting Library and Information Services in Public and Academic Libraries."[29] In an earlier analysis, I noted that the report was "an almost textbook breakdown of how . . . libraries have justified the charging of fees. For instance it was noted that 'the 1980s are a period of dramatic change in how public institutions raise and invest financial resources.'" The report cites public utilities and recreation services as positive examples of the application of fees, then defines the purpose of libraries as their relative standing in the market. The vast majority of the report (about 90%) focused on arguments justifying fees and never directly addressed the tradition of free and open access and the discriminatory nature of fees.[30] Also instructive is the parallel between England and the United States and the similar legacies of Thatcherism and Reaganism. It was noted that the ideology driving market-based school reforms in both countries was similar, and now public libraries in England have been recast in the new public philosophy mold as well. Webster has analyzed the 1997 report the *New Library: The People's Network* sponsored by Blair's New Labour government. The project described in the report received priority funding for implementation during a twenty-year era of funding cutbacks. The report operates from the assumption of the death of the book. It is to be replaced by the virtual library, itself part of the government's "much-publicised plans for a 'national grid for learning' which aims, in conjunction with British Telecom, to network schools, colleges, universities and libraries, with the primary goal of promoting lifetime learning"—crucial to maintaining a competitive economic edge as a "knowledge society."[31] To be certain, this ethos (or something like it) has been present in the ideology of public libraries from the start, but the era of the new public philosophy stands in stark ideological contrast: funding comes much easier when the "new" economy agenda is served.

Again, the themes of information capitalism and the private good are easy to identify in the policy frameworks just reviewed. Again, this insight has explanatory power as to the disjunction between the rhetoric of the importance of libraries in the information economy and society and the actual funding patterns for public libraries to be reviewed next.

## Public Library Funding Trends

The funding and expenditure trends in public libraries clearly follow the new public philosophy policy priorities just outlined. Between 1993 and 1998, the National Center for Education Statistics reported that public libraries' total operating income rose about 34% (from the 1993 base of $5 billion) or about 6.8% per year on average. In the main these increases look pretty good. However, funding was very inconsistent from year to year. For example, total operating income was about the same in 1995 and 1996 after an increase of around 11% the previous year, and 1998 saw a very large jump in operating income but, puzzlingly, not in operating expenditures ($6.7 billion vs. $6.2 billion).[32] Overall, public library operating budgets were not keeping pace with materials inflation (particularly serials, which ran at around 8.8% per year during that time). This makes the gains over general inflation (around 2.47% per year during this period) and books (around 2.15% average inflation rate for the various types of books they buy) seem a little less significant. Put another way (and without factoring in cost increases in electronic resources or salaries), *public* tax support for library operating budgets overall during this period was not increasing at the growth rate of our information economy (in which it is claimed we are a vital part and have a vital stake): the period saw an increase of over 50% in "other" support (that is, donations, fines, fees, and other nontax income). Public libraries got a bit smaller slice of a much bigger economic pie—the information sector portion of which was *much* bigger—and in order to retain even that aggregate level of funding, they increasingly turned to private funds and other (entrepreneurial and fee-related) means of raising money.[33] Given the very local, town-by-town decision nature of public library funding, it is not surprising to see the policy framework of information capitalism enacted a bit more slowly in public libraries. Nevertheless, the emergent pattern of these recent years fits well into the critical framework identified.

How was public libraries' money spent? In rough tandem, overall expenditures went up about 24% from 1994–95 to 2000–2001. However, spending on books went up about 7% less during that time, or about 2.8% per year.

Again, it was not consistent from year to year. There were pretty dramatic decreases in expenditures between 1994–95 and the next year in both the overall and book categories. What increased more? Technology. The *Bowker Annual* formerly reported expenditures on databases, and from 1994–95 to 1998–99 that category went up 70%, and it still went up in the year of decreases just noted. However, in the 1999–2000 statistical report, *Bowker* changed the category to "electronic reference" and the category went from just below an aggregate of $20 million the previous year to well over $44 million. If one looks at this redefined technology category, it represents a significant increase in technology investments over the course of seven years.[34] I think the conclusion from a different look at public library technology numbers ("only through fiscal dexterity are libraries able to deliver the latest information technologies to patrons while maintaining the breadth and diversity of their collections") is a bit of a spin on the facts. These technological resources increased in costs well beyond the inflation rate (in some cases fivefold) and over a quarter of the libraries surveyed trimmed materials budgets, hours, and staffing to pay for technology. The issue becomes a little more stark when recent data indicates that the single most common use of American public libraries is not primarily job or skill related but still to borrow materials and use the collections. Likewise English public libraries—and their print collections—remain broadly popular and well used.[35]

The technological bias of information capitalism (enacted in the processes of commodification and privatized information supply) and the new public philosophy agenda of harnessing public institutions toward private, economic ends are clearly at play in the budgeting and spending patterns of public libraries. Again, these fall well within the economic policy frameworks of the governmental reports on libraries.

## FUNDING IDEOLOGIES IN ACADEMIC LIBRARIES

Academic libraries are certainly one of the focuses of the Reagan-era reports previously noted. Both *A Nation At Risk* and *Alliance for Excellence* call for research and standards to be improved in various areas in higher education to prepare conditions for the "new" economy and the "Learning Society." Academic libraries have been most certainly enveloped in the sweep of privatizing government information and the consequent growth of the for-profit information sector that the "Public/Private Report" laid much of the groundwork for, and the "Role of Fees" report specifically identified academic libraries as a site of for-pay information services. These contexts alone would put academic library funding policy firmly in the new public philosophy framework, but there is additional evidence.

Academic library leadership has been at the ideological forefront in arguing for and justifying these changes. The breathless (and inaccurate) literature on the "paperless society" identified by Michael Harris and Stan Hannah came primarily from academic library leadership, and I have previously identified this same professional group as the source of "enthusias[m] about our technological future, or arguments for the inevitability of technological changes."[36] Reviewing the membership of the panels that produced the four Reagan-era reports outlined previously, one sees that higher education representatives are the single largest identifiable group.[37] Michael Winter's study of the sociology of librarianship concluded that these elites are "oriented toward national and international networking trends and frequently remote from the professional concerns and routine organizational problems. [They] are often openly allied with outside interests [and] not surprisingly . . . often lean toward the elite corporate culture that controls telematic technology."[38] One can certainly see all of those leanings in the writings of the prominent library administrator extensively reviewed in the first chapter. However, one does not have to read into his words: he was very much in sync with the ideological shifts of the new public philosophy in the Reagan era. He wrote in 1981 (and was subsequently consistent on this point thereafter): "I do not agree with those libraries who insist as a matter of principle that libraries should never charge fees," concluding that "those charged with the stewardship of libraries should be assured that librarians and businessmen are using electronic technology to give libraries the enhanced capabilities they need to continue to function effectively in the present mode and to make the transition to new and as yet unknown future modes."[39] By 1988, that mode had become the "crucial" need for "libraries to implement entrepreneurially oriented management structures."[40]

Writing from a prominent and influential position, this author typified much of the new public philosophy embedded in the management of academic libraries, and not surprisingly the results have again played out in the overall budgeting and spending patterns of academic libraries. They very much follow the pattern of a policy bias toward funding technology and furthering the agenda of information capitalism—precepts that still form the overall framework of funding and policy decisions in all of librarianship.

## Academic Library Funding

Albert Henderson has done an invaluable service in his review of research library spending. He has documented a general pattern of "siphoning off" resources in higher education away from libraries. While academic research has grown exponentially, "library growth slowed" and increased at only half the rate of research output. The results: a "debasement" of collections and "propped up [inadequate research libraries] by a new industry that procures hundreds of thousands of photocopies from foreign sources." Reviewing U.S. Department of Education statistics, Henderson notes that between 1945 and 1993, libraries lost 15% in spending share, the decline coming primarily after the high-water marks of the 1960s and 1970s. When he looked at specifics, even an elite Ivy League institution saw the library's share of university expenditures decline by 30% during the decade starting from 1979. A landgrant research university's library materials budget bounced up and down and ended up between $3.31 million in 1983 and $2.98 million in 1994. All the while, federal research and development dollars more than tripled during that same time.[41] Henderson basically confirms antiprint and collections bias found in the other spending patterns previously reviewed.

A review of recent academic library funding data meshes with the essential trends in Henderson's findings. Funding allocations to academic libraries increased between 1992 and 1998 by about 27% (on a base of $3.6 billion in 1992), but total volumes held increased by only 17% during that time (on a base of 749 million volumes in 1992). Again, specifics tell a story: between 1994–95 and 2000–2001, overall academic library materials expenditures increased by 57%, while book expenditures increased only 33% during the same period. Along with journal inflation, it was technology spending that skyrocketed: a 29% increase from 1994–95 to 1998–99 (when the "database" category was reconfigured), and then a quantum jump of 380% (when the category was refigured as "electronic reference").[42] Other reviews of academic library funding—and where that funding is allocated and spent—confirm this pattern. One research library quadrupled its percentage of budget spent on electronic resources in three years, another did it in four years, and it is typical for these resources to be paid for from static budgets—which means cutting the additions to the permanent collections in order to pay for them.[43] Henderson identifies another interesting trend where research money is going in academia in his analysis: "soaring increases for administration." He notes that while libraries' share of spending increased 15% in higher education between 1945 and 1992, administration grew 40%, and he further sees significant inroads into library support in the increasing trends of administrators to book high overhead costs to research funds rather than spend it on libraries.[44] Academic libraries' central role in collecting and maintaining resources for intellectual inquiry and debate is being traded off in the pursuit of resources for the "new" economy.

In sum, the broad, overall patterns established in the new public philosophy policy documents reviewed throughout this section have been carried through in all types of libraries. The context of information capitalism (and its related themes) is clearly apparent in the lack of direct discussion of the need for funding, the bias toward the technological and the private, and the reapportioning of resources (and therefore by implication, the purposes) of libraries toward those ends. The new public philosophy has had a direct—if unacknowledged in the field—effect in the ways in which we think we can *legitimately* consider funding priorities, and like the field of education, those priorities have been reshaped through high-level policy reviews with an information capitalism bias. The importance of libraries in an information society and the "new" economy and the actual level of funding that would enable libraries to fulfill their missions with adequate resources of all types and professionals to do the work are revealed when one follows the money and compares it to the rhetoric of the policy reports. Libraries have *not* prospered in the shift to an information society, and librarians "stretch" fewer fiscal resources over more formats, with a tremendous economic and social emphasis on one particular "flavor" of resource.

## THE FULCRUM OF GRANTS AND FUND-RAISING

For more than twenty years, the new public philosophy has exalted the agenda of information capitalism, the private over the public, and the market as the measure of defining public good. During this era public funding has been widely cut or squeezed for libraries.[45] As Michael Apple has written, "such is the power of language manipulation: social commitments for the common good are now made out to be 'public nuisances.'"[46] In a time of tight public monies, libraries are thrown into the funding marketplace: they must look to private and governmental granting agencies for supplemental funding. It is at this point that the ideology of the private foundations—and their influence on government grant programs—becomes important. The history of American private philanthropy is a complex one, but in the main there is a central tendency to reinforce the social and economic patterns of wealth creation and protection.[47] In the twentieth century, that has taken the form of the huge wealth of foundations and their crucial role in policy leadership for public institutions. For instance, the Ford Foundation was a key player in reshaping and directing public education policy in the 1950s and 1960s. After reviewing the foundation's policies and funding patterns, one scholar noted that Ford was fully part of the "educational establishment [having] a powerful impact on the formation of national education policy [and] favor[ing] elite universities in granting funds for the reform of teacher education. [T]he Ford philanthropies [promoted] the use of managerial and technological innovations as solutions to substantive educational problems . . . on the basis of their being cost-efficient. . . . The result was a technocratic approach."[48] Aside from national education policy, corporate and private foundation giving supported the introduction of IQ tests in schools and shaped the direction and function of social science research, to give two other examples.[49] It is into this "market" that librarianship must go in search of funding to supplement or replace increasingly scarce public dollars. In turn, the private foundations' agendas have come to characterize the priorities of fund-raising for libraries, and that "market" is now very much focused on the project of bringing about the "new" economy and furthering the agenda of wealth creation and protection under information capitalism.

## Grantmaking: Private Leadership for Libraries

The only recent private funding source for libraries worth mentioning on a national scale is Bill Gates's donation of $200 million to develop computer resources in low-income and rural libraries and Microsoft's matching pledge of $200 million worth of software. On the face of it, this seems like a pretty difficult program with which to take issue. It has been touted as the biggest thing to hit American libraries since Andrew Carnegie and the resulting net-worked resources as an equalizer for small and isolated libraries. However, it is difficult to overlook two background issues. First, saturating libraries with Microsoft software essentially sows the seeds of future consumers in a setting with a fair amount of credibility. The public libraries *were* free not to utilize Microsoft products, but they forfeited technical training and support if they did so—a key factor for poorer and more isolated libraries. There was a pow-erful built-in incentive for libraries to adopt Microsoft platforms.[50] The sec-ond background issue is Gates's agenda, which is very open. For instance, the educational program of the Gates Foundation assumes that "online courses and virtual schools . . . will change the concept of school in this century" and the Gates Foundation framework for policy is very much in the mold of the old Ford Foundation's for schools: "what are the conditions that must be in place for technology to effectively improve student learning and especially the achievement of at-risk students?" and "how can technology improve productivity in all aspects of district, school, and classroom manage-ment?"[51]

For libraries, Gates himself has also been abundantly clear: he "expects to accomplish his highest goal before he die[s, which is] to put an end to paper and books."[52] Gates is not alone here—he was just easily the biggest in recent years. Library fund-raising as a whole grew 228% in the six years up to 1999, and technology very frequently stood at the center of those efforts. The logic is simple: one asks for money for projects that are deemed marketable and catchy, and the overwhelming hype and public relations surrounding net-worked technologies fits that bill and further makes libraries seem relevant and contemporary. Typically, these efforts grew from initial searches for money to automate catalogs in tight budgetary times, but the meat and po-tatoes of building and expanding library spaces and putting books on the shelves of libraries—the mainstay of such efforts in the past—has become less of a priority of fund-raising in the process.[53] Public libraries in turn frequently use successful grants and fund-raising clout to leverage more tax support (and thus the private funding agenda is furthered with public monies). In the case of academic libraries, they often must compete for budgetary shares within universities (much like a fund-raising process) by allying themselves with well-supported technological projects like distance learning.[54] The policy frame-work of the "new" economy agenda and the new public philosophy is very clear in the funding patterns followed by private foundations.

## Grantmaking: Public Funds

Scholars have noted the governmental interconnections of private foundations and their use of "financial resources and organizational prominence to capture a national policymaking role."[55] Further, federal and state grantmaking agencies have historically not fully utilized their funding to equalize resources (in public education, for example), but rather frequently supported other (economic) priorities.[56] Public granting agencies are historically very much in a follow-the-leader role. A future head of the National Endowment for the Humanities signaled the overall climate change in an essay in 1984, declaring flatly that in the matter of arts funding, demand will always outstrip supply (of funds), so the framework in which to consider funding issues is the mix and balance of the market, public, private, and educational funding.[57] While I am not undertaking a comprehensive review of public grant programs to libraries here, there are not surprisingly strong biases in favor of technological "innovation" of the type that promotes the same agenda of information capitalism within libraries that Gates is so clear about. What follows are three brief examples:

1. The old Library Services and Construction Act, a consistently renewed federal source of funds for library buildings, renovations, collections, and "numerous programs for social, educational and economic betterment"[58] has been revamped in recent years into the Library Services and Technology Act (LSTA). The LSTA's two areas of funding (replacing the former spread of eight areas) makes the focus very clear: "information access through technology" and "information empowerment through special services."[59] Gone now are the areas of funding for buildings and collections—those now must be done entirely locally, without a hope of public funding. Nicholson Baker's review of the systematic preference in federal funding for microfilm, then for digitization of print resources[60] is a clear indication that LSTA continues and intensifies a "new" economy bias in public funding.

2. The U.S. Department of Education funneled about $20 million per year (on average for the program's first five years) into its Technology Opportunities Program, which "gives grants for model projects demonstrating innovative uses of network technology." This relatively small national program makes matching grants to states, local governments, Indian tribes, health care providers, schools, libraries, police departments, and nonprofits on a "highly competitive" basis to bring "the benefits of an advanced national information infrastructure" to the public. In even blunter language, the program description states that these "grants play an important role in realizing the vision of an information society [that] provide[s] economic and social benefits to the nation as a whole."[61]

3. An example from my own institution drives home the point of how thoroughly the policy framework and ideology of information capitalism has penetrated into the government grant process. The music library of my university sought a grant from the Department of Education's (DOE) Fund for the

Improvement of Postsecondary Education (FIPSE) program last year. Of the fourteen Congressional Priorities identified in FIPSE guidelines, more than half directly relate to technological projects, and a number of the remaining items can be interpreted in a technological vein. However, our project was to catalog the remainder of the collection of scores, sound recordings, and music books for the university's online catalog, directly addressing the Congressional Priority encouraging "applications for conversion of library catalogs to electronic formats." A review of the criteria by which proposals were judged found some areas that seemed to be at odds with applications that clearly addressed some of the Priorities. For instance, applications are judged on the basis of "replicability" or providing "new strategies." A meat-and-potatoes grant to finish cataloging valuable retrospective music materials would be downgraded on these accounts (as it was in the first unsuccessful attempt). FIPSE is quite mechanical about the awarding of grants. Scores are allocated for each area of the criteria, and the highest scores get the grants. I made a call to the program's director to see if there was a strategy to address criteria that didn't seem to apply to a legitimate Priority project. She was quite blunt: yes, our project directly addressed one of the priorities Congress set in funding the program, but no, our proposal "didn't stand a chance." The evaluation criteria were skewed to favor particular kinds of Priorities. A project such as ours would automatically get a low score, and areas like "enhanced distance learning" and "demonstration programs to establish a state of the art science and technology program" were the focus of funding.[62]

Government funding programs have consistently followed the leadership examples of private foundations, and the policy framework of economic agendas for public institutions is only thinly disguised, if at all.

## CONCLUSION: FUNDING AND THE PUBLIC SPHERE

So what's the big deal? Technology is ascendant and library funding is following that lead. There are a number of problems with these funding and spending patterns directly related to the public sphere as embodied in libraries. First of all, as an overall trend the funding of *additional* technological resources is *not* being funded with additional resources. It is not as if books and other print outlets have diminished in output, so one portion of a library's mission is being sacrificed to a degree to fund technologies. This is clearly a case where following the money reveals a set of priorities belying the high tone of much of the policy discussions of libraries. These spending and funding patterns are taking place within a framework of deep hostility to taxes— even for a general public good like libraries (or schools). Government must be "reinvented" and we must "do more with less." Basic funding for additional hours, buildings, essential repairs, and maintaining collections comes at a struggle in a time when funding for technology (from a variety of sources) comes much easier. An ideology is being pursued here because the pure logic of the "market" is not being followed (as we can see in public libraries): collections and popular services are cut to move libraries toward networked resources. It is essentially a way to "position" the library *within* the dominant new public philosophy trends. In the process, the public sphere function of libraries subtly but surely changes: from a space for research, reflection, and reading to part of a community's "social capital." One consulting firm "recommended that 'public' be dropped from 'public schools' because its similar use in conjunction with housing, libraries, radio, and assistance programs has come to have negative connotations."[63] Libraries must thus be redefined as part of a community's (or a university's or a school's) economic assets to lure wealthier homeowners or students or businesses. Though libraries are frequently memorialized for their democratic heritage and role in the public sphere, making the funding argument to support the library as a source of democratic inquiry and critique becomes something of a sidelight (or an embarrassment) when "social capital" is at stake.

Secondly, technological, multimedia resources redefine the library as a *place* in the public sphere. For instance, it has been pretty clear for some time that the Internet was *not* going to be a home for free information harnessed to the purposes of democratic debate and information inquiry. Rather, the Internet was rapidly transformed into a commercial space where entertainment is marketed and advertisements are sold.[64] When libraries absorb these media and buy these technologies, they become "entertainment centers," in the words of a widely read article in a national magazine.[65] The ability to research, read, and reflect (that is, for libraries to function as a democratic public sphere) is nonexistent in an institution so conceived. It is like studying at the mall. One moronic library commentary embraced and extended the media/entertainment center analogy even further in drawing a connection between emerging technologies, libraries, and a recent popular movie:

*The Matrix* has started already. If you stick around for a couple dozen years it may even be available at an implant near you. [T]he trend toward multimedia Web design follows the pattern [of the visual presentation of information]. Next we'll need to install sound cards and Web cams on our public access computers. [T]hat Web cam atop your monitor is not only recording your image, it will be able to tell whether you are angry or sad, reading or watching the screen, and more or less what you are doing. . . . I know this has tremendous surveillance implications, but it's not all bad.[66]

There is something of a vicious cycle here: funding is frozen or cut, except for technologically based resources that mesh with the "new" economy. They are given priority in funding because they are "popular" and therefore the library must buy them to get the traffic to justify further (or even continued) funding. The president of the American Library Association inadvertently summarized the reduction and redefinition of libraries' role in the public sphere succinctly in "rebutting" the article on libraries as entertainment cen-

ters: "America's libraries have always been great equalizers [but] faced with
a revolution in information technology, our libraries must keep pace."[67] Bill
Gates's vision to eliminate books and paper does not have to be technically
feasible at all. It only need crowd out permanent print resources in the market
and in the funding priorities of libraries. Tom Mann argues persuasively that
the Internet is designed "to bypass libraries entirely" and at a minimum, he
has identified the intellectual efficacy of full subject cataloging (as opposed
to full text key word searching) and the inherent value of subject (vs. size)
arrangement of books on library shelves—the vast amount of which will never
be digitized because of costs.[68] Libraries diminish the quality of the public
sphere within their walls in the unthinking shift to the entertainment resources and products of the "new" economy. They do not function as a
democratic space apart for inquiry and reflection, and they do not further
rational discourse—or the potential for discourse—when they become an extension of the media entertainment empire in order to "survive."

Finally, there is no question that there is more information available, but
there are fundamental questions about the quality of that information. Webster has noted that "commercial arrangements are substituting for public supply, and commerce is pioneering new informational services." The expansion
of those new resources includes "phenomena as diverse as the sales of tabloid
newspapers and the expansion in numbers of doctoral candidates in universities, subscriptions to cable sports channels and round-the-clock-stock trad-
ing, employment opportunities in advertising and research positions." In
other words, the "information" concept and its growth is not particularly
coherent. Webster's conclusion is that the increasing quantity of information
has in no way translated into quality and is now an intellectual equivalent
of the nutritional value and effects of junk food.[69] For example, Robert
McChesney[70] and Andre Schiffrin among many have identified the degrada-
tion of journalism and publishing in the era of media conglomerates. Schiffrin
writes that it is now almost beyond imagining that NBC once sponsored a
public good in the form of a full symphony orchestra or that Will and Ariel
Durant's *Story of Philosophy* was a bestseller over fifty years ago, a "middle-
brow" book compared to the likes of Steinbeck or Sinclair Lewis when they
were top sellers.[71]

The pipeline of the purported wide and democratic variety of information—the Internet—has often been cast as the saving grace for the public
purpose of libraries. However, Juris Dilevko has summarized a good deal of
research that calls that assumption into question. The Web's nonhierarchical
nature is not borne out when one analyzes the patterns of links that "point
to sites backed by fame, money and power [while] far fewer scattered links
point toward sites posted by the obscure and impoverished."[72] "Push" technology poses serious problems concerning the neutrality of search engines.
Essentially, priority placement of search results is auctioned off: the resulting

"rankings" reflect not relevance but payments. Large media outlets dominate news dissemination on the Web—in the face of claims of a more free alternative information environment. The Web is only friendly to the alternatives that have the money to "push" their resources on to search engines. These same vehicles sell customized advertising space on Web search results screens that then utilize search information to place ads relevant to your search around the results. Lastly, the purchasing of portals "has created a landscape very much like that of traditional television channels." That is, these corporate entry points "make extraordinary efforts to keep the user within the closed loops of their own worlds"—to capture and sell a ready-made market for advertisements and services. She notes that, when libraries consent to this agenda by their embrace of the Web, they have "consented to its assumptions." Those assumptions cast library users as consumers—not citizens or readers or researchers.[73] Finally, Dilevko analyzes some interesting results from a Web-based survey on the federal budget. She found that Web use is dominated by more well-off men. Among this technological demographic there is a radical antitax sentiment, a bias in favor of market and private mechanisms to address social problems, a desire to decrease social regulation of high-status illegal pleasures (heroin and cocaine), and support for technologically based government funding (like space exploration and science research). Political and ethical culture has a fundamentally antipolitical and antipublic sphere bias as it has been technologically mediated in the era of the new public philosophy.[74] Further, that bias jives perfectly with the policy framework and funding/spending patterns of libraries. As Richard Brosio noted, "it seems obvious that the concentration on information instead of knowledge is also useful to a consumer society wherein the putatively sovereign shopper decides upon the attractiveness of products, as if such a choice were an adequate substitute for bona fide democratic participation."[75]

In sum, library funding has been tied to the agenda of the "new" economy through the new public philosophy logic embedded in blue-ribbon panels and government reports. That policy framework has shaped the pattern of overall funding (and increasingly, where and how those funds are acquired) and the manner in which funds are expended in tight times. The agenda and leadership of private foundation giving and public grantmaking closely complements these developments. As a colleague of mine has said many times, budgets are assumptions, values, and priorities written in dollar signs. Those priorities very much parallel those outlined for education (in chapter 2): we are very much in the same boat, subject to the social and fiscal discipline of the "need" to turn every public resource to the service of information capitalism. The results have been inroads into the public sphere embodiment by libraries. Libraries as entertainment centers, as sites of economic (instead of democratic) value, and sites of potential customer identification are weakening libraries' embodiment of the public sphere.

## NOTES

1. For example, see Sue Curry Jansen, "Censorship, Critical Theory, and New Information Technologies: Foundations of Critical Scholarship in Communications," in *Critical Approaches to Information Technology in Librarianship: Foundations and Applications,* ed. John Buschman (Westport, Conn.: Greenwood Press, 1993), 59–81; Vincent Mosco, "Introduction: Information in the Pay-per Society," in *The Political Economy of Information,* ed. Vincent Mosco and Janet Wasko (Madison: University of Wisconsin Press, 1988), 3–26; Dan Schiller, "How to Think About Information," in *The Political Economy of Information,* ed. Mosco and Wasko, 27–43; Kevin Robins and Frank Webster, "Cybernetic Capitalism: Information, Technology, Everyday Life," in *The Political Economy of Information,* ed. Mosco and Wasko, 44–75; Robert McChesney, Ellen Wood, and John Foster, eds., *Capitalism and the Information Age: The Political Economy of the Global Communication Revolution* (New York: Monthly Review Press, 1998); Frank Webster and Kevin Robins, "Plan and Control: Towards a Cultural History of the Information Society," *Theory and Society* 18 (1989): 323–51; Sarah Douglas and Thomas Guback, "Production and Technology in the Communication/Information Revolution," *Media, Culture and Society* 6 (1984): 233–45; David Lyon, "From 'Post-Industrialism' to 'Information Society': A New Social Transformation?" *Sociology* 20, no. 4 (1986): 577–88; Jennifer Slack, "The Information Revolution as Ideology," *Media, Culture and Society* 6 (1984): 247–56; Peter Stearns, "The Idea of Postindustrial Society: Some Problems," *Journal of Social History* 17 (1984): 685–93; and Henry Blanke, "Librarianship and Public Culture in the Age of Information Capitalism," *Journal of Information Ethics* 5 (Fall 1996): 54–69.

2. Frank Webster, "Information: A Sceptical Account," *Advances in Librarianship* 24 (2000): 10. He also makes a strong argument for the essential nonliberatory, capitalist nature of the information "revolution" in this article and in two others: Frank Webster, "Knowledgeability and Democracy in an Information Age," *Library Review* 48, no. 8 (1999): 373–83; and Frank Webster, "The Information Society Revisited," in *Handbook of New Media,* ed. Leah Lievrouw and Sonia Livingstone (London: Sage, 2002), 22–33.

3. Webster, "Information: A Sceptical Account," 11.

4. Evan St. Lifer, Julie Boehning, and Adam Mazmania, "*LJ* News Report: Public Libraries Face Fiscal Challenges," *The Bowker Annual,* 41st ed., ed. Dave Bogart (New Providence, N.J.: R. R. Bowker, 1996), 3–4; Evan St. Lifer, "*LJ* News Report: Public Libraries Post Solid Fiscal Gains," *The Bowker Annual,* 43rd ed., ed. Dave Bogart (New Providence, N.J.: R. R. Bowker, 1998), 3–4; Evan St. Lifer, "*LJ* News Report: Libraries Succeed at Funding Books *and* Bytes," *The Bowker Annual,* 44th ed., ed. Dave Bogart (New Providence, N.J.: R. R. Bowker, 1999), 3; Evan St. Lifer, "*LJ* Budget Report: The Library as Anchor," *The Bowker Annual,* 46th ed., ed. Dave Bogart (New Providence, N.J.: R. R. Bowker, 2001), 406–7; Norman Oder, "*LJ* Budget Report: The New Wariness," *The Bowker Annual,* 47th ed., ed. Dave Bogart (New Providence, N.J.: R. R. Bowker, 2002), 462.

5. Norman Oder, "State Library Agency and Collection in Minnesota Gutted," *Library Journal,* 15 July 2002, 14.

6. Andrew Albanese, "UNC's 16 Libraries Face Budget Cuts," *Library Journal,* 1 May 2002, 17.

7. Norman Oder, "Tough Times for State Libraries as States Face Budget Crunch," *Library Journal,* 15 April 2002, 14–16.

8. "Drop in State Aid Behind Ohio Closings," *Library Journal*, 30 July 2002, <http://www.libraryjournal.com>.

9. Norman Oder, "The New Wariness," *Library Journal*, 15 January 2002, 55–57.

10. "Philly Cuts 16 School Librarians," *School Library Journal*, July 2002, 18.

11. "Gross Domestic Product." *FRED Gross Domestic Product and Components*. Federal Reserve Bank of St. Louis. 25 September 2002, <http://research.stlouisfed.org/fred/data/gdp/gdp>.

12. Christina Dunn, "Assessment of the Role of School and Public Libraries in Support of Educational Reform: Final Report on the Study," *The Bowker Annual*, 45th ed., ed. Dave Bogart (New Providence, N.J.: R. R. Bowker, 2000), 385–406 (a U.S. Department of Education study). A review of early Reagan-era cost/benefit analyses of librarianship (one of which was sponsored by the Public Library Association) can be found in Miriam Braverman, "From Adam Smith to Ronald Reagan: Public Libraries as a Public Good," *Library Journal*, 15 February 1982: 397–401.

13. U.S. Department of Education, Center for Libraries and Education Improvement, *Alliance for Excellence: Librarians Respond to A Nation at Risk*, (Washington, D.C.: U.S. Government Printing Office, 1984), 1–2, 4. It is well worth repeating some of the harsh and loaded language that this report was responding to on behalf of librarianship:

> We have, in effect, been committing an act of unthinking, unilateral educational disarmament.
>
> History is not kind to idlers. . . . We live among determined, well-educated, and strongly motivated competitors. We compete with them for international standing and markets, not only with products but also with the ideas of our laboratories and neighborhood workshops. America's position in the world may once have been reasonably secure with only a few exceptionally well-trained men and women. It is no longer.
>
> In a world of ever-accelerating competition and change in the conditions of the workplace, of ever-greater danger, and of ever-larger opportunities for those prepared to meet them, educational reform should focus on the goal of creating a Learning Society.

U.S. Department of Education, National Commission on Excellence in Education, *A Nation at Risk: The Imperative for Educational Reform* (Washington, D.C.: U.S. Government Printing Office, 1983), 5–6, 13.

14. U.S. Department of Education, *Alliance*, 6–7, 9–10. The "New Basics" are outlined in Department of Education, *A Nation at Risk*, 25–27.

15. U.S. Department of Education, *Alliance*, 11, 13, 16.

16. U.S. Department of Education, *Alliance*, 22, 46 (emphasis added).

17. Christina Dunn, "Assessment of the Role of School and Public Libraries in Support of Educational Reform: A Status Report on the Study," *The Bowker Annual*, 44th ed., ed. Bogart, 440.

18. For example, see Marilyn Miller and Marilyn Shontz, "Expenditures for Resources in School Library Media Centers, 1997–1998: A Region-by-Region Look at Spending and Services," *The Bowker Annual*, 46th ed., ed. Bogart, 447–58 (adapted from *School Library Journal*, November 2000).

19. Dunn, "Assessment: Final Report," 385–86, 394.

20. Dunn, "Assessment: Final Report," 390.

21. Dorothy Warner and John Buschman, "The Internet and Social Activism: *Savage Inequalities* Revisited," *Progressive Librarian* 17 (2002): 44–53.

22. "Library (institution): Funding," *Encarta Encyclopedia,* Standard ed., CD-ROM (Redmond, Wash.: Microsoft, 2002).

23. From Marilyn Miller and Marilyn Shontz, "Expenditures for Resources in School Library Media Centers, 1993–1994: The Race for the School Library Dollar," *The Bowker Annual,* 41st ed., ed. Bogart, 464–65 (reprinted from *School Library Journal,* October 1995); and Marilyn Miller and Marilyn Shontz, "Expenditures for Resources in School Library Media Centers, 1999–2000: New Money, Old Books," *The Bowker Annual,* 47th ed., ed. Bogart, 503–4 (adapted from *School Library Journal,* October 2001).

24. Data from the American Association of School Librarians and the Association for Educational Communications and Technology, *Information Power: Guidelines for School Library Media Programs* (Chicago: American Library Association, 1988), 117–23; Miller and Shontz, "Expenditures 1997–1998: A Region-by-Region Look," *The Bowker Annual,* 46th ed., ed. Bogart, 451; Dunn, "Assessment: Final Report," 387–88.

25. Jonathon Kozol, *Savage Inequalities: Children in America's Schools* (New York: Crown, 1991).

26. Dunn, "Assessment: Final Report," 395–406.

27. National Commission on Libraries and Information Science, *Public Sector/Private Sector Interaction in Providing Information Services* (Washington, D.C.: U.S. Government Printing Office, 1982), x–xi. A good example of this ideology in practice can be found in Kathryn Balint, "Public Laws Owned by the Public? Think Again, Copyright Rulings Show," *San Diego Union-Tribune,* 13 May 2001, A1.

28. Patricia Schuman, "Information Justice," *Library Journal,* 1 June 1982, 1064.

29. National Commission on Libraries and Information Science, "The Role of Fees in Supporting Library and Information Services in Public and Academic Libraries (April 1985)," *The Bowker Annual,* 31st ed., ed. Filomena Simora (New York: R. R. Bowker, 1986), 89–112.

30. John Buschman, "History and Theory of Information Poverty," in *Poor People and Library Services,* ed. Karen Venturella (Jefferson, N.C.: McFarland, 1998), 23; see also William Davis, John Swan, and Sanford Berman, "Three Statements on Fees," in *Alternative Library Literature, 1990/1991,* ed. James Danky and Sanford Berman (Jefferson, N.C.: McFarland, 1992), 127–30. Further justifications for fees can be found in Peter Young, "Changing Information Access Economics: New Roles for Libraries and Librarians," *Information Technology and Libraries,* June 1994, 103–14. Young was the former head of the National Commission on Libraries and Information Science.

31. Webster, "Knowledgeability," 375–77; and Webster, "Information: A Sceptical Account," 5–6. See also Richard Biddiscombe, "The Changing Role of the Information Professional in Support of Learning and Research," *Advances in Librarianship* 23 (2000): 70–71.

32. National Center for Education Statistics, "Highlights of NCES Surveys," *The*

*Bowker Annual,* 41st ed., ed. Bogart, 448; National Center for Education Statistics, "Highlights of NCES Surveys," *The Bowker Annual,* 43rd ed., ed. Bogart, 423; National Center for Education Statistics, "Highlights of NCES Surveys," *The Bowker Annual,* 44th ed., ed. Bogart, 448–49; Adrienne Chute, "National Center for Education Statistics: Library Statistics Program," *The Bowker Annual,* 45th ed., ed. Bogart, 24; National Center for Education Statistics, "Highlights of NCES Surveys," *The Bowker Annual,* 47th ed., ed. Bogart, 443.

33. CPI, serials, hardcover, trade, and mass market paperback average prices from Gay Danelly, "Prices of U.S. and Foreign Published Materials," *The Bowker Annual,* 41st ed., ed. Bogart, 517–27; and Sharon Sullivan, "Prices of U.S. and Foreign Published Materials," *The Bowker Annual,* 47th ed., ed. Bogart, 525–39. Figures for "Other" operating income calculated from National Center for Education Statistics, "Highlights," *The Bowker Annual,* 41st ed., ed. Bogart, 448; and National Center for Education Statistics, "Highlights," *The Bowker Annual,* 47th ed., ed. Bogart, 443.

34. "Library Acquisitions Expenditures, 1994–1995: U.S. Public, Academic, Special, and Government Libraries," *The Bowker Annual,* 41st ed., ed. Bogart, 454–55; "Library Acquisitions Expenditures, 1996–1997: U.S. Public, Academic, Special, and Government Libraries," *The Bowker Annual,* 43rd ed., ed. Bogart, 432–33; "Library Acquisitions Expenditures, 1997–1998: U.S. Public, Academic, Special, and Government Libraries," *The Bowker Annual,* 44th ed., ed. Bogart, 460–61; "Library Acquisitions Expenditures, 1998–1999: U.S. Public, Academic, Special, and Government Libraries," *The Bowker Annual,* 45th ed., ed. Bogart, 418–19; "Library Acquisitions Expenditures, 1999–2000: U.S. Public, Academic, Special, and Government Libraries," *The Bowker Annual,* 46th ed., ed. Bogart, 398–99; and "Library Acquisitions Expenditures, 2000–2001: U.S. Public, Academic, Special, and Government Libraries," *The Bowker Annual,* 47th ed., ed. Bogart, 454–55.

35. St. Lifer, "*LJ* News Report: Libraries Succeed at Funding Books *and* Bytes," *The Bowker Annual,* 44th ed., ed. Bogart, 4–5; "Highlights," *The Bowker Annual,* 44th ed., ed. Bogart, 450; Webster, "Information: A Sceptical Account," 12–13; Webster, "Knowledgeability," 376–77; see also Wayne Wiegand, "Librarians Ignore the Value of Stories," *Chronicle of Higher Education,* 27 October 2000, B20; and "Off to the Library," *Economist,* 12 September 1998, 30. Of course, one need not "rob" materials budgets to pay for technological resources if that priority is built into the process in the first place—printed materials would not be *cut* after allocation but the budget limited before allocation.

36. Michael Harris and Stan Hannah, *Into the Future: The Foundations of Library and Information Services in the Post-Industrial Era,* (Norwood, N.J.: Ablex, 1993), 33–45; and John Buschman, "Taking a Hard Look at Technology and Librarianship: Compliance, Complicity, and the Intellectual Independence of the Profession," *Argus* 23, no. 2 (1994): 17.

37. There were about eighteen academic/academic library representatives, fourteen private business/information sector representatives, and thirty-four others divided among government, professional associations, and nonprofits.

38. Winter in Buschman, "Taking a Hard Look," 17.

39. Richard De Gennaro, *Libraries, Technology, and the Information Marketplace: Selected Papers* (Boston: G. K. Hall, 1987), 63, 69–70.

40. Richard De Gennaro, "Technology and Access in an Enterprise Society," *Library Journal*, 1 October 1988, 43.

41. Albert Henderson, "The Devil and Max Weber in the Research University," *Journal of Information Ethics*, Spring 1999, 20–23.

42. National Center for Education Statistics, "Highlights," *The Bowker Annual*, 41st ed., ed. Bogart, 449–50; National Center for Education Statistics, "Highlights," *The Bowker Annual*, 44th ed., ed. Bogart, 451–52; National Center for Education Statistics, "Highlights," *The Bowker Annual*, 45th ed., ed. Bogart, 411–12; National Center for Education Statistics, "Highlights," *The Bowker Annual*, 47th ed., ed. Bogart, 446; "Library Acquisitions Expenditures, 1994–1995," *The Bowker Annual*, 41st ed., ed. Bogart, 456–57; "Library Acquisitions Expenditures, 1996–1997," *The Bowker Annual*, 43rd ed., ed. Bogart, 434–35; "Library Acquisitions Expenditures, 1997–1998," *The Bowker Annual*, 44th ed., ed. Bogart, 462–63; "Library Acquisitions Expenditures, 1998–1999," *The Bowker Annual*, 45th ed., ed. Bogart, 420–21; "Library Acquisitions Expenditures, 1999–2000," *The Bowker Annual*, 46th ed., ed. Bogart, 400–401; and "Library Acquisitions Expenditures, 2000–2001," *The Bowker Annual*, 47th ed., ed. Bogart, 456–57.

43. Andrew Albanese, "Moving from Books to Bytes," *Library Journal*, 1 September 2001, 52–54; and Scott Carlson, "The Deserted Library," *Chronicle of Higher Education*, 16 November 2001, A35.

44. Henderson, 20–23.

45. As examples of the overall climate, see Don Boroughs, "Bureaucracy Busters: Business Is Teaching Government How to Give Taxpayers More for Their Money," *U.S. News & World Report*, 30 November 1992, 49–52; and Cynthia Wagner, "The Renaissance in Government," *The Futurist*, September–October 1992, 45–46. For other reviews of libraries' overall funding situation, see Patricia Glass Schuman, "Vanishing Act: The Collapse of America's Libraries," *USA Today*, July 1992, 10–12; John Kenneth Galbraith, "Are Public Libraries Against Liberty?" *American Libraries*, September 1979, 482–85; Brian Reynolds, "Public Library Funding: Issues, Trends, and Resources," *Advances in Librarianship* 18 (1994): 159–68; Joel Rutstein, Anna DeMiller, and Elizabeth Fuseler, "Ownership Versus Access: Shifting Perspectives for Libraries," *Advances in Librarianship* 17 (1993): 50–53; and Redmond Kathleen Molz and Phyllis Dain, *Civic Space/Cyberspace: The American Public Library in the Information Age* (Cambridge, Mass.: MIT Press, 1999).

46. Michael Apple and James Beane, eds., *Democratic Schools* (Alexandria, Va.: Association for Supervision and Curriculum Development, 1995), 101.

47. Jacek Tittenbrun, "Ownership of Philanthropic Foundations," *Science & Society* 55, no. 1 (1991): 91–102; Robert Bremner, *American Philanthropy* (Chicago: University of Chicago Press, 1960); Donald Fisher, "American Philanthropy and the Social Sciences: The Reproduction of a Conservative Ideology," in *Philanthropy and Cultural Imperialism: The Foundations at Home and Abroad*, ed. Robert Arnove (Boston: G. K. Hall, 1980), 233–68; David Weischadle, "The Carnegie Corporation and the

Shaping of American Educational Policy," in *Philanthropy and Cultural Imperialism,* ed. Arnove, 363–84; Frank Darknell, "The Carnegie Philanthropy and Private Corporate Influence on Higher Education," in *Philanthropy and Cultural Imperialism,* ed. Arnove, 385–86; and "The Gospel of Wealth," *The Economist,* 30 May 1998, 19–21.

48. Dennis Buss, "The Ford Foundation in Public Education: Emergent Patterns," in *Philanthropy and Cultural Imperialism,* ed. Arnove, 357–58.

49. Fisher; David Gersh, "The Corporate Elite and the Introduction of IQ Testing in American Public Schools," in *The Structure of Power in America: The Corporate Elite as a Ruling Class,* ed. Michael Schwarz (New York: Holmes & Meier, 1987), 163–84; and Peter Seybold, "The Ford Foundation and the Transformation of Political Science," in *The Structure of Power in America,* ed. Schwarz, 185–98.

50. See Katie Hafner, "Gates's Library Gifts Arrive, But with Windows Attached," *New York Times,* 21 February 1999, A1; Renee Olson, "*SLJ* News Report: I Spy—Librarians in the Public Eye," *The Bowker Annual,* 43rd ed., ed. Bogart, 12; Barbara Ford, "American Library Association," *The Bowker Annual,* 43rd ed., ed. Bogart, 150; and Lisa Guernsey, "Corporate Largesse: Philanthropy or Self-Interest?" *Chronicle of Higher Education,* 24 April 1998, A28–29.

51. "Research on Computers and Education: Past Present and Future (Executive Summary)." 2000. Bill & Melinda Gates Foundation. 8 March 2000, <http://www.glf.org/learning/education/executivesummary.htm>. See also William Gates, "Multimedia Technology and Education: Progressive Products and Powerful Promises," *Booklist,* 15 May 1994, 1705.

52. Gates in Richard Flanagan, "The Wonder & Glory of Books," *Waterstone's Books Quarterly* 5 (2002): 34.

53. Robert Wedgeworth, "Donor Relations as Public Relations: Toward a Philosophy of Fund-Raising," *Library Trends* 48, no. 3 (2000): 530–39; Reynolds; Edwin Clay and Patricia Bangs, "Entrepreneurs in the Public Library: Reinventing an Institution," *Library Trends* 48, no. 3 (2000): 606–18; John Bertot, Charles McClure, and Joe Ryan, "Study Shows New Funding Sources Crucial to Technology Services," *American Libraries,* March 2002, 57–59; and Dwight Burlingame, "The Small Library and Fund-Raising for Automation," *Library Hi Tech* 7, no. 2 (1989): 49–52.

54. Terry Collings, "Books, Bytes, & Believers: Seattle's Grassroots Fundraising Campaign," *American Libraries,* September 1998, 40–42; Deborah Jacobs, "Private Funding Ensures Public Support," *American Libraries,* September 1998, 42; Kevin Starr, "The Politics of Success," *Library Administration and Management* 15, no. 3 (2001): 152–54; Reynolds; Joan Hood, "Past, Present, and Future of Library Development (Fund-Raising)," *Advances in Librarianship* 22 (1998): 123–39; Ron Chepesiuk, "Internet College: The Virtual Classroom Challenge," *American Libraries,* March 1998, 52–55; John Buschman and Michael Carbone, "Technocracy, Educational Structures and Libraries: Historical Notes from the United States," *Journal of Education Policy* 11, no. 5 (1996): 561–78; Linda Pratt, "Liberal Education and the Idea of the Postmodern University," *Academe,* November–December 1994, 46–51; Dan Carnevale, "Survey Finds 72% Rise in Number of Distance-Education Programs,"

*Chronicle of Higher Education,* 7 January 2000, A57; Scott Carlson, "Wired to the Hilt: Saint Joseph's University Stakes Its Future on a $30-Million Bet," *Chronicle of Higher Education,* 29 March 2002, A33; and "Ball State Creates Wireless Campus," *Ball State Alumnus,* September 2002, 6.

55. Weischadle, 363.

56. Stephan Michelson, "The Political Economy of Public School Finance," in *Schooling in a Corporate Economy,* ed. Martin Carnoy (New York: David McKay, 1972), 140–74.

57. Sheldon Hackney, "Supply, Demand, and the University," in *Paying for Culture,* ed. Patricia McFate (Beverly Hills, Calif.: Sage, 1984), 74–83.

58. Jean Key Gates, *Introduction to Librarianship,* 2nd ed. (New York: McGraw-Hill, 1976), 126; see also Barbara Weaver, "Federal Funding for Libraries: A State Library Perspective," *The Bowker Annual,* 41st ed., ed. Bogart, 214–15.

59. Weaver, 216.

60. Nicholson Baker, *Double Fold: Libraries and the Assault on Paper* (New York: Random House, 2001).

61. "Program Overview." Technology Opportunities Program, National Telecommunications and Information Administration. 5 January 2000. U.S. Department of Commerce. 8 March 2000, <http://www.ntia.doc.gov/otiahome/tiiap/General. general.html>. See also Ron Southwick, "Scholars Fear Humanities Endowment Is Being Dumbed Down," *Chronicle of Higher Education,* 6 October 2000, A29–A31.

62. Fund for the Improvement of Postsecondary Education, "Professional Priorities Program Review Form (and) Proposal Review Criteria," U.S. Department of Education, 3 August 1999. For this topic generally, see also Southwick.

63. Apple and Beane, 101. See Nancy Kranich, "Libraries Create Social Capital," *Library Journal,* 15 November 2001, 40–41; St. Lifer, "The Library as Anchor," *The Bowker Annual,* 46th ed., ed. Bogart, 406. See Steve Fuller, "A Critical Guide to Knowledge Society Newspeak: Or, How Not to Take the Great Leap Backward," *Current Sociology* 49, no. 4 (2001): 177–201; on the "big government" bias, see Michael Harris, Stan Hannah, and Pamela Harris, *Into the Future: The Foundation of Library and Information Services in the Post-Industrial Era,* 2nd ed. (Greenwich, Conn.: Ablex, 1998), 69–71; Molz and Dain.

64. Robert McChesney, *Rich Media, Poor Democracy: Communication Politics in Dubious Times* (New York: New Press, 1999), 128–35, 171–75; Ronda Hauben, "Privatizing the Internet? A Call to Arms!" *Counterpoise* 2, no. 4 (1998): 5–19; Suzy Shaw, "The Internet as an Entertainment System," *Bulletin of the American Society for Information Science,* October/November 1994, 9–11; Jack Kessler, "International Entertainment on the Internet: Customer Needs-Based Networking," *Bulletin of the American Society for Information Science,* October/November 1994, 12–14.

65. Sallie Tisdale, "Silence, Please," *Harper's,* March 1997, 65–74. The metamorphosis of library buildings, environments, and purposes is explored further in sections of chapters 5, 6, and 8.

66. Michael Schuyler, "A Look at What's on the Horizon," *Computers in Libraries,* January 2001, 62.

67. Mary Somerville, letter to the editor, *Harper's,* June 1997, 4.

68. Thomas Mann, "The Importance of Books, Free Access, and Libraries as Places—and the Dangerous Inadequacy of the Information Science Paradigm," *Journal of Academic Librarianship* 27, no. 4 (2001): 274; Thomas Mann, *The Oxford Guide to Library Research* (New York: Oxford University Press, 1998); and Thomas Mann, "Height Shelving Threat to the Nation's Libraries," in *Alternative Library Literature, 1998/1999: A Biennial Anthology,* ed. Sanford Berman and James Danky (Jefferson, N.C.: McFarland, 2001), 338–57.

69. Webster, "Information: A Sceptical Account," 7, 11; see also Webster, "Knowledgeability"; and Webster, "The Information Society Revisited."

70. McChesney, *Rich Media.*

71. Andre Schiffrin, *The Business of Books* (New York: Verso, 2000), 9–11; and Andre Schiffrin, "Public-Interest Publishing in a World of Conglomerates," in *Alternative Library Literature, 1998/1999: A Biennial Anthology,* ed. Berman and Danky, 237.

72. E. Mendelson in Juris Dilevko, "Why Sally Tisdale is *Really* Upset About the State of Libraries: Socio-Political Implications of Internet Information Sources," *Journal of Information Ethics,* Spring 1999, 40.

73. Dilevko, 40–47; see also David Corn, "Anatomy of a Netscam," *Washington Post,* 7 July 1996, C5.

74. Dilevko, 49–50. A similar point is made about another "democratic" media/medium: talk radio. Both instances point back to Habermas's thesis on the refeudalization of the public sphere. Carl Boggs and Tina Dirmann, "The Myth of Electronic Populism: Talk Radio and the Decline of the Public Sphere," *Democracy & Nature* 5, no. 1 (1999): 65–94.

75. Richard Brosio, "Pixels, Decenteredness, Marketization, Totalism, and Ingmar Bergman's Cry for Help," *Philosophy of Education* (1996), 3 March 2000, <http://www.ed.uiuc.edu/PES/96_docs/brosio.html>.

# 5

## CO-OPTED OR ROLLING OVER? FOLLOW-THE-LEADER LIBRARY MANAGEMENT AND THE NEW PUBLIC PHILOSOPHY

### INTRODUCTION

The literature of library management does not have a new public philosophy subtext. Rather, it is the *text* of that literature: there is no critical distance between economic/business management themes and those in librarianship. Mark Day has extensively reviewed and synthesized library management literature and he finds that it is directly derivative of business management fashions and that "library administrators . . . only follow the ideological super-highways that have been ripped through the management theory jungle."[1] Which is to say, there is very little evidence of skepticism or skillful adaptation (or possible rejection) of business management themes, but there is a pattern of wholesale adoption of dominant fads and fashions. Day has identified the strong links between the assumptions of the broader management literature and its derivative in librarianship. He writes that business management literature defines "core concepts such as the consumer, employee, manager, and professional [and] the basic nature of the . . . environment within which these social roles are enacted. That environment is characterized by . . . 'creative destruction' in which heroic capitalistic entrepreneurs apply innovative technology to continuously reengineer production and create new consumer markets, thereby increasing wealth and promoting progress." This has evolved into "market populism," the assumption that "free market consumer choices not only always result in more rational decisions and better organizational choices, but also produce decisions that are more democratic."[2] Library managers have in turn adopted an Alvin Toffler-like "transformational discourse" that takes "as valid the core argument of th[is] paradigm [to] enhance competitiveness, performance, and productivity as well as improve the quality of working life" and results in the recasting of library users as "customers," the library manager as "entrepreneur," the acceptance of information commodification, and the "imperative" to "reinvent" libraries— all buzzwords that (along with other fashionable terms) consistently appear in librarianship's management literature.[3] Thus does a privatized and economic vision of the public cultural institution of the library come to dominate discussions and assumptions about its future, and thus does information capitalism come to define the purposes of libraries, enacting the new public philosophy?

The jargon of the business moment all appear in the library management literature, as if passing through a frictionless tube after a short delay: total quality management, the learning organization, empowering teams, service quality, network "literacy," transforming the organization, flattening hierarchy, branding and marketing the institution, "informating" work, knowledge management, information consulting, cultivating imagination and organizational creativity, the lifelong learning workforce, and perhaps most insidiously, the library user as "customer" and the resulting "customer service." The language of imperatives abounds: "breathtaking" is often paired with "change" and the literature frequently poses an "adapt or die" metaphor for libraries, again lifting a theme directly from the business literature. Day patches together a humorous sentence consisting of popular management guru titles and slogans that, I would argue, applies to librarianship seamlessly: "we live in a *turbulent age of discontinuity* and *unreason* that requires managers to strive for *excellence* and to become *change masters* who use tools such as the *fifth discipline* of systems thinking, *organizational learning*, business process *reengineering*, and *smart machines* to create the *new organization*, which will be infused with *information* and thereby give us a *competitive advantage*."[4] There is, he notes, an increasing trend toward radical and shrill rhetoric and transformational recommendations in business management literature in response to core cultural contradictions, institutional resistances to change, and the shorter cycles of management fashions.[5] I would argue that this has come to characterize much of the library management literature too, and it has contributed a good deal to the crisis culture identified in the first chapter. Furthermore, this has been going on a *very* long time: the fundamentally different, "turbulent" business environment, the "paperless" and networked society, and the consequent demise of libraries (all themes with innumerable subsequent variations) have been declared and predicted for over a quarter of a century.[6]

There is no requirement for subtle analysis to ferret out the overwhelmingly dominant themes of library management literature. Quite apart from the analyses just noted, even a cursory glance through a few issues of one of the journals that publish these pieces confirms the obvious saliency of the new public philosophy characterization.[7] The core issues of library management need to be reframed. To adapt the ideas of Manfred Stanley, "executives are currently among the most unavailable audiences for reasoned discourse about the nature and obligations of power. [D]iscussions of management take on an unhistorical technocratic veer" when they do not take place within a framework of debate over the proper role of institutions like the library in society. In the end, Stanley notes (like Day) that "management 'theories' after all, are disguised political ideologies" and in a democratic culture, questions of the direction and fate of our public institutions are not—and should not be—the exclusive domain of its managers.[8] If war is too important to be left to the generals, the fate of libraries is too important to be left just to library administrators. The purpose of this chapter is to raise such questions and extend the critical examination of library management through a brief examination of three concepts prominent in its literature: information, postindustrialism, and knowledge management. The chapter will then identify some of the ways in which library management is making the unsound and faddish adaptation of business management ideologies a permanent feature of libraries. The chapter will conclude with a review of the associated problems in light of librarianship's role in the public sphere.

## INTELLECTUAL SLOPPINESS AND LIBRARY MANAGEMENT LITERATURE

The management literature of librarianship is shot through with ill-defined and ill-used concepts, paradigms, and notions that lack coherence. Formed as it is from a shallow understanding and simplistic aping of business management trends, library managers tell "unbelievable stories based upon bad rhetoric using unsupported theories of social change."[9] This literature therefore cannot form an intelligible framework in which to intelligently analyze (let alone guide) the historical mission of libraries in the long run, but that does not necessarily mean that its dominant ideas do not hold sway in the field. It is not necessary to undertake a comprehensive review here since others in the field have done fine work critically analyzing library management themes. In addition to the seminal work of Mark Day in this area, Bernd Frohmann and Tom Mann have pulled apart many of the assumptions of the "information science" framework and its consequences for libraries.[10] My own work has pointed out the utter lack of connection to the longstanding scholarship concerning intellectual and power questions within the agenda of wholesale adoption of information technology.[11] Roma Harris's analyses have correctly put gender issues at the core of library leadership's proposed changes for the profession and clear preferences for technology.[12] And finally, the disastrous management pursuit of technological forms of materials "preservation" has been explored most famously by Nicholson Baker and also by some in the field.[13] In the remainder of this section I wish to incrementally

extend this work by reviewing some questions raised about three key terms/
concepts widely ill-used in the library management literature.

## The Use of "Information"

"Information" is a concept that is shot through the management literature.
Examples abound: "we must focus on the core mission of the profession,
namely, making it possible for people to get information. . . . We should be
willing to sacrifice any organizational model or specific practice in order to
better carry out our mission."[14] One library systems corporate vice president
noted that "information is expanding at an exponential rate [and] the value
of that information is becoming more and more time-sensitive," along the
way declaring that it really doesn't matter what information and services libraries provide—just so long as they do provide it.[15] Information (in a variety
of meanings) was listed in each of five outlined aspects of the future of librarianship in one management review, and library leaders now position their
institutions as equalizers between "the information 'haves' vs. the information 'have nots.'"[16] Library school leaders (egged on by their universities)
have dropped the word "library" from their names and picked up the information moniker, in the words of one hyperventilating article, "like the pri-
mates who escape from subservience to take over the world in *Planet of the
Apes* . . . crawling out from behind their card catalogs to rule the global
datasphere."[17] Clearly, library leaders have an "information paradigm" in
mind (in the words of one early analysis[18]), but there are some problems with
the underlying concept.

Roszak notes that the word itself has become a "godword," something
that means "all good things to all people. Words that come to mean everything may finally mean nothing; yet their very emptiness may allow them to
be filled with a mesmerizing glamour."[19] I would argue that this statement
characterizes much of the library management literature. For example: "the
information networks of today are the railways of yesterday";[20] "organizations
are increasingly viewing information as central to their competitive position
in the marketplace [and] the role and place of these information centers of
tomorrow are undergoing considerable debate";[21] "we can no longer perpetuate romantic myths about the quality of services we provided in the
past. . . . The confluence of increased expectations for customer service and
the accelerated pace of integrating information technologies spurred much
of the recent discussion [of] the reference function";[22] "does the proliferation
of information in electronic form require a new breed of information professional? Yes."[23] Frank Webster notes that 400 different definitions and conceptions of information have been identified in scholarly literature, which
themselves divide between nonsemantic concepts and those that assume the
data has inherent meaning.[24] I count at least five different concepts in the
previous quotes from library managers: information as system or technique,

as economic "matter," as "stuff" to be collected and organized, and as a basis of occupation. One could easily add information as technology/machinery and information as social and economic infrastructure or "fabric" to that short list.

Positioning libraries to survive in the "turbulent" economy and the evolving "information society" is at the core of much of the library management literature.[25] Definitions of an Information Society are elusive. The notion can be broken down into six separate categories according to Webster, based on technology, occupation shifts, economic concepts of information, data flow, and symbolic expansion. For instance, if the uncontroversial fact that there is more information around now means that we have therefore created the Information Society, then it could just as easily be argued that we live in an "automobile society" or an "antibiotic age" since both of those product clusters (among many) have rapidly increased in number and social/environmental/health effects as well. Webster points out that defining and explaining the Information Society by occupational shifts is at odds with the concept of the Information Society as defined by technological innovation and diffusion. The "bundling" of all these concepts under one term both homogenizes extraordinarily different activities and spheres (counting the growth in economic value of "information" vs. analyzing the shift in symbolic communication, for instance) and collapses the meaning of the word itself.[26] He concludes that the notion and use of the language of information and the Information Society is so diffuse as to be of very little help in understanding what is happening in the economy and in communities.[27]

Phil Agre describes our concept of information as captured in stories or a mental model "that builds a bridge between the states of artifacts and meanings in people's lives." He identifies three overarching stories or themes: information processing (information as industrial material); information as the fabric of a perfect society ("masculine transcendentalism"); and information professionalism (organizing and distributing large bodies of data and text).[28] Remarkably, our prominent library administrator quoted earlier in chapter 1 just about manages to weave all three themes into a few (nostalgic) paragraphs:

I am confident that libraries and librarians are going to survive, and that they will continue to . . . carry out their traditional functions—to select, organize, preserve, and provide access to the records of human knowledge *in whatever form they take*. [A]s a young librarian at Harvard . . . using computers and reprography [I wanted] to transform the library. My goal was to combine the library's computer systems and photographic services into a single new department that would be the library's principle vehicle for change. I was convinced that the marriage of these two technologies would give us the tools we needed to bring about a revolution in library operations and services to users.[29]

None of these stories/metaphors are adequate to analyze and plan for the future of libraries Agre notes, but each has a recognizable and persistent place in library management literature. What is missing in those discussions are "key questions such as what information is to be delivered, of what quality, for what purposes and on what terms?"[30] Taking the particular issue of the quality of information, Webster pulls apart the blithe assumption that more information equals a reinvigoration of democracy. To say that as a society we are better (and thus more democratically) informed because sports, soap operas, *Jerry Springer,* and sound bite news are massively available through the media all the time is to "empty . . . the concept of democracy of any notion of seriousness and responsibility. . . . When one looks [at] the USA—which is the direction of all [media]—one cannot but be struck by the low quality of content co-existing with the highest quality technique. [But] sophisticated technique cannot substitute for high-quality content."[31] I would contend that this has also been a problem at the very core of the library management literature: there is virtually no serious questioning or investigation of the validity, permanence, integrity, or value of the information so avidly (and transformationally) funded and piped into libraries. All of the identified intellectual problems with the definition and concept of information are a near-constant presence in library management literature, and what is also present is the sometimes-acknowledged and sometimes-not assumption that the "information" concept of libraries means making them "players" in the information capitalism economy.

## The Public Good and Postindustrial Society

It is not necessary to review the connections made between postindustrialism and the Information Society concepts and its translation into librarianship. Harris and Hannah and others have thoroughly reviewed this linkage and fruitfully analyzed it.[32] The "ceremonial" and breathless rhetoric of an Alvin Toffler or a John Naisbitt (postindustrialism's popularizers) finds a ready and sincerely imitative audience in library managers. Mark Day combed the literature and found postindustrial "reality-transcending visions . . . in which robots run our libraries while we roam the universe embodied as immortal silicon intelligences."[33] I would like to focus on one particular tenet in postindustrialism and how it has been turned on its head by librarianship's leaders. Daniel Bell's original thesis posited a new class of information technocrats in control of the economy. No longer would business cycles and their disruptions be the hallmark of capitalism in a new era of affluence: "if class strife was born of industrial society, a newly differentiated and integrated workforce would issue from post-industrial society."[34] In so theorizing, Bell was nominally against unfettered, free-market capitalism. Laurence Veysey notes Bell's "embrace of technocratic planning and [the] prediction that the dominance of the planners is the inevitable trend of recent history," his contention that the "central conflict is between the economy and the culture" and that culture held the "initiative," and that the old-style capitalism is thus in decline—all point to this conclusion. Though Bell's ideas and writings are contradictory and "slapdash," Veysey identifies him as a "conventional New Deal liberal" who asserts the primacy of the polity, advocates an expansion of the public sector and environmental protection, and worries about corporate power and the need to limit its extension.[35] Postindustrialism and the Information Society were therefore conceived as a planned, rational economic structure *limiting* unfettered market capitalism and solving its historical problems. In Bell's words, we live in "an increasingly communal society wherein public mechanisms rather than the market become the allocators of goods [through] the subordination of economic function to societal goals."[36] Information was most certainly counted as one of those goods to be (at least partially) exempted from the market.

That is the idea that has been turned on its head by library administrators. After initial resistance to the new public philosophy framework of information-as-private-capital,[37] librarianship's leaders have adopted the new paradigm (some with gusto). James Govan was an early and most acute commentator on the ensuing development of "entrepreneurial librarianship," and Mark Day has identified some dominant trends in the library management literature that incorporate "formal economic theories which stress the influence of a market system and that treat all organizations as if they were 'firms' whose primary reason for existence is to lower 'transaction costs.' [Others] are pursuing a more radical strategy of cultural revolution [in libraries] within a strong corporate culture."[38] He notes that the single most-cited work in the library and information science (LIS) literature is a work on information as a commodity, driven by the market. Other closely related authors in his study pursue the business management theme of the "competitive advantage" theory of information. These authors stand alongside widely cited non-LIS manager/authors who act as popularizers of business fashions, which themselves situate libraries firmly in the information capitalism sphere.[39]

Specific examples among librarianship's leaders are not difficult to find. Our prominent library administrator wrote in 1987 that predictions were "that information technology will put libraries out of business. But the evidence is that technology is, in fact, putting libraries into business."[40] Thus the redefinition of library schools to "schools of information" is specifically designed to adapt librarianship's skill base for high-tech business applications.[41] Arnold Hirshon provides us with a near-perfect example of aggressive acquiescence to this concept:

Internet commercialization will change the strategic directions for library customer services. Librarians typically have given away expertise for free. The Internet is creating a new venue for fee-based access and retrieval information services that could provide the necessary capital to continue funding high-cost technology. Ultimately [it] may be what makes libraries more expensive, more lucrative, and, ironically, more customer-service oriented because it will be the marketplace that will determine which services are essential.[42]

The (rightfully deposed) former head of the San Francisco Public Library, Ken Dowlin, bluntly declared that, in building an information infrastructure in the New Main library, "we intend to generate revenue off this pipeline."[43] Perhaps the most alarming management proposal came from one library school dean who decried our "obsession" with the privacy of library records, declaring that we should not delete them but rather use them to demographically sort library users for "competitive opportunity."[44] A twisted version of that very scenario came to pass when Ken Starr subpoenaed the records of two Washington, D.C., bookstores to find what Monica Lewinsky may have purchased or read in his hunt for anything incriminating about President Clinton.[45] However, the relationship between this development and its ramifications for library intellectual values was not a topic of widespread discussion in the library—or library management—literature. Nor was it a cause for reflection concerning our historical missions and the possible tensions with using such records for "competitive advantages" as far as I know.

It is perhaps not surprising that library managers have turned this particular aspect on its head. In a piece reprinted in an early volume on postindustrialism and libraries, Bell asserted the need to nurture creativity and enrich education as seedbeds of theoretical knowledge-workers (and the affluence they will bring) in the Information Society. He noted that "a major political problem will be the post-industrial society's information policy"—meaning the fate of information as a public good or a private resource, subject to the market.[46] Rather than function in the public, social, and communal role in information policy matters (as Bell envisioned), library leaders reached for the status candy embodied in Bell's ascendant economic (knowledge manager and organization) concepts, consistently ignoring the broader meanings of that shift.[47] Likewise, the implications of management theorists who have stressed the uniqueness (and thus the separation) of nonprofit organizations from mainstream management fashions (and the economic bases of their methods) have been widely overlooked in the field.[48] If library administrators have not wholesale transformed libraries into for-profit institutions, they have most certainly made the selective movement of the institution toward that model respectable—and fashionable.

## Knowledge Management

Knowledge management is another concept that runs through much of writing of librarianship's leaders. The essential idea is contained within Bell's ascendant technocratic class of the postindustrial Information Society (just reviewed). Day's literature study confirms the prevalence of the concept[49] and it is very easy to find it embedded within current management literature under disparate terms like "information professional," "information manager," "knowledge specialists," or managers and analysts of the "information component," and sometimes simply in the descriptions of the combination of technical, analytical, and management skills needed to be a "chief information officer," and so forth.[50] Again, the concept has been rather simplistically and crudely utilized, typically as a necessity in order to adapt or transform librarianship. However, a brief review of the work of Steve Fuller illustrates the complexity of the idea and its implications in contrast to its use in library management literature. Fuller breaks knowledge management (a compromise term that coincides with Day's investigation) into three classical orientations: wage, rent, and profit.[51] To greatly simplify his analysis, the wage orientation of knowledge management is most closely associated with information as a public good and the pursuit of academic knowledge. The underlying assumption is that the value of the knowledge managed will not be diminished as it is distributed, used, and shared but rather may increase in social/ economic value. This conception accepts the "unpredictable relation between the effort expended . . . and the ultimate impact of the knowledge produced" and places a high value on upholding standards: "Left to their devices, businesspeople and other professionals may prefer a free market environment, where knowledge claims are made willy-nilly and the consumer is simply told 'Let the buyer beware!'" The valuable *public* role of the academic truth-seeking ethic of wage-orientated knowledge management can not be easily replaced.[52] Librarianship has traditionally fit within the wage orientation of knowledge management—which itself squares nicely with Bell's original notions of the public-good nature of information resources.

The rent orientation of knowledge management is best typified by our concept of intellectual property (as in collecting "rent" by licensing the use of an idea or invention). As it was classically formulated in the eighteenth century, intellectual property was rooted in *new* information and discoveries. Fuller sees a problem in that the concept of this "property" (and the orientation of its knowledge managers) has been radically and recently extended to patenting things that *already* exist (like people's genetic codes or reformulations of public facts like laws). Fuller calls this "an open invitation to privatize public goods or . . . to convert the marketplace of ideas to a feudal regime of 'virtual real estate.'" He concludes that "the most obvious lesson to be drawn . . . is that economistic conceptions of [intellectual property] are bound to support pernicious policies, if they are disembedded from the actual political economies in which they are meant to apply."[53] The rent orientation of knowledge management characterizes the growing emphases on fees and entrepreneurial funding strategies in the library management literature.

The third—profit—orientation of knowledge management is "the most removed from the academic ethos." In this conception, McDonald's is a "smart" knowledge organization in that systems are in place to control variables and squeeze high productivity out of low-skilled and low-paid staff through knowledge management. Universities are "dumb" organizations in their high "human capital" costs, unpredictable variables, and unsure outcomes. Fuller notes that the "intrinsic unpredictability of new knowledge renders a planned increase in innovation close to a logical impossibility." Profit-oriented knowledge managers have a Realpolitik attitude: "there is nothing especially sacrosanct about knowledge that makes it worthy of indefinite promotion [or protection. It] is always the moral equivalent of a necessary evil."[54] This final variation—the profit orientation of knowledge management—represents the "cutting edge" of library management theory and its literature in proposals to completely realign the institutions along the lines of the private, profit-seeking sector.

In concert with Fuller's analysis, I would argue that the rent and profit orientations of knowledge management are clearly ascendant in librarianship. Public goods (like information) are being "demystified" in the current environment (their costs being highlighted in public "debate"—like identifying "wasteful" public spending—and then cut) while public support for the needs of capital (like subsidizing broadcasting and Internet commerce) remain hidden—and funded. He suggests that knowledge management and production "may be capitalism's final frontier," and he points to the increasingly stringent management of nonprofit institutions as evidence. They "have begun to mimic some of the institutional features of profit-oriented corporations" through adopting rent and profit knowledge management orientations—very much like the themes Day has uncovered in library management literature. Finally, Fuller points out that, once the knowledge management paradigm has run its full course, expert systems may well put information workers (like librarians) out of a job. The machinery need not replace humans by *exactly* replicating the work they do but rather by lowering the cost of similar results. In such a case (for instance, of sophisticated medical diagnostic systems), "it is not clear that the human touch is worth the additional cost and hassle for most individuals and most institutions."[55] Given the previous discussions on the new public philosophy and business bases of library management, it is not difficult to see the connections here. The simplistic adaptation of Bell's concept of the postindustrial technocrat (knowledge manager) to libraries by our leadership is not a small matter of professional adaptation and preservation as is often blithely asserted. Fuller's work explicates the underlying orientations and ideologies inherent in adopting this as a metaphor for library management and librarianship, and its dominant orientations are in fundamental conflict with much of our stated values like public information, preservation, and free access. Like the concept of information and postindustrialism, much library management thinking (as embodied in its literature) about knowledge management is a sloppy and shallow adaptation of concepts, requiring more careful thought and study before moving us further into a new public philosophy vision of librarianship.

## BUILDINGS AND COLLECTIONS: SETTING THE NEW PUBLIC PHILOSOPHY IN STONE

The new public philosophy orientation of library management does not exist purely as a discourse: it is used to frame and organize decisions about libraries. There are two areas of management decision that will have long-term (perhaps even permanent) impact on libraries' public role that I would like to briefly review: buildings (new or renovated) and outsourcing selection. In both cases the fashionable management "transformation" rhetoric of the moment *and* the intellectual sloppiness of library management literature is being put into action in substantive, concrete ways: it is making manifest and, at times, literally setting into stone the new public philosophy theme of libraries as economic units. The "digital future" is taken as a fact of the present in plans for both buildings and future collections (and how they are assembled) in the management literature: "librarians may no longer safely identify themselves solely with the *library as a site or collection*";[56] "*a reexamination of where we work* for the near future will require modification of the physical environment [and] libraries must provide innovative new services that exploit the native environment of the virtual workplace";[57] "today the academic library serves a university that . . . is less bricks and mortar and more a system of connections through which data stream constantly";[58] "it is not a given that ownership is less costly [than access, and] if libraries are to take on the role of information brokers . . . they must look beyond their own catalogs and collections."[59]

The Kellogg Foundation produced a widely publicized "research" report on the future of libraries (*Buildings, Books, and Bytes*[60]) that illustrates this theme. Michael Gorman reviewed the report and concluded that the dubiously selected library administrators who produced "vision statements" for the future had a clear agenda: "fueled by fear and desire to be with-it, library leaders are telling us that we have to take the trust of decades and the faith and confidence of our users and sacrifice them on the altar of the digital age."[61] Though the public loves libraries and *is* willing to pay for them, their traditional-but-evolving institutional image "makes it difficult politically for libraries to remake their image and surge forward," in the words of the report, and two analyses strongly suggest that some of the polling and focus group data (legitimate in themselves) were badly misinterpreted to point to the "leaders'" conclusions.[62] Nicholson Baker (again) has perhaps captured this bias best in his writing on the preference for defense and intelligence information-retrieval projects among the Library of Congress leadership during the Cold War and the consequent foot-dragging in lobbying Congress for the funds to build buildings and house the library's collections.[63] But it is his battles with Ken Dowlin over the New Main library in San Francisco and his passionate defense of the value of card catalogs that have brought out Baker's clearest explication of this point:

Library administrators (more often male than female) want so keenly to distance themselves from the quasi-clerical associations that surround traditional librarianship [that] they think (rightly), hasn't received the respect it deserves. [T]he lowly, meek-and-mild public librarian as she exists in the popular mind [is an] archetype, [and] though they know it to be cheap and false, [it] shames them. [I]f they are disemburdened . . . they will be able to define themselves as Brokers of Information and Off-Site Hypertextual Retrievalists instead of as shy, bookish people. [L]ibrary managers are encouraged to forget—are eventually frightened even to admit—that their principal job is to keep millions of used books dry and lend them out to people. [W]e may think that the new, more "visionary," more megatrendy definition embraces the old, but in fact it doesn't: [it] allows misguided administrators to work out their hostility toward printed history while the rest of us sleep.[64]

What follows is a brief look at some management trends in buildings and selection of collections (outsourcing) that illustrate the depth of the new public philosophy's hold in library management.

## "Transformative" Buildings

From the outset I want to be clear that many in librarianship (including administrators) still demonstrate a sensible and reasonably clear-headed approach to the future through the process of renovating and building libraries.[65] There must be something about staring a provost or a library/school board in the face—when asking for several millions of dollars to be spent on a project that many people will walk through for many years and evaluate the results (sometimes loudly)—that unnerves some of the purveyors of that normally boundless (and baseless) transformative rhetoric. Of course, it is not the fundamentally sound-but-unspectacular building projects that usefully serve their campuses and communities for many years that are the stuff of media attention. Rather, it is the "transformative" building (and its library administrator) which is the up-and-coming trend receiving notice.

What is such a building? At its most basic, such a project literally builds trendy management shibboleths into the design in the form of a number of priorities. First, there is an emphasis on "rebranding" libraries as cool, "modern, forward-looking places"[66] through dramatic design features like space-eating atria designed as a "highly visible forum for changing exhibitions and receptions" and "sweeping expanses of carpeting, multistory works of public art, . . . and uninterrupted sight lines in almost every direction."[67] There is a conscious effort to make manifest the transformation of the library as "an architectural and symbolic presence" through "the most advanced applications of technology and communication systems for administrative management [and] state-of-the-art infrastructure and distribution systems for digital information."[68] This is done by "announcing" the library's advanced technology by having "reference desks with LED signage strips running along the edge of the desk canopies" and through the grander (and more expensive) building of exteriors such as an "articulate, glass sheathed, sculptural crystal volume that . . . establishes an extended and dynamic 'place marker' [and] a massive presence of information technology . . . combining computer literacy and library literacy."[69] While these are expressed as design concepts, they become manifest in the bricks and mortar of library buildings and the functions they give preference to. Two recent projects will illustrate this point.

There are obvious messages built into the "language" of library buildings (like a high-tech "look"), but there are also more radical "reconceptualizations." The Cerritos, California, Public Library building was conceptualized as an "experience library." What exactly that jargon means is unclear to me, but it appears to have included a number of assumptions about appealing to "customers" with "concierge-style service" by staff and librarians equipped with telephone headsets and digital assistants. The library boasts a "multi-sensory learning environment," conveying "information graphically as well as in words" in "layered" information layouts and manifested by a "futuristic exterior [that] sports a titanium skin that changes color in response to atmospheric conditions" and a giant replica of a T-Rex. It was dubbed "a Club Med for the mind," and makes manifest Sallie Tisdale's critique of the library-as-entertainment-center.[70] The Cerritos Public Library sounds very much like a formulaic upscale description of an information broker "arcade" at a trendy mall, complete with corporate-sounding buzzwords to convey the capturing of its "market" and "target audience."

Seattle Public Library's project turned on a postmodernist course of design with Rem Koolhaas's nano-hip "vision":

The Library represents, maybe with the prison, the last of the uncontested moral universes [and] the moral goodness of the Library is intimately connected to the value of the book. . . . In this scheme, the Electronic is identified with the Barbaric [and] the Library's insistence on one kind of literacy has blinded it to the other emerging forms that increasingly dominate our culture, especially the huge efficiencies (and pleasures) of visual intelligence. Our ambition is to redefine/reinvent the Library as an institution [and] unless the Library transforms itself wholeheartedly into an information storehouse. . . . its unquestioned loyalty to the book will undermine the Library's plausibility at the moment of its potential apotheosis.[71]

(One can almost hear the Foucauldian "discourse of fear" in those statements.) Rather than challenge convention (as he bravely claimed to be doing), Koolhaas simply extended the conformism of shallow management fashion trends. The result was an admixture of deconstructive and transformative management jargon in public discussions of the building, and the consequent privileging of information capitalism's foundational tenets. It all came through in the library's design, built as a spiral, with "roving librarians," certain collections and services housed in retail-like environments (dubbed "the store"), and "interstitial spaces." Koolhaas intended the building to be "iconic" of Seattle's high-tech economy, with money lavished on the exterior again: "the face of the building has given way to a kind of interface . . . in which activities are inserted and hyper-energized [and] all media and the professionalism of their presentation and interaction that will make the library new." The new Seattle Public Library is indeed a postmodern "receptacle for irony and data," as one critic observed.[72] In both of these (and other) projects, the echoes of the new public philosophy and management bias toward viewing libraries as economic instruments within information capitalism are clear. The language may be a kind of architect-hip, but the recasting of library buildings as "hyper-energized" postmodern entertainment centers with librarians as concierges to "customers" (to give a few of the most egregious examples) has a clear information capitalism subtext.

What is frequently *not* "conceptualized" in new library buildings is enough space for collections (let alone growth), while space is lavished on technology and grand interior design spaces and buckets of money further spent on exterior architectural "statements." Numerous high-profile projects have notably "forgotten" or neglected this aspect of libraries (like the new national libraries in France and England), with sometimes disastrous results.[73] One library architect put the issue plainly: "as we reinvent the library for the future [and] the impact of paperless information is felt. . . . we are revising our planning methodology [from] a 20-year projection of rising collections . . . to a 12-year model aimed at zero-growth collections."[74] Tom Mann has called this a "*de facto* abandonment of [our] professional responsibility to preserve knowledge records in stable formats," making permanent the fashionable management trend to assume "everything will soon be electronic." He notes that the "persistence of copyright law alone precludes the possibility" and that output of print materials continues apace.[75] A recent review of some library building projects supports Mann's view: many of the newer universities who grandly announced that they would not build libraries or collections (relying instead on "virtual" libraries) are now (quietly) building them. Those distance learning students we all constantly hear about ("independent learners") are often found using the collections of nearby colleges and large public libraries for their courses.[76] After visiting San Francisco's New Main and its corporate-sponsored rooms and cut-up design, Nicholson Baker and Sallie Tisdale both concluded that the library administration and design team "hated" books and were devoted to the information paradigm. Certainly the tenaciousness with which the library bureaucracy there defended the building—only at the end admitting the lack of stack space and the consigning of a significant portion of the collections to the landfill—gives some credence to their conclusion.[77] These projects garner much attention, and library administrators blithely expend millions of dollars and the rare opportunity to build or renovate a library building on fashionable and easily discredited notions of a "transformed" institution. As such, they set in stone the new public philosophy discourse of librarianship's essential "home" within the functions and boundaries of information capitalism.

## Outsourcing and McLibraries

Janet Swan Hill has reviewed the issue of outsourcing and came up with some rather sensible distinctions. She notes that almost all libraries engage in some form of outsourcing. For instance, the uniformity of catalog records is (in part) ensured through outsourcing and sharing of catalog records through bibliographic utilities. Tasks for which there is no in-house expertise (special collections cataloging or preservation/binding) are routinely contracted out, and systems work often must be done by companies that have the expertise and computing power to carry out local decisions on database management (like authority control). In other words, outsourcing is a limited, sensible, and routine solution to a number of mundane professional issues and problems faced in librarianship. She contends that there *is* a difference, on the other hand, in the radical extension of the concept of outsourcing by some library managers. When core services and professional competencies are outsourced, the local, professional control (by librarians) is shifted to administrators who negotiate the long-term contracts for the service, and sometimes it is even beyond oversight control of the local administrator. She further contends that there is a big difference between a one-time project (an opening-day collection, catalog disaster recovery, or a special project) and the shifting of the work permanently to a vendor: the "difference between the pieces and the pie." Outsourcing as an extension and aid to the work of librarians is a different story from wholesale outsourcing of librarians' jobs and competencies. This kind of "reengineering" has sometimes met with widespread protest and resistance in the profession.[78]

The controversy over the complete outsourcing of selection in Hawaii is *the* classic example of trendy management slogans and the new public philosophy at work in this area. The state librarian (Bart Kane), in response to budget cuts, declared that he had "created the model for the 21st century" by enacting "customer service" at the core of the library system. He did this by contracting out all selection (and technical) services, and then moving all staff whose job had been eliminated into the public services, thus "reengineering" the state's public library system.[79] Remarkably, Kane's own language is very much like that of his critics: he very much wants "a Wal-Mart approach" to libraries[80] and that is the core of the problem. Quite apart from the inherent de-skilling and de-professionalization of librarians, such an economistic approach leads to library homogeneity across very different communities and campuses—just as Wal-Mart has made uniform the retail goods and services in the small towns they move into and economically dominate. One critic has dubbed this the "McDonaldization" of libraries in that such selection systems (knowledge management approaches) will seek safe, "predictable," and uncontroversial choices of *content* for all libraries. It is not in the interest of companies contracted to "select" for a community or campus to expand the public realm through controversial (or even unusual) materials that would call their business decisions into question, so such schemes inevitably homogenize the resulting collections.[81]

Under such a regime it is not clear where the intellectual freedom responsibilities of libraries (if any) would rest if materials were challenged—with the vendor, a committed/interested librarian (who would not have formal responsibility for selection) if there happened to be one, the management, or perhaps no one. Under homogenous "selection" profiles, the viewpoints in the alternative press—already underrepresented—will stand even less of a chance to make it to the shelves of local public and academic libraries.[82] The whole essence of a library does not lie in the portion of their collections that they have in *common* but rather the *differences* and the continual shaping of the collections around local campus/community interests. With real Wal-Marts (and other such chains) homogenizing so many communities, libraries remain one of the few expressions outside the market realm where communal identity can be somewhat realized. The radical—and complete—extension of outsourcing would make permanent the "predictable" corporate economic model of the McLibrary, complete with the "reengineered' workforce and "customer" service. It is another path to setting in stone (this time in the form of collections) trendy library management fashions that ape the business world, and again, its partial success has paved the way for this tactic to become respectable in the field.

## CONCLUSION: MANAGING AWAY THE PUBLIC SPHERE

If the public founding of American libraries as a social institution helped to make it the embodiment of the public sphere (as I have argued), the trajectory of library administration is to manage away the public sphere. I have given clear indications of this throughout the chapter: the language of library administration encompasses an information capitalism view of the institution with users as "customers" and "markets" to be "captured." Along the way, inappropriate business concepts are applied to libraries and cavalierly misused. Trends in buildings and collections have made this discourse concrete in some "transformed" and "reengineered" institutions. When the future of the library is talked about so incessantly in the language of economics, its public (nonprofit) orientation slowly slips away. One is reminded of Wolin's formulations that "all public questions can be converted into economic terms" and "when the economy becomes the polity, *citizen* and *community* become subversive words."[83] Under such a management discussion regime it *appears* absurd to defend libraries' public sphere role in democracy, public memory, embodying organized and rational discourse, and fair and free information as a democratic safeguard. The library-as-public-sphere is being managed out of existence.

A recent development highlighted the disastrous direction in which librarianship is being lead. A study by the Middle States Commission on Higher Education reported on a survey of library administrators on the question of the existence of a library as a prerequisite for a degree-granting college or university. Following business management fads and jargon, many administrators replied to the survey that distance learning was the future of education and that a library was "irrelevant" for some students and not a necessary measure of educational quality. The report found that these library leaders "were approximately equally divided on whether or not a library as a physical place" was really necessary for the legitimacy (and accreditation) of a college or university, and not surprisingly the commission began exploring means of reviewing institutions without libraries and has dropped the requirement that a librarian be a part of reaccreditation teams.[84] It was a highly interesting process to see business rhetoric rebound back as a direct threat to academic libraries (and the jobs of managers) and the consequent reaction "not out of self-protection, but in defense of student satisfaction and learning productivity" (this from a library director who has pursued vigorously the technological vision of a distributed library).[85] A council of academic library directors suddenly became quite careful with language, quibbling that the "survey was a perception study of library administrators, not a use study" and asserting the library as the "intellectual commons" of higher education.[86] How quickly baseless management rhetoric flips back to public sphere visions of the good of libraries when the logical conclusions are drawn and the logical questions are asked based on library administrators' own careless "futuring." This would be an amusing case in point if the very existence of libraries (and their public mission) were not put in danger by "unbelievable stories based upon bad rhetoric using unsupported theories of social change"—to repeat a phrase.[87] It seems clear to me that fashionable management rhetoric about libraries constitutes a form of managing away the public sphere in librarianship—and possibly managing away the institution itself. It is a discourse shallowly conceived and logically incapable of defending the field long term. Such formulations can—and should—be routinely challenged.

## NOTES

1. Mark Day, "Discourse Fashions in Library Administration and Information Management: A Critical History and Bibliometric Analysis," *Advances in Librarianship* 26 (2002): 284. I am grateful to the author for sharing the manuscript version of this article in preparation for this chapter. Day's work is excellent and the only system-

atic, critical analysis of the library management literature that I know of, filling a very important gap in the overall analysis of librarianship.

2. Day, "Discourse Fashions," 235, 279. Day notes that, ironically, far from being "heroic" individual innovators, most managers are under "extreme social pressure to conform" to current fashions, are driven by reputation considerations as much as performance, and are therefore frequently conformists (277).

3. Mark Day, "Transformational Discourse: Ideologies of Organizational Change in the Academic Library," *Library Trends* 46, no. 4 (1998): 638; Day, "Discourse Fashions," 279.

4. Day, "Discourse Fashions," 274 (emphasis in original).

5. Day, "Discourse Fashions," 284–85.

6. Day, "Discourse Fashions," 279–80; Richard De Gennaro, *Libraries, Technology, and the Information Marketplace: Selected Papers* (Boston: G. K. Hall, 1987), 49–52.

7. For example see three literature reviews: LAMA/LOMS Comparative Library Organization Committee (CLOC) and CLOC Bibliography Task Force, "Required Reading for Library Administrators: An Annotated Bibliography of Influential Authors and Their Works," *Library Administration & Management* 16, no. 3 (2002): 126–36; Donald Riggs, "What's in Store for Academic Libraries? Leadership and Management Issues," *Journal of Academic Librarianship* 23, no. 1 (1997: 3–8; and Terence Huwe, "Libraries and the Idea of the Organization," *Advances in Librarianship* 21 (1997): 1–24.

8. Manfred Stanley, "The Mystery of the Commons: On the Indispensability of Civic Rhetoric," *Social Research* 50, no. 4 (1983): 867–68.

9. Mark Day, "Challenges to the Professional Control of Knowledge Work in Academic Libraries: A Proposed Agenda for Organizational Research and Action," in *Choosing Our Futures: Proceedings of the 8th National Conference of the Association of College and Research Libraries.* 1997. <http://www.ala.org/acrl/papers.html#C24>.

10. Bernd Frohmann, "The Ethics of Information Science Theory" (Information Democracy session, 55th Annual American Society for Information Science Meeting, Pittsburgh, 27 October 1992); Thomas Mann, "The Importance of Books, Free Access, and Libraries as Places—and the Dangerous Inadequacy of the Information Science Paradigm," *Journal of Academic Librarianship* 27, no. 4 (2001): 268–81.

11. John Buschman, ed., *Critical Approaches to Information Technology in Librarianship: Foundations and Applications* (Westport, Conn.: Greenwood, 1993).

12. Roma Harris, *Librarianship: The Erosion of a Woman's Profession* (Norwood, N.J.: Ablex, 1992); Roma Harris, "Service Undermined by Technology: An Examination of Gender Relations, Economics and Ideology," *Progressive Librarian* 10/11 (1995/1996): 5–22; Juris Dilevko and Roma Harris, "Information Technology and Social Relations: Portrayals of Gender Roles in High Tech Product Advertisements," *Journal of the American Society for Information Science* 48, no. 8 (1997): 718–27; and Roma Harris, "Leadership, Professionalism, and Librarianship" (25th Annual Conference of the Corporation of Professional Librarians of Quebec, InterContinental Hotel, Montreal, 26 May 1994).

13. Nicholson Baker, *Double Fold: Libraries and the Assault on Paper* (New York: Random House, 2001); Dorothy Warner, "'Why Do We Need to Keep This in Print? It's on the Web . . . ': A Review of Electronic Archiving Issues and Problems," *Pro-

*gressive Librarian* 19/20 (Spring 2002): 47–64; and Alexander Stille, "Overload," *New Yorker,* 8 March 1999, 38–44.

14. Jerry Campbell, "Choosing to Have a Future," *American Libraries,* June 1993, 560.

15. Bruce Park, "Libraries Without Walls; Or, Librarians Without a Profession," *American Libraries,* October 1992, 747.

16. Richard Biddiscombe, "The Changing Role of the Information Professional in Support of Learning and Research," *Advances in Librarianship* 23 (2000): 63–64; and Susan Kent, "The Public Library Director in the Dot (.) World," *New Library World* 103, no. 1/2 (2002): 49.

17. Brian Caufield, "Morphing the Librarians." *Wired* Archive 5.08 (August 1997), 2 pp., 22 May 2001, <www.wired.com>. See also Katherine Mangan, "In Revamped Library Schools, Information Trumps Books," *Chronicle of Higher Education,* 7 April 2000, A43–44.

18. Richard Apostle and Boris Raymond, "Librarianship and the Information Paradigm," *Canadian Library Journal* 43 (December 1986): 377–86.

19. Theodore Roszak, *The Cult of Information: The Folklore of Computers and the True Art of Thinking* (New York: Pantheon, 1986), x; Theodore Roszak, "Politics of Information and the Fate of the Earth," *Progressive Librarian* 6/7 (1993): 3–14; see also Norman Stevens, "The History of Information," *Advances in Librarianship* 14 (1986): 1–48.

20. Biddiscombe, 66.

21. James Matarazzo, "Bites, Bits, and Video Games: The Changes Ahead," *Journal of Academic Librarianship* 27, no. 3 (2001): 171.

22. Arnold Hirshon, "Running with the Red Queen: Breaking New Habits to Survive in the Virtual World," *Advances in Librarianship* 20 (1996): 2–3.

23. Campbell, 566.

24. Frank Webster, "The Information Society Revisited," in *Handbook of New Media,* ed. Leah Lievrouw and Sonia Livingstone (London: Sage, 2002), 28.

25. Day, "Discourse Fashions"; and Day, "Transformational Discourse."

26. Frank Webster, "Information: A Sceptical Account," *Advances in Librarianship* 24 (2000): 2–3, 6–7.

27. Webster, "The Information Society Revisited," 22–23.

28. Phil Agre, "The End of Information & the Future of Libraries," *Progressive Librarian* 12/13 (1997): 1–3.

29. De Gennaro, 3, 5 (emphasis in original).

30. Frank Webster, "Knowledgeability and Democracy in an Information Age," *Library Review* 48, no. 8 (1999): 378.

31. Webster, "Knowledgeability," 380.

32. Michael Harris and Stan Hannah, *Into the Future: the Foundations of Library and Information Services in the Post-Industrial Era* (Norwood, N.J.: Ablex, 1993); John Buschman, "Myths of the Information Society: A Guide for Librarians," *Urban Academic Librarian* 9, no. 1 (1994): 4–17; see also Daniel Bell, "Welcome to the Post-Industrial Society," in *Libraries in Post-Industrial Society,* ed. Leigh Estabrook (Phoenix, Ariz.: Oryx, 1977), 3–7; and David Lyon, "From 'Post-Industrialism' to 'Information Society': A New Social Transformation?" *Sociology* 20, no. 4 (1986): 577–88.

33. Day, "Transformational Discourse," 635.

34. Steve Fuller, "Why Post-Industrial Society Never Came," *Academe,* November–December 1994, 22; see also Michael Harrington, "Post-Industrial Society and the Welfare State," in *Libraries in Post-Industrial Society,* ed. Estabrook, 19–29; Steve Fuller, "A Critical Guide to Knowledge Society Newspeak: Or, How Not to Take the Great Leap Backward," *Current Sociology* 49, no. 4 (2001): 177–201; Lyon.

35. Laurence Veysey, "A Postmortem on Daniel Bell's Postindustrialism," *American Quarterly* 34, no. 1 (1982): 51, 58–59. Bell later backed away somewhat from the prediction of capitalism's being tamed by a technocratic information society and advocacy of economic regulation: "the world of the postindustrial society requires new modes of social organization, and these are only now being fashioned by the new entrepreneurs of the new technology" In Daniel Bell, "The Third Technological Revolution," *Dissent* 36, no. 2 (1989): 175.

36. Bell in Harrington, 20.

37. See Harris and Hannah, 78–80; Herbert Schiller and Anita Schiller, "Libraries, Public Access to Information, and Commerce," in *The Political Economy of Information,* ed. Vincent Mosco and Janet Wasko (Madison: University of Wisconsin Press, 1988), 146–66; Patricia Glass Schuman, "Information Justice," *Library Journal,* 1 June 1982, 1060–66.

38. James Govan, "The Creeping Invisible Hand: Entrepreneurial Librarianship," *American Libraries,* January 1988, 35–38; Day, "Transformational Discourse," 640.

39. Day, "Discourse Fashions," 239, 242–44, 274–76. See also Riggs and CLOC for examples.

40. De Gennaro, 17.

41. Mangan, "Revamped"; Margaret Thomas, "Crossing Over . . . to the Corporate Sector," *Library Journal,* 1 September 2001, 48–50.

42. Hirshon, 19–20. The same essential point is made in Joel Rutstein, Anna DeMiller, and Elizabeth Fuseler, "Ownership Versus Access: Shifting Perspectives for Libraries," *Advances in Librarianship* 17 (1993): 52–53.

43. Dowlin in Nicholson Baker, "The Author vs. the Library," *New Yorker,* 14 October 1996, 51.

44. Leigh Estabrook, "Sacred Trust or Competitive Opportunity: Using Patron Records," *Library Journal,* 1 February 1996, 48–49. For a more thoughtful consideration of the issue, see Rhoda Garoogian, "Librarian/Patron Confidentiality: An Ethical Challenge," *Library Trends* 40, no. 2 (1991): 216–33.

45. Nicholas Basbanes, "Controversy Redux," *Biblio,* August 1998, 8–9. The article is a profile of Nicholson Baker, whose erotic novel about phone sex (*Vox*) was purchased by Lewinsky, thus putting him in another high-profile, controversial situation. His indignant comment on the investigation has again put librarianship's inaction on the issue into high relief: "it is appalling that the legal system is being employed to squeeze out what works of fiction a person who has not been charged with any crime may have read at a certain point in time" (8).

46. Bell, "Welcome," 7.

47. Harris and Hannah, 28, 33–58.

48. Day, "Discourse Fashions," 273, 281–82, 284–85.

49. Day, "Discourse Fashions," 257–60. He notes that this is one of two dominant themes in library management connected to the information society concept that do not have direct links to fashionable discourses in the business management literature. That is, they are certainly themes related to business functions translated into libraries,

but they are framed in specific language that isolates the discourse within librarianship. See also Michael Harris, Stan Hannah, and Pamela Harris, *Into the Future: The Foundation of Library and Information Services in the Post-Industrial Era*, 2nd ed. (Greenwich, Conn.: Ablex, 1998), 40–43.

50. See CLOC; Huwe; Biddiscombe; Terrence Mech, "Leadership and the Evolution of Academic Librarianship," *Journal of Academic Librarianship* 22, no. 5 (1996): 345–53.

51. Fuller, "Critical Guide to Knowledge Society Newspeak."

52. Fuller, "Critical Guide to Knowledge Society Newspeak," 181–82.

53. Fuller, "Critical Guide to Knowledge Society Newspeak," 179–83; see also James Love, "A Primer on WIPO & Database Extraction Rights," *Progressive Librarian* 12/13 (1997): 18–31; see also Kathryn Balint, "Public Laws Owned by the Public? Think Again, Copyright Rulings Show," *San Diego Union-Tribune*, 13 May 2001, A1.

54. Fuller, "Critical Guide to Knowledge Society Newspeak," 180–84.

55. Fuller, "Critical Guide to Knowledge Society Newspeak," 178–83.

56. Huwe, 21 (emphasis in original).

57. Hirshon, 24 (emphasis added).

58. Kevin Starr, "The Politics of Success," *Library Administration & Management* 15, no. 3 (2001): 153.

59. Rutstein, DeMiller, and Fuseler, 50–51. See Stille, "Overload" for a particularly acute analysis of the cost issue as it relates to archiving electronic resources.

60. Benton Foundation, *Buildings, Books, and Bytes: Libraries and Communities in the Digital Age* (Washington, D.C.: Benton Foundation, 1996).

61. Michael Gorman, "Living and Dying with 'Information': Comments on the Report *Buildings, Books, and Bytes*," *Library Trends* 46, no. 1 (1997): 4.

62. Benton in Gorman, 4. See also two good analyses of the report: Bryce Allen, "The Benton Report as Research," *Library Trends* 46, no. 1 (1997): 5–18; and Douglas Zweizig, "How Firm a Foundation?" *Library Trends* 46, no. 1 (1997): 19–27.

63. Baker, *Double Fold*.

64. Nicholson Baker, "Discards," *New Yorker*, 4 April 1994, 78.

65. See, for example, William Miller, "The Library as a Place: Tradition and Evolution," *Library Issues* 22, no. 3 (January 2002); Charles Forrest, "Building Libraries and Library Building Awards—Twenty Years of Change: An Interview with Anders C. Dahlgren," *Library Administration & Management* 16, no. 3 (2002): 120–25; Christine Hage, "Books, Bytes, Buildings, and Bodies: Public Libraries in the 21st Century," *American Libraries*, January 1999, 79–81; Mary Thomas, "Redefining Library Space: Managing the Coexistence of Books, Computers, and Readers," *Journal of Academic Librarianship* 26, no. 6 (2000): 408–15; and Norman Stevens, "Research Libraries: Past, Present, and Future," *Advances in Librarianship* 17 (1993): 79–109.

66. "Freedom of Information?" *Economist*, 18 May 2000.

67. *The New York Public Library: The Science, Industry and Business Library (SIBL). New York, New York* (New York: Gwathmey Siegel & Associates Architects LLC, n.d.); Baker, "Author," 54–55.

68. *Ferris State University: FSU Library for Information, Technology and Education (FLITE). Big Rapids, Michigan* (New York: Gwathmey Siegel & Associates Architects LLC, n.d.); and *Akron Summit County Public Library. Akron, Ohio* (New York: Gwathmey Siegel & Associates Architects LLC, n.d.).

69. *The City University of New York: The Graduate Center Library. New York, New*

*York* (New York: Gwathmey Siegel & Associates Architects LLC, n.d.); and *The New York Public Library: Mid-Manhattan Library, Renovation and Expansion Project. New York, New York* (New York: Gwathmey Siegel & Associates Architects LLC, n.d.).

70. Joan Williams, "Shaping the 'Experience Library'," *American Libraries,* April 2002, 70–72; and Sallie Tisdale, "Silence, Please," *Harper's,* March 1997, 65–74.

71. Koolhaas in Shannon Mattern, "A Receptacle for Irony and Data: Rem Koolhaas's Vision for Seattle Public Library" (Society for the History of Authorship, Reading, and Publishing 2001 Conference, College of William and Mary, Williamsburg, Virginia, 21 July 2001).

72. Mattern.

73. Baker, *Double Fold;* Baker, "Author"; Mann, "The Importance of Books"; "New Room for Readers," *Economist,* 27 November 1997; Patrice Higonnet, "Scandal on the Seine," *New York Review of Books,* 15 August 1991, 32–33; and Melissa Riley, "Notes from the Front Line at San Francisco Public Library," *Progressive Librarian* 12/13 (1997): 60–62. Lehigh University in Pennsylvania built a new library wing around 1983, and the brand new structure was *purposefully* built not to hold more than a few years worth of normal book and journal growth. The idea was to force the library (already very technically oriented at a highly focused sci-tech university) toward the electronic future and to the cutting edge of electronic information. Needless to say, they overestimated that electronic future twenty years ago, and by the time of my conversations with the director in 1985, they were already near the limits of the building.

74. Geoffrey Freeman, "The Academic Library in the 21st Century: Partner in Education," in *Building Libraries for the 21st Century: The Shape of Information,* ed. T. D. Webb (Jefferson, N.C.: McFarland, 2000), 169–70.

75. Mann, "The Importance of Books," 272. Mann's general thrust concerning copyright and misplaced priorities is confirmed in an edited summation of a very long e-mail discussion concerning digital audio reserves and copyright: Darwin Scott, comp., "War and Peace II (aka audio reserves)," distributed on MLA-L@listserv.indiana.edu on 6 October 2000 (approx. 25 pp.), with a short follow-up: Ralph Papakhian, comp., "Re: War and Peace II," distributed on MLA-L@listserv.indiana.edu on 7 October 2000 (approx. 2 pp.).

76. Miller, 2–3.

77. Tisdale; Baker, "Author."

78. Janet Swan Hill, "Outsourcing: Understanding the Fuss," *The Bowker Annual,* 46th ed., ed. Dave Bogart (New Providence, N.J.: R. R. Bowker, 2001), 218–32. She notes that *cataloging* is usually the target of more complete outsourcing management strategies (like Hirshon—again—at Wright State University Library), and that this is generally less contested in the profession. Mann, "The Importance of Books" (and others) vigorously argue for cataloging standards and against the descent of book records into an assumed full text key word searching future; see also Thomas Mann, *The Oxford Guide To Library Research* (New York: Oxford University Press, 1998), 140–41. Hill notes that the outsourcing/privatizing of federal libraries was widely protested among librarians to little avail; see also R. Lee Hadden, "Outsourcing Federal Libraries," *Progressive Librarian* 14 (1998): 44–46.

79. Kane in Norman Oder, "Outsourcing: Model—or Mistake?" *Library Journal,* 15 March 1997, 28–29.

80. Marilyn Smithson, "By You, for You, or in Spite of You: Outsourcing and the Demise of the Public Library," *SRRT Newsletter,* March 1997, 16.

81. Brian Quinn, "The McDonaldization of Academic Libraries?" *College & Research Libraries,* May 2000, 248–61; see also Patricia Wallace, "Outsourcing Book Selection in Public and School Libraries," *Collection Building* 16, no. 4 (1997): 160–66; John Charles and Shelley Mosley, "Keeping Selection In-house," *Library Journal,* 15 March 1997, 30–31; and Karen Schneider, "The McLibrary Syndrome," *American Libraries,* January 1998, 68–70.

82. Rita Marinko and Kristin Gerhard, "Representations of the Alternative Press in Academic Library Collections," *College & Research Libraries,* July 1998, 363–76; and Charles Willett, "Consider the Source: A Case Against Outsourcing Materials Selection in Academic Libraries," *Collection Building* 17, no. 2 (1998): 91–95.

83. Sheldon Wolin, "The New Public Philosophy," *Democracy* 1, no. 4 (1981): 27, 36 (emphasis in original).

84. Oswald Ratteray, *A Survey of Librarians in the Middle States Region on the Role of the Library, Electronic Resources, and Information Literacy Training in Higher Education* (Philadelphia: Middle States Commission on Higher Education, November 1999); and New Jersey Council of Academic Library Directors, *NJ Council of Academic Library Directors Position Paper,* January 2000.

85. Richard Sweeney, "Middle States Survey & Library Accreditation Guidelines," e-mail to nj_libdir@email.rutgers.edu, 15 November 1999.

86. New Jersey Council of Academic Library Directors.

87. Day, "Challenges to the Professional Control of Knowledge Work."

# 6

## ON CUSTOMER-DRIVEN
## LIBRARIANSHIP

### INTRODUCTION

Within librarianship there has developed a number of themes or subthemes that, at first glance, would seem to have very little in common: accountability/ measurement of quality, libraries and the bookstore-with-a-Starbucks model, and public relations/marketing in libraries. This chapter will argue that each recasts the library user as "customer" and is a different facet of customer driven librarianship. This is the one central idea that links them all, and they represent institutional and professional acquiescence to the new public philosophy climate. In this sense, these three trends (some have been around long enough to become established practices) are not just disparate reflections of the dominant themes of public discourse. Rather, these themes and practices have come together in a kind of professional stew that both responds to and reinforces an economic vision of librarianship at its base, culminating in the "customer" concept. I have called this redefinition customer-driven librarianship.

To give one illustration, accountability as a trend for public institutions (public schools are the earliest example) was a self-imposed response to conservative questions concerning the value (in both the economic and qualitative meanings of that term) received for the tax dollars spent.[1] The idea has since become much more crudely economic in the intervening years, with direct threats to cut or withhold funding or privatize all or part of public institutions that are not "performing."[2] In turn, accountability has given rise to research on qualitative measures as a means to justify budgets or encourage private donations.[3] This reorientation of the profession represents a philosophical change in outlook, as John Budd argues. When talked and written about this way, the presupposition is that libraries provide collections and services (and "account" for and evaluate them) not as an end but *in exchange* or as a *means,* and the "desired end is really the material success of the library."[4] Such practices are not harmless, trendy adaptations to altered circumstances but a reorientation of librarianship along the lines of the new public philosophy, with significant contradictions to the public sphere role of libraries. What follows is a brief review of librarianship's versions of accountability/measurement of quality, the bookstore-with-a-Starbucks model, and public relations/marketing. It will not be an exhaustive review of each issue because (as I will argue) it quickly becomes clear in a sampling of the literature that new public philosophy reconceptions of the library are at the heart of each of these trends/practices. The chapter will conclude with a critique of this professional stew in light of patrons recast as "customers" and the significant dismantling of the public sphere that these developments represent.

## ACCOUNTABILITY/QUALITY MEASUREMENT

Unlike the case of public education, the rise of accountability in librarianship did not have even a temporary mediating factor of a debate or questions concerning the quality of collections and services. Justification of funding was the focus from the beginning: "Accountability has been one of our society's major concerns in the 1980's, with . . . academic libraries scrutinized as perhaps never before. Demands for accountability come from . . . administrators as well as from legislators and governmental agencies [and] within the library, the growing use of technology, increasing costs of materials, and the labor-intensive nature of library services all conspire to increase costs."[5] Nor is it limited to the trends that have swept through educational institutions: "in today's era of tightening library budgets based upon competition for fewer local dollars, it is more important than ever for public libraries . . . to identify changing population characteristics and needs, in order to provide the most desired and effective services and materials."[6] Peter Hernon and Charles McClure see accountability as an objective to determine "the degree to which the activity or service can be justified to external funding bodies."[7]

As noted, the accountability trend has given rise to a research agenda to measure "quality." The language about assessing quality can be very high-sounding: "we . . . need to take a positive view of measurement as a means of ensuring the relevance and quality of our services. Measurement tools and techniques will evolve over time, but they will eventually form the basis for evidence-based practice in [the field] and provide a continuing source of data for innovation and improvement." However, the very next paragraph indicates the core of the issue. Evaluating quality is "not just self-preservation," but it *is* a way to communicate value to "senior management" who are, of course, in charge of the levers of funding.[8] Hernon and McClure's volume on evaluation and library decision making is also clear: "there is likely to be increased pressure on librarians to maintain or cut costs, while, at the same time, increasing both the range and quality of services and programs. To accomplish this seemingly paradoxical set of objectives, librarians must be better able to evaluate library services."[9] Indeed, the funding theme is a blatant part of the highly publicized (and marketed) LibQUAL+ evaluation project. The pilot at Texas A&M University Libraries is being used and tested as a means to measure and justify student support of the library through approved fees.[10] Identifying, measuring, and documenting "quality" is therefore not pure as its proponents would have you believe, and it is in fact a search for—or a way of protecting—funding by other means.

Am I suggesting that there is something inherently bad in a search for higher quality or more effective services and collections? No. But I *am* suggesting that the economic roots of the very much related accountability/quality measurement trends has shaped more of this agenda than the rather neutral language surrounding it would lead one to believe. It is *not* a simple matter of being for or against "quality" and its measurement. Henry Mintzberg (a management guru) sensibly lays out the central issues at stake, which can easily be adapted to libraries. Public institutions do not conform to the business-based models that these approaches presuppose. Accountability assumes, among other things, that there are "clear, unambiguous policies" (that is, agreed-upon purposes for the institution in the public/political sphere) "for the implementation in the administrative sphere. In other words, policies have to be rather stable over time" and social/political factors must be kept "clear of the execution of those policies." Mintzberg asks the appropriate question: "how common is that?" and answers in return that isolated, autonomous functioning of public institutions is an assumption bound to "collapse in the face of what most [of them] do and how they have to work."[11] Public institutions face political and social pressures and interference all the time. To give just two examples, libraries are often renamed and given a different purpose—like "learning and leisure centers"—by local boards trying to catch a trendy wave, and museums have frequently had to respond to political pressures (Mayor Guiliani vs. the Brooklyn Museum and the Smithsonian's proposed Enola Gay display are two good examples).[12] Accountability as a scheme to justify and guide libraries is based on inappropriate premises, as Mintzberg notes. "The belief that politics and administration [in public institutions] can be separated [in the same way as] formulation and implementation in corporate planning . . . is another old myth that should be allowed to die a quiet death." If this premise is wrong, as he argues, then accountability is not a guiding principle for effective management but rather an inappropriate management model for public institutions, recasting their purpose as new public philosophy economic entities in the process since the modus operandi is the search for funding.[13]

Mintzberg also identifies the key weakness in measuring quality: the assumption that "performance can be fully and properly evaluated by objective measures." Again, he asks the proper question: "how many of the real benefits of [public institutions] lend themselves to such measurement? Many activities are in the public sector precisely because of measurement problems." He goes on to give a wonderful example of different calculations of the "success rate" of an organ transplant, which vary from nine out of eleven (by the surgeon who only counts patient survival), to six out of ten (by a hospital administrator who reviews the costs vs. the benefits), to three out of ten (by the nurses who take quality of postoperative life as the major criterion). Decisions in public institutions can not be nailed down as measurable quantities. They require, in his words, "soft judgement."[14] One can see easily the assumption that Mintzberg has identified shot through the literature on quality.[15] As Neil Postman observed, to a person with a hammer, everything looks like a nail. To the person out to measure "quality," what is/can be measured—and for what purposes—becomes the reality.

William Starbuck has identified how this becomes a kind of self-generating trend in organizations. Much simplified, his research led him to the conclusion that decisions in organizations are not based upon objective phenomena but rather upon ideologies that come into play when a "crisis" is seen, envisioned, made up and simply declared, sought, or genuinely thrust upon an institution from external factors. Actual problem solving as an organizational response is not typical. What *is* typical is an "action generating mode [where] people watch the results of their actions, appraise these results as good or bad, and propose needs for action. Whether [they] are real is decided by [means] which . . . are phrased as clichés about causation." Ideologies (which are "integrated clusters of beliefs, values, rituals, and symbols") form the basis of those explanations of the causes of crisis and guide further action and research in a closed—and dysfunctional—loop.[16] I would characterize "quality" measurement as just such a response to the crisis culture of librarianship identified in the first chapter. What is measured in response to our variously declared "crises" is "quality" from a particular ideological (in Starbuck's definition of the word) point of view: recasting libraries in the new public philosophy mold. The basis of this research means that what is identified and defined as "quality" is that which will pay off, and therefore, the lack of quality is defined as those aspects of librarianship that do not provide a return—or do not or pay off soon enough. If Mintzberg is right (and I believe he is), then we are changing the mission of librarianship with a "quality" research focus that ignores the very reason libraries are public institutions in the first place: the public (sphere) good of our institutions is difficult to quantify. The result can only be a redefinition of the purpose of the institution, and a patently inadequate one at that.

## LIBRARIES AND THE BOOKSTORE-WITH-COFFEE-SHOP MODEL

Recently, a small cottage industry within librarianship has developed in the form of articles on the "discovery" of the success of plush, superchain bookstore outlets (like Barnes & Noble) as a place to browse for and read books. In this scenario, bookstores are seen as more successful "competitors," and a key to their success is their more open and welcoming atmosphere in the form of Starbucks and other coffee shops. One article went so far as to suggest that Barnes & Noble's staffing and pay structure, the quasi-catalog of inventory control systems, and the "reference" knowledge of staff was in all ways more effective than local libraries: "if comfortable chairs alone aren't enough of a lure, bookstores now offer a calendar of book talks, book signings, discussion groups, demonstrations, and performances unrivaled by all but the largest urban libraries [and they] even started imitating the most sacrosanct of all public library services: story time and summer reading programs"— selling good coffee to boot, which you can actually have with the materials.[17] In typical lemming-like fashion, library administrators have added coffee shops to libraries to "compete" and bring people back into libraries.[18] The result has been a quick reversal of the rhetoric of the "virtual" library and an almost obsessive focus on actual bodies coming into the buildings.[19] As one author put it, "considering how intently librarians have attempted to drive services out of their libraries in order to make them more readily accessible online [outside their walls], it would be remarkable if foot traffic were not down."[20]

In other words, library managers are trying to "innovate" their way out of the logical end to their approach to information technologies and its hype by adding coffee shops to increase traffic. The emphasis on foot traffic contradicts the management fad/trend of evaluating the *quality* of collections (and denigrating quantitative issues like size of the collection, reference transactions, total items circulated—and yes, gate count).[21] As a particularly shallow piece put it: the "former paradigm" is of the library as a "place where customers must come physically ; . . . an organization steeped in tradition [with] a presumption of 'goodness.'" The "emerging paradigm [is] of a library as the sum of its services focus[ed] on customer needs and convenience and an acknowledgement that support . . . must be earned through demonstration of benefits."[22] However, the focus on the number of people in the library betrays the shallowness of all the pronouncements about the importance of quality vs. quantity, and in the end, it appears that the "value-added" and "customer" approach to users and electronic resources will not suffice either. The library/coffee-shop fad has resurrected the quantitative, traditional gate count approach.

The actual coffee-shop issue itself represents some contradictions. Far from being an *alternative* model of "competition," the bookstore superchains actually *imitate* the library atmosphere—as has been acknowledged by the chains themselves.[23] Second, the resulting increase in gate count does not necessarily mean more use of collections, better use of better electronic resources, or better student research,[24] and there is some evidence that in fact the widely discussed *Chronicle of Higher Education* article on this topic was skewed to sensationalize the "death of the library" angle.[25] There is no question that such renovations are given funding priority in an era when collections, services, and more mundane aspects of library buildings all very much need finances, and such enterprises *are* intended to generate revenue off of "library" users.[26] It would appear that getting a well-equipped Starbucks, a higher gate count, and a return on a building investment is what constitutes "quality" library services among these administrations. What I find perhaps most astonishing and insulting in all of this is two underlying assumptions built into the arguments in favor of this minitrend. First is the implicit claim that librarians (and local library administrators) *don't* want to make libraries comfortable, well stocked, inviting, clean, and well decorated. That represents the clearest distortion of a reality that I can think of. Such funds are extraordinarily hard to get because they do not represent one of two types of preferred investments: technology or capital improvements. Everyone knows that furniture and maintenance in such a facility represents a temporary improvement that will wear out. *All* public institutions are routinely directed to squeeze the maximum life out of furniture, carpeting, lighting, and so forth. Chapter 4 was about the siphoning *away* of resources from print collections to create the "virtual" library, and chapter 5 was about the elaborate library management justifications for those trends. Money can simply be reapportioned toward print if we want to "compete" with the superchains in terms of titles offered. Second, the bookstore/coffee-shop model represents a near-total denigration of the value of intelligent selection and cataloging of retrospective collections, ignoring the value of the investment in and maintenance of a collection (print, electronic, or otherwise) available over time. To equate the turnover and stock of a good bookstore and its inventory control system and salespeople with a library demonstrates a breathtakingly shallow understanding of what a library is and does. The principal effects (as far as I could tell) cited in the other widely publicized article that advocated this approach would be to slash staff pay while increasing their work hours and the amount of time open and to raise the average manager's salary by about 13%.[27] In sum, the library as bookstore-with-a-coffee-shop model represents a contradictory, slapdash, "crisis" approach to planning for libraries, and as such it fits well with the trendy "solution" of the moment approach among administrators. In so doing, the model of the library (not so subtly) changes without real debate. A focus on foot traffic, revenue-generating renovations, and "competing" with bookstores bears all the hallmarks of a store at the mall and the new public philosophy economic conception of librarianship.

## MARKETING AND PUBLIC RELATIONS TO LIBRARY "CUSTOMERS"

Though some in the field have attempted to make a distinction between marketing and public relations in librarianship, I am at somewhat of a loss to distinguish between the two. When large research libraries were recently surveyed on their marketing/public relations activities, classic definitions of the two were quoted and they indicated how closely related the areas were: "marketing . . . fulfills the organization's mission and, like public relations, inspires public awareness and educates."[28] There is a clear link between them that has been present from the beginning, but there is a more important connection as well. Like the epiphenomena previously noted, they are also firmly rooted in the search for funding, and most specifically, the fiscal problems of public cultural institutions that date from the Reagan era and the acceleration of the new public philosophy during that time.[29] For instance, in 1984 the editor of a special journal issue on marketing wrote that "libraries need to adopt marketing to prosper. In my opinion it is much more likely that the battles most library administrators face for relatively scarce resources will intensify rather than diminish. The only hope that [they] have of winning their fair share of those battles is to be able to . . . provide persuasive evidence that dollars invested in libraries are well-spent."[30] This perspective has become a bedrock of marketing/public relations in libraries in the intervening years, despite the initial lip service given to the core mission when these functions are discussed: "when libraries are expected to do even more with less, marketing and public relations play an increasingly important role in . . . funding strategies. . . . New titles such as director of marketing and publishing . . . reflect the more active role libraries play in fundraising [and these] activities have repaid the initial investment. Most indicated that . . . library funds have increased—sometimes by a substantial percentage."[31]

With this essential financial basis, marketing and public relations in libraries has laid claim to the older function (and language) of outreach. Highlighting new or useful services of benefit to the library's community[32] has come to be redefined as public relations, and in this redefinition there is an almost effortless slide over to funding issues: "there is some evidence that the relatively small step of providing service to those who are not directly affiliated with the institution brings tremendous public relations benefits to the library. [In] its efforts to provide information for local businesses [one academic library was] so successful that the college administration even increased the library's budget."[33] There is even some sense in the field that this connection has gone too far and a shift away from a pure funding focus back to a broader sense of outreach is due.[34] However, this represents a decided minority of opinion within librarianship, and the overwhelming prevalence of funding as the basis of these professional practices would appear to point in the opposite direction. Outside of the management literature, perhaps nowhere else is the language

of business more evident and more dominant in librarianship. Library marketing now includes concepts of "brand identity," "merchandizing and media
partners," and "co-branding" in the quest for public and corporate support.[35]
These efforts are now conceived of as central to entrepreneurial efforts within
the field where new or extended services are tied to funding support.[36] The
formulation that libraries do financially well by doing good is firmly in place.

However, the most intense rhetorical focus in the public relations and marketing literature in librarianship is in defining the library user as a "customer."
While this most certainly has been a not-terribly subtle subtext of the previous
areas reviewed, it is an overwhelming theme within this particular literature
in the field: "the best and most important public relations activity for a library
is providing consistently excellent customer service";[37] "the main purpose of
the library services is to create and deliver customer needed services in a
customer satisfying manner";[38] "all library staff wear name tags to make themselves easily identifiable to the customers [and] the library has regular and
formal mechanisms to receive customer feedback";[39] "accumulated statistics
about [library users] was put through consumer product software [to find]
for every branch, the characteristics of the population that a facility is trying
to serve";[40] "each customer evaluates the quality of service received and decides when (or if) there will be further interaction with that organization.
That some librarians reject the idea of users as customers is equally irrelevant.
Most people do not focus on a label."[41] The "customer" metaphor—and the
resulting customer driven librarianship—is arguably a near obsession (and a
faddish one at that) in the field.[42] It was the prime reasoning behind the total
outsourcing of cataloging and collection development where it has been
tried,[43] and in coming full circle back to the epiphenomena noted in the first
chapter, market research is now equated with assessing quality, which is
equated with meeting customer demands. Among many notable examples,
the International Federation of Library Associations (IFLA) ran a full pre-
conference on "using market research to improve customer satisfaction" with
a lengthy bibliography of background publications.[44] Under the shibboleth
of library "customers" and their "service," public relations and marketing
have laid claim to several related areas, replete with imitative business jargon
of "competitive advantage," "target markets," "market segmentation," "repositioning," a focus on "the competition"[45] all the way to absorbing Ranganathan's Laws into this metaphor.[46] All the while, John Budd's essential
point about the nature of the (economic) exchange with "the customer" is
present, sometimes in a fairly crude form: "the amount of [financial] support
received is viewed as somehow 'owed' to the library because of the library's
inherent value as an institution. [T]his is yesterday's thinking and it is imperative that library staff adopt a new attitude: that funding and other forms
of support need to be earned, based on documented quality and value to
customers [and not] passively rel[ying] on external good will."[47]

The redefinition of library users as customers (who receive customer service) is the culmination of library marketing and public relations and it completes the professional stew that I have called customer-driven librarianship. There is little depth of analysis required to identify its economic basis in library funding and most specifically its new public philosophy themes. All together, this stew represents another of the dominant discourses in our field that define libraries in economic (vs. democratic) terms. I will address this overall trend—and its "customer" culmination—in the conclusion of this chapter, but there are a few specific issues to be taken with this "new" paradigm and its underlying assumptions. First, Budd is correct in pointing out that the "customer service" trend is only a tactical renaming of longstanding professional values, and the pretense that these values have only been recently discovered is both ahistorical and masks an economic definition of librarianship inherent in its language.[48] Like the example of outreach, this service orientation is merely poaching and renaming. In the process, the language in which the essential purpose and framework of service is expressed has taken on economic and businesslike hues. Second, the underlying assumption that the business model is the heart and soul of the correct way to provide service is, at best, not well supported by the evidence. As one article tartly put it, in our

adoration of the corporate value system [we] are made to engage in a grotesque dance that apes the movements and moods of private enterprise. . . . Those who ceaselessly sing the praises of private industry's superior customer service must believe the rest of us are visiting here from Mars [and] anyone who has spent an hour standing in a bank line, or waiting for days for the telephone company's service personnel knows this. To say that public service in libraries needs to be improved presupposes that it is lacking or inadequate in the first place [and the] assumption seems to be based on yet another effort to ape private industry.[49]

Finally, there is more than rhetorical evidence that these practices distort the purposes—and therefore the practices—of libraries. For instance, a review of the literature on the evaluation of bibliographic/library instruction sessions and programs concluded that librarianship has produced only "persistently shallow instruments to evaluate that teaching [and these problems] have received no sustained research attention." There is virtually no correlation between the level at which our instructional evaluation methods actually assess and evaluate and the broad, overhyped claims made in our literature that argue for the critical importance of our role in teaching information literacy and our teaching role in distance learning and distributed information resources. Instead, what these consistently inadequate methods do seem to correlate to is a facile professional response to fads and trends of accountability, quality, and marketing/public relations along with the search for ways to justify funding and to stake a claim to some of the investments being made in technologies.[50] In other words, the underlying connection of our instructional evaluation methods/instruments to those practices that are intimately connected to the search for funding means that there is a built-in incentive not to find the shortcomings with our practices and seek ways to improve on them. Rather, the incentive is to continue to assess and evaluate with facile and surface methodologies and instruments to identify and document "quality" and "successes" that support the arguments for funding and the rhetoric of repositioning of libraries within the new public/philosophy information society. How we look at our services—and how we seek to improve them— is closely connected to the framework of institutional purpose in which we discuss our libraries. That framework has been consistently moved toward the new public philosophy conception of libraries, and it has filtered through to professional practices. The argument that business models and language are merely different ways to speak about the same unaltered public ends is a specious one, and our professional practices are in turn conforming to our repositioned purposes.

## CONCLUSION: CHIPPING AWAY AT THE PUBLIC SPHERE

In putting forward this critique and analysis, I am not suggesting that librarianship must operate in a "pure" manner, completely apart from any worldly influences by the business sector. That is clearly not realistic—or even desirable. Almost all who have critiqued these trends have done so with the full acknowledgment that public cultural institutions have—appropriately— benefited from adopting some business practices, and that these institutions do engage in some forms of "business" as they expend funds, make plans, build buildings, buy supplies, and so on.[51] Nor am I suggesting that librarianship alone is facing these trends, nor is the field singular in its reaction to them. The work by Mintzberg that was previously cited was an analysis of business fashions dominating the discussions of the proper workings of *government*. The size of our field—as economic entities *or* as a public projects— pales by comparison. Unlike the totality of the domination of library management literature by business fashions, there exists within librarianship some evident resistance to these trends. The essential point is that, outside of a more comprehensive view of what is happening to public institutions, reacting to specifics (like library users as "customers") without recognizing the interconnections among such trends in librarianship and similar developments in other parts of the public sphere is futile. Almost all public institutions and areas of public life have experienced similar effects from the dominance of the new public philosophy, and they have accelerated throughout the past twenty or more years.

The rather odd combination of Henry Mintzberg and Neil Postman have both put their fingers on the core issue for libraries. While Postman articulated the concept first, Mintzberg has given it a particularly contemporary ring. He notes the self-satisfaction with which the West has trumpeted the "victory" of capitalism with the fall of Communism in Eastern Europe and Russia. However, Mintzberg contends that

> the conclusion itself is wrong. . . . Capitalism did not triumph at all; balance did. [Unlike] the countries under communism [where] the state controlled an enormous proportion of all organized activity . . . we in the West have been living in balanced societies with strong private sectors, strong public sectors, and great strength in the sectors in between. The belief that capitalism has triumphed is now throwing the societies of the West out of balance. . . . When the enterprises are really free, the people are not. Indeed, there is a role in our society for different kinds of organizations and for the different contributions they make.[52]

More than twenty years before Mintzberg, Postman put forward the same basic point in what he called an "ecological" or "thermostatic" view of public institutions. In so doing, he posed cogent questions along similar lines: "what specific cultural biases, if left unchecked, will leave [society] distorted . . . to what extent [are public cultural institutions] competent to deal with those biases [and] how may [they] oppose, both emphatically and constructively, such biases?" Postman did not intend by this a "mindless opposition" to *every* current in society at the moment: not every trend *should* be opposed and the public would not continue to support such contrary institutions that are themselves not equipped to carry on massive and continual opposition. Rather, he invokes the ecological concept that "the stability and vitality of an environment depend not on what is *in* [it] but on the interplay of its elements; that is, on their diverse and dynamic complementarities." This view of public institutions is "not ideology-centered. It is balance-centered [and] its aim . . . is to make visible the prevailing biases of a culture" and oppose the damaging consequences of a society out of balance.[53] (Hence, the thermostat metaphor of providing heat when it is too cold and cooling when it is too hot.) In this review, I am suggesting that Postman's and Mintzberg's ideas frame our field's accommodations to those trends and how this contributes to the lack of balance in our culture, in the process furthering the reconception of public cultural institutions in economic terms and chipping away at the public sphere role of libraries. Alternatives *are* possible—and necessary.

As noted, librarianship is not alone. The "customer" metaphor has hit education as well—from elementary schools all the way up through universities and graduate education.[54] However, a colleague of mine argues that, even on its own merits, the metaphor is wrongly used. As commonly used in education, it assumes that the student is the customer, the school is the business providing the service, and the end product is a degree that the student receives. The logical conclusion of that approach is that "the only acceptable practice would be to teach the requested subjects and use the appropriate pedagogy to entertain and reward the students for coming to class."[55] Or, as my colleague more bluntly puts it, following that assumption through in a college would mean, in exchange for tuition, the school provides students with free telephones, cable television, pornography, junk food, booze, and privacy for four years with little or no academic requirements, and then at the end of four years sends them away with a very high grade point average and a degree of their choice.[56] The "customer" would most surely be happy—for a short time—under such circumstances, but I rather suspect that public and private support for colleges would not persist under such a model. If one insists on using this analogy, then the proper formulation is that society is the customer, buying the "good" in the form of an educated individual, produced (i.e., educated) by the school/university. Certainly the vast public subsidy of education at all levels would give primacy to society's claim as the ultimate "customer" who pays for the "products" of the educational system, or as yet another colleague puts it, "in reality we're all on welfare."[57]

The customer metaphor in librarianship appears in many guises: the quest for instantaneous and correct information delivery and the related quantification of customer "satisfaction," and "give 'em what they want" librarianship, to name just two. Each is subject to similar pitfalls, as noted previously, and each contributes to chipping away at the public sphere role of libraries. To take the first example, Budd cites a number of authors who argue that libraries should be more like a hardware store or the "McDonalds of information," presupposing that there is an awareness of content and knowledge available to formulate expectations (like similar approaches in education), and the "product . . . is as readily definable as the[se] examples and the 'customers' know what they want and what the library has to offer."[58] Our quest to meet (somewhat self-generated) expectations for instant, complete, and correct information provision is a manifestation of the hardware store customer metaphor.[59] The quest to improve customer service (i.e., give instantaneous and better answers) is itself based on widely held premises like "half-right reference," which has been called into question by recent research.[60] Budd argues that just under the surface of customer-driven librarianship is the notion that libraries deal in commodities,[61] which abandons the public notion of the library as a sharer of information and a place of creativity: "the unregulated, organic, spontaneous interactions among connected people" where information's value does not erode because it is shared, and in fact, can sometimes increase in value.[62] Further, instant delivery of the commodity of information simply isn't the same thing as actually learning something about what is being looked up, let alone real research that can be the focus of years worth of work.[63] I have repeatedly witnessed the disbelief of students who could not imagine that the statistic, fact, or image they dreamt up did not exist somewhere on the Internet and further watched them struggle for long periods trying to tease a needed bit of information out of this "faster" resource when there existed a readily available and intellectually more reliable print source for the information needed. The democratic public sphere roles of libraries as disseminators of rational, reasoned, and organized discourse, as a source of verifying or disputing claims, and as a space for the inclusion of alternative views of society and reality have no place in the vision of the library as the instant-satisfaction, fast-food equivalent of information.

Another version of the customer focus has been called "give 'em what they want" librarianship. Essentially the idea is to ignore merit or lasting value in selection and put a large number of "hot" items on the shelf to compete with the bookstore chains. This approach has what one author called "an associated set of predilections [for] a library manager," among them abandoning the practice of making available—and trying to introduce children and adults to—works of merit, acknowledging that "libraries are middle class institutions staffed by middle-class people for middle-class people," that "libraries should stop trying to be all things to all people," and the reliance on "fees for 15 percent of current income even if that prices out many low-income users."[64] Again, this approach lacks balance and assumes that the value of a library collection can and should *only* be quantified through the popularity of its titles. While I am not making the argument that a library and its librarians should be unresponsive to the desires of its community, such customer-driven librarianship abandons a number of public sphere roles. The first of these is (again) our role in organized social memory and rational discourse in a democracy. As Albert Henderson notes, "the potential value of a library collection is unrelated to its cost; it cannot be estimated in any way similar to the value of [other] services or facilities."[65] This is a point borne out over and over again: the "ephemera" of one age is the source of sometimes immense insight in another.[66] If our field has been accused of arrogance in knowing what is best (and safest) for people to read (and it has), this version of librarianship is guilty of the arrogance of asserting that what is best is exclusively what is popular at the moment. Such an approach by definition abandons the public sphere goal of a plurality of "voices" and viewpoints on our shelves and in our services, and it abandons the notion of the value of anything not "hot" to a present or future reader. At this point it is worth recounting Mintzberg's observation that there is a reason some services are in the public sector: their value is very real but difficult to measure and requires a different kind of judgment and management.

Further, libraries have never tried to be all things to all people. For instance, the vast majority of libraries have never attempted to systematically preserve and catalog the seventy-five to eighty years of radio broadcasts (or other broadcast media) that have served as information sources. Nor have they widely catered to tastes for pornography, erotica, underground music, or a myriad of other examples that would undoubtedly be popular and even increase gate count or server "hits." Libraries have not endeavored to provide simple, practical information in foreign languages to aid immigration or to successfully acquire social services. The complaint from some in the profession is that, if libraries truly do not overtly censor (as they claim), they have still managed to widely underrepresent or omit much information from their

shelves. The all-things-to-all-people charge is a straw man, essentially designed to mask a "competitive" version of librarianship, abandoning even the
pretense of fairness and rounded representation in services and collections.
This is most evident in the related ethic of fees and the abandonment of the
poor, who don't pay off in terms of taxes and money. Sanford Berman has
been indefatigable on this point for many years: "it is a lie to talk about 'free
public libraries' and 'equality of service'" under such circumstances, and
when poor patrons are regarded as "problems," we perpetuate inequalities.[67]
Budd has identified this who-can-pay, customer approach as a model in which
a *part* (that is, the library user who will pay off as a customer) comes to stand
for the group as a *whole*. Under such circumstances, collections and services
are winnowed to serve the "customer" and the "privileged customers will be
those who, in some way, contribute to the [fiscal] end of the library."[68] For
good measure, the bookstore-with-a-coffee-shop model is librarianship's me-
too response to the overt commercialization of public spaces for its "customers" and represents a trend much like advertising in classrooms to a captive
audience.[69]

In the end, customer-driven librarianship contributes to the changeover
from "a democracy of citizens [to] a democracy of consumers"[70] because it
is only those who can "vote" with money or tax support who are meaningfully
addressed by libraries. Henry Giroux contends that "within this new public
philosophy there is a ruthlessly frank expression of doubt about the viability
of democracy" and a "disdain [for] the democratic implications of pluralism."[71] Librarianship—which has prided itself on its vital role in democracy—
is turning that credo into empty lip service through its avid adoption of the
customer-driven model and in the process chipping away at what remains of
the public sphere in our institutions. It is worth returning to the idea of
balance that Postman and Mintzberg explored, and Giroux has linked that
with the diminution of the public sphere. This is a good point at which to
revisit his critique and his vision of the democratic public sphere and the role
of public cultural institutions:

[A] narrow redefinition of freedom as a private good may actually present a threat to
democracy. . . . Markets don't reward moral behavior, and as corporate culture begins
to dominate public life it becomes more difficult for citizens to think critically and act
morally. [This] necessitates that [we] create organizations capable of mobilizing civic
dialogue, provide an alternative conception of the meaning and purpose of [public
institutions, and] challenge corporate power's ascendancy over . . . mechanisms of civil
society. This project requires . . . institutional spaces that highlight, nourish, and
evaluate the tension between civil society and corporate power while simultaneously
. . . prioritiz[ing] citizen rights over the consumer rights. [Public institutions must]
nourish the proper balance between democratic public spheres and commercial power,
between identities founded on democratic principles and identities steeped in forms

of competitive, self-interested individualism that celebrate their own material and ideological advantages.[72]

Those values exist within librarianship or it could never be seriously argued that our institutions enable, enact, and embody much of the public sphere. But under customer-driven librarianship, democracy—and one of the necessary foundations of democracy in the form of a public sphere in which alternatives are possible to envision—is surely leaking away.

## NOTES

1. Joel Spring, *The American School: 1642–1985* (New York: Longman, 1986), 320–23.
2. One of the best examples of the new and blunt approach has been the case of the Philadelphia public schools. With widespread failure and collapse and longstanding fiscal crises in the city's schools, the Commonwealth of Pennsylvania sought to take over the system, awarding a no-bid contract to Chris Whittle's Edison Schools to study the system and make recommendations. Edison unsurprisingly recommended private management of many of the schools, and the state promised more aid as a result. Unsurprisingly, Edison was awarded a very large share of the contract with their promises of accountability through raising student test scores. In the ensuing controversy, protests, and negotiations with the city, state government officials were quite blunt about withholding funding until/unless the privatization was seen through. Mayor John Street was in the end able to blunt (but not stave off) the depth of the state/private control of the school system and the number of schools awarded to Edison under the contract while maintaining the extra state funds. See "School Building Blocks," *Philadelphia Inquirer,* 2 August 2002, A22; Larry Eichel, "Phila. Schools on Track?" *Philadelphia Inquirer,* 2 August 2002, A23; Dale Mezzacappa, "School Official Misses Deadline," *Philadelphia Inquirer,* 16 August 2002, B2; Jacques Steinberg and Diana Henriques, "Complex Calculations on Academics," *New York Times,* 16 July 2002, A10; and Jacques Steinberg, "Buying in to the Company School," *New York Times,* 17 February 2002, A24. For a good overview of how Philadelphia's schools came to this point, see William Kashatus, "Public Education in Private Hands," *New York Times,* 2 February 2002, A19. For a very probusiness and privatization view of these developments (and for the similarity to the ways in which librarianship is discussed), see "City of Brotherly Thugs," *Wall Street Journal,* 2 December 2001, A18; and "Philadelphia's Loss," *Wall Street Journal,* 19 April 2002, A18.
3. John Buschman and Dorothy Warner, "A Slip Between the Cup and the Lip: Practical and Intellectual Problems of Marketing U.S. Academic Libraries," in *Education and Research for Marketing and Quality Management in Libraries,* ed. Rejean Savard (Munich: K. G. Saur, 2002), 267–78. For a jargon and business cliché-filled piece that emphasizes this connection, see Darlene Weingand, "Managing Outside the Box: Marketing and Quality Management as Key to Library Effectiveness," in *Education and Research for Marketing,* ed. Savard, 8–17.
4. John Budd, "A Critique of Customer and Commodity," *College & Research Libraries,* July 1997, 313. This point is again inadvertently strengthened by Weingand.
5. Nancy Van House, Beth Weil, and Charles McClure, *Measuring Academic Li-*

*brary Performance* (Chicago: American Library Association, 1990), vii, 3. A similar volume was previously developed for public libraries. See LAMA/LOMS Comparative Library Organization Committee (CLOC) and CLOC Bibliography Task Force, "Required Reading for Library Administrators, Part Two: An Annotated Bibliography of Highly Cited Library and Information Science Authors and Their Works," *Library Administration & Management* 17, no. 1 (2002): 11–20.

6. Christie Koontz, "Continuing Education for Library and Information Professionals: A Practical Approach," in *Education and Research for Marketing*, ed. Savard, 128; for school libraries see also Paula Montgomery, "Evolution of School Library Media Programs in the 1990s," *The Bowker Annual*, 42nd ed., ed. Dave Bogart (New Providence, N.J.: R. R. Bowker, 1997), 249–50.

7. Peter Hernon and Charles McClure, *Evaluation and Library Decision Making* (Norwood, N.J.: Ablex, 1990), 6.

8. Joanne Marshall, "Determining Our Worth, Communicating Our Value," *Library Journal*, 15 November 2000, 28. See also Peter Hernon, "Editorial: The Practice of Outcomes Assessment," *Journal of Academic Librarianship* 28, no. 1 (2002): 1–2; a number of entries in the CLOC bibliography indicate that major works in the field revolve around this principle as well.

9. Hernon and McClure, xv.

10. Carolyn Snyder, "Measuring Library Service Quality with a Focus on the LibQUAL+ Project: An Interview with Fred Heath," *Library Administration & Management* 16, no. 1 (2002): 4–7. This perspective is pervasive in the volume edited by Savard, *Education and Research for Marketing*; see also Karen Chapman and Kate Ragsdale, "Improving Service Quality with a Library Service Assessment Program," *Library Administration & Management* 16, no. 1 (2002): 8–15.

11. Henry Mintzberg, "Managing Government, Governing Management," *Harvard Business Review*, May–June 1996, 78–79.

12. See CLOC; Elaine Harger, "The 'Enola Gay' Controversy as a Library Issue," *Progressive Librarian* 10/11 (Winter 1995/96): 60–78; and Kathleen Baxter, "In the Headlines," *American Artist*, August 2001, 66.

13. Mintzberg, 79.

14. Mintzberg, 79–80.

15. Again, see Savard, *Education and Research for Marketing*.

16. William Starbuck, "Congealing Oil: Inventing Ideologies to Justify Acting Ideologies Out," *Journal of Management Studies* 19, no. 1 (1982): 3–27.

17. Steve Coffman, "What if You Ran Your Library Like a Bookstore?" *American Libraries*, March 1998, 40–46. The caption to this story asks the leading rhetorical question "what's wrong with more service hours, bigger collections and great coffee?" It is also worth noting that this was the feature on the cover of that issue of *American Libraries*, again with a leading headline in the form of a question (Why can't a library be more like a bookstore?) and a mock advertisement circled in red, for an "Information Manager, 21st-Century Public Information and Popular Culture Center seeks dynamic customer service-oriented professional to direct strategic visioning at technologically advanced facility. Bookstore experience required. MLS helpful." See also Benton Foundation, *Buildings, Books, and Bytes: Libraries and Communities in the Digital Age* (Washington, D.C.: Benton Foundation, 1996).

18. Mark Clayton, "Food for Thought," *Christian Science Monitor*, 22 January 2002, 12; Scott Carlson, "The Deserted Library: As Students Work Online, Reading

Rooms Empty Out—Leading Some Campuses to Add Starbucks," *Chronicle of Higher Education,* 16 November 2001, A35; and Teresa Lindeman, "Would You Like a Latte with That Bestseller?" *Pittsburgh Post-Gazette,* 18 February 2001, <http://www.post-gazette.com/businessnews/20010218library2.asp>.

19. See Clayton; Carlson; "Should We Worry if Some Libraries Seem to Be Attracting Fewer Students?" (Letters to the Editor) *Chronicle of Higher Education,* 21 December 2001, B4; and "no.2104—Declining Use Measures," distributed 26 August 1999 by John Abbott on Colldv-l@usc.edu.

20. William Miller, "The Library as a Place: Tradition and Evolution," *Library Issues* 22, no. 3 (January 2002).

21. See Hernon and McClure; Budd, 317–18; and John Sumison, "Library Statistics for Marketing," *IFLA Journal* 27, no. 1 (2001): 221–32.

22. Weingand, 9.

23. William Birdsall, "A 'New Deal' for Libraries in the Digital Age?" *Library Trends* 46, no. 1 (1997): 52–67; Benton; Coffman.

24. Clayton; Lindeman; "Should We Worry"; Carlson.

25. "Should We Worry." See in particular the letter by Diane Graves.

26. Clayton.

27. Coffman. For another defense of cataloging, see Michael Gorman, "The Corruption of Cataloging," *Library Journal,* 15 September 1995, 32.

28. Evelyn Smykla, *Marketing and Public Relations Activities in ARL Libraries* (Washington, D.C.: Association of Research Libraries, 1999) in Flyer 240: 1.

29. See Redmond Kathleen Molz and Phyllis Dain, *Civic Space/Cyberspace: The American Public Library in the Information* Age (Cambridge, Mass: MIT, 1999), 28–33; Robert Wedgeworth, "Donor Relations as Public Relations: Toward a Philosophy of Fund-Raising," *Library Trends* 48, no. 3 (2000): 530–39; Edwin Clay and Patricia Bangs, "Entrepreneurs in the Public Library: Reinventing an Institution," *Library Trends* 48, no. 3 (2000): 606–18; and Brian Reynolds, "Public Library Funding: Issues, Trends, and Resources," *Advances in Librarianship* 18 (1994): 159–68.

30. Gary Ford, "Introduction," in *Marketing and the Library,* ed. Gary Ford (New York: Haworth Press, 1984), 3.

31. Smykla.

32. Jean Key Gates, *Introduction to Librarianship,* 2nd ed. (New York: McGraw-Hill, 1976), 156, 198–99; and John Buschman, "History and Theory of Information Poverty," in *Poor People and Library Services,* ed. Karen Venturella (Jefferson, N.C.: McFarland, 1998), 20.

33. Nancy Marshall, "Public Relations in Academic Libraries: A Descriptive Analysis," *Journal of Academic Librarianship* 27, no. 2 (2001): 117; see also Clay and Bangs; and Albert Tabah, "Marketing Electronic Services: The One-on-One Approach," *Argus* 22, no. 1 (1993): 25–28.

34. Michele Russo and Nancy Colborn, "Something for (Almost) Nothing: Public Relations on a Shoestring in an Academic Library," *Library Administration & Management* 16, no. 3 (2002): 143.

35. Martin Gomez, "Marketing Models for Libraries: A Survey of Effective Muses from Far Afield," *Library Administration & Management* 15, no. 3 (2001): 169. See also Susan Kent, "The Public Library Director in the Dot (.) World," *New Library World* 103, no. 1/2 (2002): 48–54.

36. See Clay and Bangs; Wedgeworth; and Reynolds.

37. Russo and Colborn, 142.

38. Dinesh Gupta, "Making Relationship with Customers: An Agenda for 21st Century Library and Information Services" (Academy of Marketing Conference 2000, University of Derby, England, 5–7 July 2000).

39. Arnold Hirshon, "Running with the Red Queen: Breaking New Habits to Survive in the Virtual World," *Advances in Librarianship* 20 (1996): 4. This author's rhetoric is arguably pitched at the most extreme and hysterical level among all those cited.

40. Lindeman.

41. Ellen Altman and Peter Hernon, "Service Quality and Customer Satisfaction Do Matter," *American Libraries,* August 1998, 53–54.

42. See Budd; Teresa Omidsalar and Mohmoud Omidsalar, "Customer Service: A View from the Trenches," *American Libraries,* February 1999, 24–25; William Fisher, "Library Management: The Latest Fad, a Dismal Science, or Just Plain Work?" *Library Acquisitions: Practice & Theory* 20, no. 1 (1996): 49–56; and John Lubans, "'I Borrowed the Shoes, but the Holes Are Mine': Management Fads, Trends, and What's Next," *Library Administration & Management* 14, no. 3 (2000): 131–34. Among many examples, see the volume edited by Savard, *Education and Research for Marketing;* Hirshon; Susan Hahn, Pat Weaver-Meyers, and Michal Bolin, "Assessing Customer Demands: Making Changes That Count," *Library Administration & Management* 16, no. 1 (2002): 16–23; Richard Dougherty, "Being Successful (Nimble and Agile) in the Current Turbulent Environment," *Journal of Academic Librarianship* 27, no. 4 (2001): 265–66; Rivkah Sass, "Marketing the Worth of Your Library," *Library Journal,* 15 June 2002, 37–38; Charles Robinson, "The Public Library Vanishes," *Library Journal,* 15 March 1992, 51–53; Blaise Cronin, "Customer Satisfaction," *Library Journal,* 15 October 2000, 44; John Lubans, "'To Save the Time of the User': Customer Services at the Millennium," *Library Administration & Management* 15, no. 3 (2001): 179–82; and Altman and Hernon.

43. Norman Oder, "Outsourcing: Model—or Mistake?" *Library Journal,* 15 March 1997, 28–29; and Janet Swan Hill, "Outsourcing: Understanding the Fuss," *The Bowker Annual,* 46th ed., ed. Dave Bogart (New Providence, N.J.: R. R. Bowker, 2001), 218–32.

44. "IFLA Pre-Conference Seminar: Using Market Research to Improve Customer Satisfaction." 2002. International Federation of Library Associations and Institutions. 5 June 2002, <http://dis.shef.ac.uk/sheila/ifla>, <http://dis.shef.ac.uk/sheila/marketing/sources.htm>. See also Altman and Hernon; Hahn, et. al.; Sumison; Dinesh Gupta and Ashok Jambhekar, "On the Link Between Marketing and Quality," in *Education and Research for Marketing,* ed. Savard, 205–20; Waldomiro Vergueiro and Telma de Carvalho, "Quality Indicators and Marketing," in *Education and Research for Marketing,* ed. Savard, 236–46; Sheila Webber, "Teaching of Marketing and Quality Management in Schools of Library and Information Science (LIS) in the UK: A Review and Report of Findings," in *Education and Research for Marketing,* ed. Savard, 43–68; and Dinesh Gupta, "A Focus on Customers: Imperative for Delivering Quality Library and Information Services," *Proceedings of the Conference on Delivering Service Quality: Managerial Challenges for the 21st Century,* ed. M. Raghavachari and K. Ramani (London: Macmillan, 2000), 401–6.

45. Judith Broady-Preston and Emma Barnes, "Creating and Sustaining Competitive Advantage in Libraries: Wales, Case Study," in *Education and Research for Mar-*

*keting,* ed. Savard, 309–16; and Diane Mittermeyer, "Repositioning the Library with Two Lines of Information Services for a Target Market: The Virtual Customers," in *Education and Research for Marketing,* ed. Savard, 281–92.

46. Lubans, "To Save"; Dinesh Gupta, "Quality Management in Library and Information Services: Is Ranganathan Revisited?" *ILA Bulletin* 36, no. 2 (2000): 52–55; and Dinesh Gupta, "User-Focus Approach: Central to Ranganathan's Philosophy," *Library Science with a Slant to Documentation and Information Studies* 36, no. 2 (1999): 123–28.

47. Weingand, 9.

48. Budd, 310.

49. Omidsalar and Omidsalar.

50. Buschman and Warner, "A Slip"; John Buschman and Dorothy A. Warner, "Wider Access to Higher Education in the United States: An Evaluative Case Study of the Library," in *Researching Widening Access: International Perspectives,* ed. Mike Osborne and Jim Gallacher (Glasgow, Scotland: Center for Research in Lifelong Learning, Glasgow Caledonian University, 2001), 60–65; John Buschman and Michael Carbone, "Technocracy, Educational Structures and Libraries: Historical Notes from the United States," *Journal of Education Policy* 11, no. 5 (1996): 561–78; John Buschman and Michael Carbone, "De-Politicized Technology and Intellectual/ Economic Problems of Information Technology: Notes on a U.S. Higher Education Case History," in *Managing Learning Innovation: The Challenges of the Changing Curriculum,* ed. Geoff Windle (Lincoln, England: University of Lincolnshire and Humberside, 1999), 22–28.

51. See, for example, Geoff Whitty, "The 'Privatization' of Education," *Educational Leadership* 41, no. 7 (1984): 51–54; and Budd.

52. Mintzberg, 75.

53. Neil Postman, *Teaching as a Conserving Activity* (New York: Delta, 1979), 18, 20, 24–25. Henry Giroux, "Vocationalizing Higher Education: Schooling and the Politics of Corporate Culture," *College Literature* 26, no. 3 (1999): 147–61 makes a series of similar points to Mintzberg and Postman.

54. Caralee Adams, "School Choice," *Better Homes and Gardens,* March 2001, 88–90; Howard Buchbinder and Janice Newson, "The Service University and Market Forces," *Academe,* July–August 1992, 13–15; Henry Giroux, "Schools for Sale: Public Education, Corporate Culture, and the Citizen-Consumer," *Educational Forum* 63 (Winter 1999): 140–49; John Palatella, "Ivory Towers in the Marketplace," *Dissent,* Summer 2001, 70–73; and Arthur Bayer, "What is Wrong with Customer?" *College Teaching* 44, no. 3 (1996): 82.

55. Bayer.

56. Though Bayer is quoted on this point, my colleague Dr. Jeffrey Halpern in the Sociology Department of Rider University has vociferously been attacking this notion for more than a decade.

57. Palatella, 71. My other colleague who presses home the point to students of how heavily subsidized all middle-class activities are is Dr. Joe Gowaskie in the History Department of Rider University.

58. Budd, 312.

59. For a good analysis, see David Isaacson, "Instant Information Gratification," *American Libraries,* February 2002, 39. For examples of such an approach in the literature, see Richard Dougherty, "Reference Around the Clock: Is It in Your Fu-

ture?" *American Libraries,* May 2002, 44, 46. Judith Trump and Ian Tuttle, "Here, There, and Everywhere: Reference at the Point-of-Need," *Journal of Academic Librarianship* 27, no. 6 (2001): 464–66; Joel Rutstein, Anna DeMiller, and Elizabeth Fuseler, "Ownership Versus Access: Shifting Perspectives for Libraries," *Advances in Librarianship* 17 (1993): 48; a particularly vapid example that advocates the "weightless" instant library is Phyllis Spies, "Libraries, Leadership, and the Future," *Library Management* 21, no. 3 (2000): 123–27.

60. For example, Hernon and McClure, 205 (the originators of the 55% rule) contend that thirty studies conducted over twenty years confirm their original findings. This is disputed by John Richardson, "Reference Is Better Than We Thought," *Library Journal,* 15 April 2002, 41–42, who "found a lack of agreement on the definition of reference service and inconsistent operational definitions" in the literature reviews. The research on twelve California public libraries showed a much higher success rate (90%) when the nature of the actual questions was more carefully classified, vetted, and examined. Interestingly on another well-worn research justification for changing libraries, Albert Henderson, "The Devil and Max Weber in the Research University," *Journal of Information Ethics,* Spring 1999, 27, attacks the continuing use of the "Pittsburgh study," which claimed to prove that a small proportion of any library's collection accounted for the vast majority of circulation items. He notes that the study "openly declared that its purpose was to justify reduced library expenditures" and cites a number of studies and analyses that overturned its findings. Nevertheless, it continues to be cited, as "half-right reference" will undoubtedly continue to be as well.

61. Budd.

62. Siva Vaidhyanathan, "The Content-Provider Paradox: Universities in the Information Ecosystem," *Academe,* September–October 2002, 36–37.

63. Isaacson; Budd, 312.

64. Patricia Wallace, "Outsourcing Book Selection in Public and School Libraries," *Collection Building* 16, no. 4 (1997): 160–61; Robinson is the "guru" of this approach, which he made the centerpiece of the Baltimore County Public Library. He is also the source of the "McDonalds of information" model.

65. Henderson, 23.

66. Among countless examples: Robert Darnton, *The Great Cat Massacre and Other Episodes in French Cultural History* (New York, Basic Books, 1984), used a printing society's wage book, a semifictional autobiography of a print shop worker, and an odd, obsessively complete "inventory" of the city of Montpellier to reconstruct a view of eighteenth-century French society from the ground up; Wayne Wiegand, "Main Street Public Library: The Availability of Controversial Materials in the Rural Heartland, 1890–1956," *Libraries and Culture* 33, no. 1 (1998): 127–33, has studied old (and increasingly rare because they are routinely thrown out) accession/de-accession books used in public libraries to identify censorship patterns in small-town libraries; Jonathon Katz, ed., *Gay American History* (New York: Harper Colophon, 1976) used word of mouth, remembered copies, and unearthed diaries—much of which was still privately held—to make an early compilation of documentation on the suppressed history of gays and lesbians; Nancy Wicklund, "The Erik Routley Collection of Books and Hymnals at Talbott Library, Westminster Choir College of Rider University," in *The Hymn* 53, no. 4 (2002): 46–49, notes that some of the most valuable pieces of documentation in music start out as ephemera; Edward Ball, *Slaves in the Family* (New York: Ballantine, 1998), was able to track down extensive original

family plantation documents scattered among far-flung libraries and archives in the South and in turn trace and find descendents of the slaves his family owned. In a few rare instances, with a specific location he was able to trace those black families' roots back to an African ancestor.

67. Sanford Berman, "Libraries, Class, and the 'Poor People's Policy'," *American Libraries,* March 1998, 38. See also Karen Venturella, ed., *Poor People and Library Services* (Jefferson, N.C.: McFarland, 1998).

68. Budd, 314.

69. See, for example, Henry Giroux, "Education Incorporated?" *Educational Leadership,* October 1998, 12–17; Alex Molnar and Joseph Reaves, "Buy Me! Buy Me!" *Educational Leadership* 59, no. 2 (2001): 74–80; and Geov Parrish, "Ad Creep in the Classroom," *Working for Change,* 6 February 2002, <http://www.workingforchange.com/article.cfm?ItemId = 12769>.

70. G. Grace in Giroux, "Education Incorporated," 12.

71. Henry Giroux, "Liberal Arts Education and the Struggle for Public Life: Dreaming About Democracy," *South Atlantic Quarterly* 89, no. 1 (1990): 117, 119.

72. Giroux, "Vocationalizing," 148, 157–58.

# 7

## DRIFTING TOWARD THE CORPORATE MODEL: A BRIEF LOOK AT ALA

### INTRODUCTION

The American Library Association (ALA) always proudly announces itself as "the oldest and largest library association in the world," "a leader in defending intellectual freedom," and "the voice of U.S. libraries and the millions of people who depend on them."[1] There is more than a grain of truth to those assertions. For instance, it is notable that the benchmark "Library Bill of Rights" preceded the American Association of University Professors' landmark "Statement of Principles on Academic Freedom and Tenure" by a year,[2] and our policy has historically been backed up by deeds with concrete results. The incremental extension of intellectual freedom principles over the years has resulted in some progress in equalizing access to libraries, information, and learning opportunities,[3] and in his critical review of American librarianship, Wayne Wiegand concludes that ours has been the *only* consistent voice in our society advocating equal access to information, preservation and representation of minority points of view, and organization of texts around the *principles* of access.[4] He notes elsewhere that the "mere existence [of] massive collections . . . check[s] the tendency of society's problem solvers to declare that they have arrived at the 'final answer,' that they have discovered an 'absolute truth' about human behavior."[5]

This is not only an historical legacy. A quick review of recent ALA reports written for *The Bowker Annual* indicates the association's continued help to libraries with challenged materials and publicity campaigns to highlight banned books and honoring those who advance the Freedom to Read policy.[6] The legacy of access and equity policies has been extended to cover networked information resources like the Internet,[7] and ALA has consequently been at the center of court battles fighting censorship issues in federal legislation like the Communications Decency Act and the Children's Internet Protection Act.[8] ALA has consistently lobbied hard to maintain the E-rate discount for libraries and again fought for them in court in order to promote equal access to information along with fair and fair-use copyright principles for electronic resources.[9] Lastly, recent ALA presidents have put democracy, the digital divide, diversity, and information equity at the center of Association activities.[10] This record—both historical and in recent years—represents an honorable legacy for ALA and librarianship, and its importance should not be minimized.

There are, however, signs that ALA is drifting toward a new public philosophylike corporate model. By this I mean an emphasis on stabilizing the "business climate" (that is, not offending members, donors, businesses, and foundations) through avoidance of hot-button issues (irrespective of their centrality as a professional principle at times) and a leadership/management emphasis on delivering a more "unified" message from the field. This chapter is by no means a comprehensive review of ALA activities. However, a sampling of issues, positions (or lack of positions) and actions (or lack of actions) that have occurred within ALA can be seen as representing a drift toward a more corporate, businesslike approach to association matters. It is worth remembering that those matters are, in principle, governed democratically and organized around the stated values of the profession (like the "Library Bill of Rights" and Freedom to Read). The chapter will proceed by reviewing—in brief—two broad categories of ALA issues—those representing inaction and those representing action—and finish with a summary conclusion.


## INACTION

There have been a number of recent issues on which ALA has been remarkably inactive. It is not that the association is unaware of the issues or that there is not a subunit (like SRRT—the Social Responsibilities Round Table or GODORT—the Government Documents Round Table) attempting to raise the issue. Rather, the analogy to newspaper coverage is a good one: is the story on the front page and above the fold or buried in the middle of the paper? Is it relegated to the "Lifestyles" or "Weekend" section (and therefore a lesser matter)? The same can be said for ALA activities. Though a committee or a task force is set up, how quickly, how thoroughly, and in what manner the issue is taken up by the association is the question, and the results have reflected a political shift toward a corporate model. The following brief review represents important issues that have not risen to the top of the association's agenda in terms of action or even as a matter of debate.

## Outsourcing

This is the one issue that took a place of some prominence within ALA, though from a distinctly minority source. It was centered on the ham-handed actions to totally outsource selection in Hawaii by Bart Kane (see summary in chapter 4). It was introduced to ALA Council (the association's democratic governing body) by the Hawaii Working Group, which was formed out of the Alternatives in Print Task Force, which is itself appended to the SRRT. In other words, outsourcing as an issue of debate did not come from ALA leadership; it came to the formal attention of the association from an ad hoc group, formed from a subgroup of an affiliated round table. The resolution of censure failed to pass Council because it was deemed "inappropriate to take a stand on what was viewed as a local management issue."[11] (This is an approach within ALA that we will encounter again.) However, the extensive debate over the resolution did result in the formation of a task force and a research project. The Outsourcing Task Force, however, could not come up with a consensus definition of privatization, stated that there is a "complete lack of consensus in the field as to what constitutes a core service," (i.e., that which should not be outsourced or privatized), and "concluded that there was insufficient evidence that outsourcing per se represents a threat to libraries."[12] (We will encounter the results of the related research project later on.) In other words, in the face of vehement librarian protest, eloquent arguments on the nature of communities and services and the differences with business, the cancellation of the Hawaii selection contract with Baker & Taylor, the resignation of Kane, and the introduction of state legislation dealing with the issue, the American Library Association could identify no core value or practice in the field to defend against the business model of librarianship that total outsourcing of selection and privatization represents, and therefore took no action or stated no principle on the issue.[13]

## Consolidation of Publishing, Distribution, and Media Ownership

This is an issue that has consistently received sustained scholarly attention and documentation. The essential point of these critiques comes down to the viability of a democracy in the face of an oligopoly of global media and information resources. Related issues of market censorship, the debasement of journalism, disinformation, the lowest common denominator of entertainment, and the bread-and-circus aspects of sports, politics, and news have all been thoroughly examined.[14] The parallel themes as they relate to censorship, collecting alternative publications and media, the nature of diversity on library shelves in the face of corporate control of cultural output, and selection criteria have all been extrapolated from this work and applied directly—even compellingly—to libraries in our own literature.[15] However, the primary sources of this vein of scholarship come from increasingly marginalized groups within ALA (or those only loosely affiliated with it): members of the previously mentioned Alternatives in Print Task Force, the Progressive Librarians Guild, and SRRT are three primary (and closely related) sources of this work. ALA has never seriously dealt with the issue. In fact, when the noted media scholar Mark Crispin Miller spoke on this topic at the 1998 American Library Association Annual Conference in Washington, D.C., he specifically requested that ALA join—or create a liaison with—his Project on Media Ownership during the question-and-answer period after his talk.[16] If this has happened (and I believe it has not), it has had no discernable impact on discussion or action within ALA. The ramifications of consolidated, global media ownership for libraries and public information remain an invisible topic within ALA.

## The Aftermath of the September 11th Terrorist Attacks

Librarianship has faced quite a number of challenges since the World Trade Center and Pentagon were attacked. Librarians have been ordered by the federal government to purge government document items from their collections, the FBI was given the power to get a search warrant for library records without probable cause, and the Patriot Act allows the government to monitor library circulation records and library Internet use.[17] A survey done not long after the attacks showed that indeed, some small proportion of libraries had received requests for information from law enforcement (8.3%) and some had become more restrictive with Internet use (10%). More alarming, very few respondents to the survey (3%) knew of the procedures to put off or fight a Patriot Act search warrant to protect patron confidentiality.[18] Despite the notable McCarthyist overtones of the federal government's actions and the wide-ranging nature of this challenge to our professional values in a democracy, ALA's response to all of this has been pallid. The association did not join the American Civil Liberties Union, the Electronic Privacy Information Center, and the American Booksellers Foundation for Free Expression in filing an expedited Freedom of Information Act request on the use of the Patriot Act to gather information from booksellers, libraries, and so forth.[19] For the better part of a year, ALA did not produce documentation on how to fight or slow such requests for information but rather provided links to other organizations that did—not through the main Web page but through ALA's Washington office site.[20] It wasn't until June of 2002 that the ALA Council passed a resolution affirming the public's privacy rights in their use of libraries and "implicitly" guided library staff to try and protect patron's privacy, providing some guidance and documentation on how to do so.[21] All of this follows a cautious initial statement written in October of 2001 that ALA did not release alone but with two other library associations—primarily questioning the need for more legal authority to acquire library records in an investigation.[22] Tom Paine mocked the "summer soldier and the sunshine patriot" who shrank from defending principles in difficult times, and ALA has come very close that example in this case.

In sum, ALA has at times displayed an overabundance of overcaution, and not exclusively on these issues.[23] I think the explanation for this fits Michael Apple's description and analysis of textbook publishers. It is easily and, I would argue, efficaciously adaptable to ALA's pattern of inaction under such circumstances. The association's nonresponse in these cases is "a selection . . . that often represents the values of more powerful groups in society" and an orientation "to the minimization of risks, followed by a [financial] strategy." In other words, in the presence of a direct relationship to professional practice or principle (which is the case in each of these instances) there is a calculation as to whether or not pursuing the issue is worth the candle. Apple in turn asks the pertinent questions: How do economics affect such social/cultural decisions, and "which publics do [we] consider most important? How do the internal politics [affect those decisions]? Complaints about the vapid quality of [our nonresponses] ring false unless we place them back into the economic and political situations in which they exist."[24] I would suggest that these instances indicate that ALA is beginning to behave in the broad manner of these businesses and in the process moving toward that model.

## ACTION

In contrast to the previous examples, there are instances where ALA—or a significant subunit like the Council or the Association of College & Research Libraries (ACRL—ALA's largest division)—have taken specific actions, and they have incrementally moved the association toward a corporate model and put into question ALA's institutional commitment to its principles. Again, the relevant questions are ones of emphasis, where energy and resources are going instead, and toward what ends. What follows is a number of relevant examples.

### "One Voice"

ALA has taken a number of actions over the last decade that, in their totality, point toward the corporate model of speaking for the profession. Some of these have come in the form of internal policies, the manner in which the terms of a debate have been cast, and bureaucratic changes that have effectively eliminated much of the possibility for items to officially come before the association as an item of business. I am using "one voice" as an umbrella phrase to characterize a number of such actions and proposals. It is borrowed from my colleague Mark Rosenzweig, who is a highly active member of ALA Council and who has critiqued a specific policy to this effect.[25] Many of the

examples listed as discreet items have in fact arisen from the highly interconnected political tangle of ALA and attempts to get the association to take
action on some of the progressive policies already in place or to take a stand
on issues that the association could make a difference on.[26] The responses to
those proposals (that is, the various actions taken) can be characterized as a
corporatelike attempt to impose one voice speaking for the profession. For
example:

- The quorum for a membership meeting at the annual conference was raised, effectively meaning that previous membership resolutions like the Poor People's Policy,
censuring a library publisher for censorship and disciplining an author, and stating
a position on the Columbus quincentennial could no longer be officially considered
by ALA Council without the higher quorum. Such issues were placed on the agenda
of ALA's governing bodies from this venue—with the accompanying responsibility
to deal with the issue (as directed in the ALA Constitution). The higher quorum is
exceedingly difficult to achieve with competing meetings, poor time slots, and the
attractions of the large cities in which ALA meetings must be held, and critics hold
that this was a purposeful move to disable the membership meeting, taken specifically in response to ALA's involvement in a controversial issue—Israeli censorship.
Since it was raised, no membership meeting has met the quorum, and thus no
controversial issues have come out of it.[27]

- ACRL has passed a policy that directs that it should *only* act on social and political
issues when it relates "directly" to the division's mission and strategic plan *and*
where they are recognized as having some authority on the subject. The strategic
plan is itself a leadership-driven document. Again, this came about as part of a
backlash and has effectively stopped many controversial issues of principle from
being considered by ACRL in the first place.[28]

- ALA has become consistently more legalistic—and threatening of legal action—
toward those *portions of the association* that do choose to speak on issues well within
their purview and purpose. The pretext is often to make sure that a required dis-
claimer is used noting that the round table (or task force, or working group, etc.)
does not speak for the association as a whole. However, the aggressive tactics used
(speaking through lawyers, making internal policies and political preferences appear
to be legal positions, etc.) speak more to attempts to bully and cow the round tables
and so forth to get them to drop the issue or to disassociate themselves entirely
from the profession and ALA in the taking of—and publishing of—those positions.[29]

- There was a serious proposal in 2001 to limit discussion, topics, language, and
debate on ALA's Council listserv—which is used to facilitate between-meeting communication among the councilors. In response, many (myself among them) pointed
out the (apparently overlooked) untenable irony in *any* ALA forum imposing communicative limits, censoring, and ruling dissenting arguments out of order while
publicly defending intellectual freedom and fighting censorship in libraries. While
the limits were not imposed, it is worth noting that this proposal came from a
member of ALA's governing body.[30]

- The previously mentioned Outsourcing Task Force also had a funded research
agenda, which was combined with another group within ALA. The combined pur-

pose was to clarify the much muddied "core values" of the profession that were so "unclear" as revealed in the outsourcing debate. The result—a "Statement on Core Values"—was, as I have written, "a bland homogenization of euphemisms vaguely pointing at ALA policies already on the books. [It was] just a bureaucratic layer of wording which allows some policies to be more equal than others, by proxy and interpretation," including such core issues as "free and open access." Further, the statement contained no direct reference to intellectual freedom, and the base of authority as to who gets to interpret (and thus determine) what is a "core value" when the issue at hand is raised was a question never answered. Most probably, it would have been the association's Executive Council, and most probably it would have been interpreted in a restrictive way. In a dramatic Council debate and meeting, it was barely defeated.[31]

In sum, though not monolithically successful, such efforts speak to a growing corporate sense of the need for ALA *not* to behave like a democratic professional organization but rather to speak with one voice—with consequent results in the form of actions taken against those instances where the association's "message" does not come through as unified. The corporate nature of this approach will be explicated shortly in the section on ALA's publicity campaign and business affiliations.

## Limiting the Meaning of Intellectual Freedom

The association has consistently acted, in a number of venues, to limit the scope and the meaning of intellectual freedom in the profession. This was not always the case. Previously, ALA has linked this principle to a version of academic freedom (since 1946), stating that "academic freedom means for the librarian intellectual freedom [, which] implies freedom in the selection of books, in the presentation of material on all sides of controversial questions, and in the dissemination of information on all subjects. [This] makes it possible for librarians to devote themselves to the practice of their profession without fear of interference or of dismissal for . . . unjust reasons." This was followed up by a joint statement with the American Association of University Professors (AAUP) on academic freedom for librarians and a "Security of Employment" policy—both of which reinforce the essential intellectual freedom of librarians within their workplace.[32] A preliminary survey by a co-author and myself found strong support for this principle as a core value of the profession (much prior to the "Statement on Core Values" noted previously). Our survey also found an often shallow understanding of the concept and a lesser estimate of the depth of these principles in the workplace when responses from administrators were factored out of the results.[33]

However, ALA's Office for Intellectual Freedom (under the leadership of one person for well over thirty years[34]) has consistently ruled that any violation of workplace intellectual freedom is an "internal matter" in which the association cannot interfere, despite the fact that there are clear policies supporting it. This was precisely the reasoning used in not taking a position in the outsourcing case, and it ignores the highly effective practices of the AAUP, which has formed a Committee on Academic Freedom and Tenure precisely to investigate, publicize, and censure academic freedom violations in colleges and universities. This process gives such principles weight and has been used in the courts as legal precedent.[35] ALA's (or perhaps more accurately, one powerful person's) basic deferral to library administrative authority essentially evacuates the association's workplace intellectual freedom policies (which are, it is worth emphasizing, already on the books) of any meaning. The association (or again, one person) will not even *consider* investigating such violations (or nonviolations, as is often the case in with the AAUP) of principle—and therefore establishing a baseline of facts, presumably because such facts would then have to be dealt with. This contrast is especially jarring in light of how hard the Office for Intellectual Freedom fights on those issues that it does take up and how doctrinaire it can be in its positions at times.[36]

Apart from these issues, ALA and ACRL have both acted to limit intellectual freedom's meaning in important new policies like "Access to Electronic Information, Services, and Networks" (an extension and interpretation of the Library Bill of Rights) and "Libraries: An American Value." I want to state clearly that both of these, in the main, represent important extensions and clarifications of principle, and both have been approved by the association. However, the process of discussion and revision—and what was omitted— was revealing. I have examined the documentation and drafts of "Access to Electronic Information" that were distributed and discussed between ACRL's Intellectual Freedom Committee and its Executive Board, and subsequently adopted by ALA,[37] and I found a number of startling omissions and perspectives on the policy in those documents:

- Any references to information equity and the public good were omitted from early drafts by the ACRL Executive Board—including James Madison's famous statement on "a popular government without popular information."

- A specific endorsement of the rights of children to information in the electronic context was opposed by the ACRL Board.

- The ACRL Board took a draft statement that "libraries and librarians should not limit access to information on the grounds that it is perceived to be frivolous or lacking value" and turned it into a fiscal issue of requiring academic libraries to fill professor's book requests "no matter how esoteric." The President of ACRL at the time claimed that this would draw ALA into intellectual freedom championing of "unrealistic acquisitions expectations in a narrow area [like] the Classics."

- There was a veiled push by the ACRL Board for rationing of electronic services and fees.

- Most disturbing, the Board and president decried this important extension of the "Library Bill of Rights" as not "address[ing] the realities of academic life" and putting administrators in "untenable positions." One thinly veiled criticism compared this extension to "the laws and prophets of the Old Testament [that] were interpreted into literally thousands of minor regulations . . . put[ting] compliance beyond all but a very small group." (The subsequent actions of the federal government vis-à-vis libraries post-September 11th have effectively shown just how short-sighted and management centered this position was.)

The development of "Libraries: An American Value" indicates similar actions to limit the extent of the meaning of intellectual freedom. An analysis of proposed drafts and the final document shows the omission of specific mention of opposition to censorship, inclusion of published alternative points of view, opposition to privatization of libraries, and the UN's Universal Declaration of Human Rights section on freedom of information from the final document. All were proposed in previous drafts.[38] I believe the processes of adopting both policy statements (again, both of which represented progress in the main) bespeaks a growing corporate approach to the profession and its principles. As I wrote at the time,

we are clearly struggling in finding our voice amid a renegotiated and economically-driven public commitment to social goals. A large part of our leadership seeks to "save" libraries as institutions by situating them at the center of the information economy. I believe this drives much of the caution in extending . . . intellectual freedom . . . perhaps in fear of undermining libraries' potential economic utility. . . . It is essential that we question our leadership when we are encouraged to finesse our professional commitments.[39]

## Public Relations and Corporate Partnerships

ALA has begun a five-year marketing plan called "@ Your Library." This high-profile—and expensive—campaign is a very high priority within ALA, and with it the association has joined library administrative fashions (in aping the business management trends) by branding, labeling patrons as consumers, and linking libraries to the image of technology.[40] Though there have been previous corporate links with ALA (which drew protests[41]), this public relations campaign has dramatically expanded that practice: the World Wrestling Federation, NASCAR, Hershey's, and New Line Cinema are in the roster along with library-related companies like 3-M and Barnes & Noble.[42] There are indications from those on ALA's Council (again, the association's democratically elected governing board) that questions about the campaign, how it was undertaken, and under whose authority have been ignored. It would appear to contradict policy not to "imply ALA endorsement of their policies, products, or services" and falls under the jurisdiction of a number of oversight committees and offices. For instance, one of the initial sponsorships was a 3-M sponsored "Check-it-out Yourself Day @ your library," complete with a pitch for people to become "more self-sufficient in the library" by using the 3-M SelfCheck System. ALA leadership's responses to these questions have

been to ignore them, the overlaps in oversight authority, and the contradictions of policy[43] and assume centralized, corporatelike authority for the campaign and its related policy issues under its Public Information Office. While
the "core values" statement may have been hotly debated, this office and the
campaign's director have assumed the mantel of speaking for the profession
through the campaign by developing substitute "core messages" through the
marketing strategies of focus groups and public opinion surveys. Perhaps
most disturbing, this program is the genesis of the "one voice" policy,[44] the
ramifications of which have been dissected as inimical to the democratic functions of ALA.[45] Clearly, the "@ Your Library" campaign represents a very
large step forward in ALA's movement toward corporate models of management and away from a democratic model of a professional organization.

## CONCLUSION

The American Library Association is most certainly not alone in its steady
drift toward a business model of representing the profession. Thirteen years
ago, *Library Journal* embarked on a series of changes that were "explained"
(read justified) through a series of "Publisher's Letters." In them, the argument was made that libraries should be looked at as a market (i.e., a powerful
purchaser) and to have advertisements pitched to librarians was sort of flat-
tering, that libraries should be looked at as a huge retail book chain—"more
ubiquitous than McDonald's," and a plea was made for a greater understanding of the business world and its practices along with some not-so-veiled
warnings to get over our reticence concerning all of the previous.[46] The publisher noted that there would consequently be changes in the magazine, and
they are readily identifiable since that time: advertisements abound, articles
are shorter—and technology and management are the prominent themes,
graphics and color predominate, titles and blurbs are more catchy. There will
be no more wide distribution of seminal (if somewhat short by necessity) and
still-cited scholarly pieces like those of Michael Harris or Miriam Braverman.[47]
In short, the magazine is adapting and aping the mass market magazine tactics
like those in *People* and *Newsweek*.

Other library organizations have themselves committed acts that cut away
at the core of library institutions and their purposes, perfectly in tune with
the new public philosophy and the information society push. For instance,
Albert Henderson notes that the Association of Research Libraries (along
with ALA and ACRL) has allowed standards for collections and for federal
funding of collections to be gutted.[48] IFLA went through similar contortions
of revision and political carefulness in developing policy statements on human
rights in the country in which its annual conference was being held.[49] Leslie
Campbell has written and compiled a comparison of the social responsibility
debates—a flashpoint that has usually been about core public values of the
profession and a drift toward business models—in three related professional

organizations (ALA among them). One cannot help but conclude after her comparison of librarianship, law librarianship, and the legal profession that defining and defending a public role and a public purpose against a creeping corporate model for any number of professions is a similar—and vital—struggle.[50] Those social responsibility debates have been going on intermittently in librarianship for quite some time. The business/corporate model of the field tends—in the main—to be advanced by (mostly male) administrators of, shall we say, a certain generation. The arguments from this camp tend toward distorting language and principles in favor of a "no-nonsense," "business-like" approach to what's good for the profession—and they frequently invoke a false, ahistoric neutrality.[51] There is also a certain amount of brutal cynicism involved, not unlike that which Henry Giroux identified (at the end of chapter 6): "Unlike lots of things that ALA Council passes in its futile effort to reform the world and eradicate some of the more evil aspects of American society, the 'Decade of the Librarian' document may very well cost our professional association lots of money";[52] and "Don't underestimate the importance of alliteration to public policy. The euphonious Digital Divide has caught the fancy of policy wonks as much as the information community."[53]

In reading the yearly summary report for ALA published in *The Bowker Annual*, one cannot but help be struck by the fact that a goodly portion of the association's resources must go toward maintaining its Washington office, and the vast majority of the (reported) activities of that office are in lobbying for and protecting technology funding. This alone—the environment of power, the nature of lobbying, the amounts of money involved—would invoke a certain caution and a return-on-investment approach within the bureaucracy of ALA (not to mention tying it firmly to the agenda of information capitalism, as I have argued). It also serves to take the association away from its public principles, and the instances outlined in this chapter give an indication of this not-so-subtle trend. However, ALA's message is mixed and still not yet one of undiluted market worship and business imitation. A recent president of ALA (the same one who ignored councilor questions about the publicity campaign) has written frequently on libraries and democratic dialogue, libraries as civic spaces, and civil society.[54] A former president of the American Bar Association caught much of the essence of the issue and the reason to remind ALA of the need to keep our professional principles at the association's core:

Not everyone will be pleased when any organization [has] taken stands. . . . It is not a role for "Willie Lomans" because you are not going to be well liked by every customer. . . . But you will create discussion and that is the point. . . . It is a whirlpool of confusion in which we all are spinning and from which we cannot find escape. I believe . . . that the reason for this frightening and threatening state of affairs is that we will not discuss the issues of the day. . . . We must discuss, we must debate, we must talk . . . in our homes; in our churches, synagogues, and mosques; in our schools;

in our professions; and in our organizations. [And,] disagreement will become debate [and] debate will then become considered judgment.⁵⁵

This—not a "one voice" corporate model—should be the modus operandi of ALA, and it describes eloquently the democratic public role in debate, discussion, and thought that our professional associations and our institutions should play. We have an honorable professional legacy to uphold, and the new public philosophy-inspired corporate model for ALA should not be *the* voice of our profession and its values.

## NOTES

1. Betty Turock, "American Library Association," *The Bowker Annual*, 41st ed., ed. Dave Bogart (New Providence, N.J.: R. R. Bowker, 1996), 135; and Mary Somerville, "American Library Association," *The Bowker Annual*, 42nd ed., ed. Dave Bogart, (New Providence, N.J.: R. R. Bowker, 1997), 141.

2. The "Library Bill of Rights" began initially as the "ALA Bill of Rights" in 1939, in Jean Key Gates, *Introduction to Librarianship*, 2nd ed. (New York: McGraw-Hill, 1976), 82. The American Association of University Professors articulated their Academic Freedom Statement in 1940, in *Policy Documents and Reports* (Washington, D.C.: American Association of University Professors, 1990). Both standards have been used by the courts, as professional guidelines often are.

3. See, for example, summaries in John Buschman, "History and Theory of Information Poverty," in *Poor People and Library Services*, ed. Karen Venturella (Jefferson, N.C.: McFarland, 1998), 17–20; and John Buschman, "Historical Notes on Reading and the Public: A Skeptical View from Librarianship" (Society for the History of Authorship, Reading, and Publishing 2001 Conference, College of William and Mary, Williamsburg, Virginia, 21 July 2001).

4. Wayne Wiegand, "The Structure of Librarianship: Essay on an Information Profession," *Canadian Journal of Information and Library Science*, 24, no. 1 (1997): 33–35.

5. Wayne Wiegand, "The Role of the Library in American History," *The Bowker Annual*, 33rd ed., ed. Filomena Simora (New York: R. R. Bowker, 1988), 75.

6. See, for example, the summary in Sarah Long, "American Library Association," *The Bowker Annual*, 45th ed., ed. Dave Bogart (New Providence, N.J.: R. R. Bowker, 2000), 130. A good summary of some of the intellectual freedom issues that have come before and been debated in ALA between the historical period identified and the current era can be found in Patricia Latshaw, "Beyond Censorship: Issues in Intellectual Freedom," *The Bowker Annual*, 36th ed., ed. Filomena Simora (New Providence, N.J.: R. R. Bowker, 1991), 67–74. Prominent voices within the profession were also fighting the privatization and outsourcing of federal libraries, as noted in previous chapters.

7. See *Access to Electronic Information, Services, and Networks: An Interpretation of the Library Bill of Rights*, (Chicago: American Library Association, 24 January 1996); John Buschman, "A House Divided Against Itself: ACRL Leadership, Academic Freedom & Electronic Resources," *Progressive Librarian* 12/13 (1997): 7–17; and American Library Association, *Libraries: An American Value*, reprinted in Sanford

Berman, Carol Reid, and Charles Willett, "The American Library Association, Intellectual Freedom, the Alternative Press, and 'Libraries: An American Value'," *Counterpoise* 2, no. 4 (1998): 28.

8. Barbara Ford, "American Library Association," *The Bowker Annual,* 43rd ed., ed. Dave Bogart (New Providence, N.J.: R. R. Bowker, 1998), 149; John Berry, "American Library Association," *The Bowker Annual,* 47th ed., ed. Dave Bogart (New Providence, N.J.: R. R. Bowker, 2002), 126–27; and Somerville, 143.

9. Long, 128–29; Ford, 148; Berry, 129; and Ann Symons, "American Library Association," *The Bowker Annual,* 44th ed., ed. Dave Bogart (New Providence, N.J.: R. R. Bowker, 1999), 155.

10. Nancy Kranich, "American Library Association," *The Bowker Annual,* 46th ed., ed. Dave Bogart (New Providence, N.J.: R. R. Bowker, 2001), 116–19; and Berry, 124–25.

11. Janet Swan Hill, "Outsourcing: Understanding the Fuss," *The Bowker Annual,* 46th ed., ed. Bogart, 225.

12. Hill, 220, 230. It is worth noting that, unlike other such significant reports, the Outsourcing Task Force report itself never made it to the pages of *The Bowker Annual*—a good measure of how buried the issue was.

13. For a good summary of the controversies and arguments in addition to Hill, see Patricia Wallace, "Outsourcing Book Selection in Public and School Libraries," *Collection Building* 16, no. 4 (1997): 160–66; and Norman Oder, "Outsourcing: Model—or Mistake?" *Library Journal,* 15 March 1997, 28–29.

14. See, for example, Mark Crispin Miller, "What's Wrong with This Picture?" *Nation,* 7–14 January 2002, 18–22; Robert McChesney and John Nichols, "The Making of a Movement: Getting Serious About Media Reform," *Nation,* 7–14 January 2002, 11, 13–15; "The Big Ten" (chart insert tracing media ownership), *Nation,* 7–14 January 2002; Barbara Fister, "Trade Publishing: A Report from the Front," *portal: Libraries and the Academy* 1, no. 4 (2001): 509–23; Andre Schiffrin, *The Business of Books* (New York: Verso, 2000); Robert McChesney, Ellen Wood, and John Foster, eds., *Capitalism and the Information Age: The Political Economy of the Global Communication Revolution* (New York: Monthly Review Press, 1998); Robert McChesney, *Rich Media, Poor Democracy: Communication Politics in Dubious Times* (New York: New Press, 1999); Michael Apple, "Textbook Publishing: The Political and Economic Influences," *Theory into Practice* 28, no. 4 (1989): 282–87; Sue Curry Jansen, "Censorship, Critical Theory, and New Information Technologies: Foundations of Critical Scholarship in Communications," in *Critical Approaches to Information Technology in Librarianship: Foundations and Applications,* ed. John Buschman (Westport, Conn.: Greenwood Press, 1993), 59–81; Herbert Schiller, "The Global Commercialization of Culture," *Progressive Librarian* 2 (1990/1991): 15–22; and Herbert Schiller, *Culture Inc.: The Corporate Takeover of Public Expression* (New York: Oxford University Press, 1989).

15. See, for example, John Buschman, "Issues in Censorship and Information Technology," in *Critical Approaches to Information Technology in Librarianship: Foundations and Applications,* ed. Buschman, 125–50; John Buschman, "Information Technology, Power Structures, and the Fate of Librarianship," *Progressive Librarian* 6/7 (1993): 15–29; Peter McDonald, "Corporate Inroads & Librarianship: The Fight for the Soul of the Profession in the New Millennium," *Progressive Librarian* 12/13 (1997): 32–44; Henry Blanke, "Libraries and the Commercialization of Information:

Towards a Critical Discourse of Librarianship," *Progressive Librarian* 2 (1990/1991): 9–14; Henry Blanke, "Librarianship and Public Culture in the Age of Information Capitalism," *Journal of Information Ethics* 5 (Fall 1996): 54–69; Mark Crispin Miller, "Reading in the Age of Global Media" (with a response by John Buschman), *Progressive Librarian* 18 (2001): 18–28; Rory Litwin, "Issues of Inside Censorship and the ALA," *Counterpoise,* January 1998, 11–13; and John Haar, "The Politics of Electronic Information: A Reassessment," in *Critical Approaches to Information Technology in Librarianship: Foundations and Applications,* ed. Buschman, 197–210.

16. Mark Crispin Miller, "Reading in the Age of Global Media" (American Library Association Annual Conference, Washington, D.C., 28 June 1998; the transcription of this session that appeared in *Progressive Librarian* included only an edited portion of Miller's comments during the extensive discussion period).

17. Greg Kline, "Information at Risk," *Champaign (Ill.) News-Gazette,* 20 January 2002, <http://www.news-gazette.com/ngsearch/story.cfm?number-10892>; Jennifer Radcliffe, "Orders to Purge Records Have Librarians Worried," *Fort Worth (Texas) Star-Telegram,* 8 December 2001, 1; Bill Sammon, "Web Sites Told to Delete Data," *Washington Times,* 21 March 2002, <http://asp.washtimes.com/printarti . . . = print&ArticleID = 20020321-16859342>; "A Chill in the Library," *St. Petersburg Times,* 23 July 2002, <http://www.sptimes.com/2002/07/23/A_chill_in_the_librar.shtml>; Eric Lichtblau, "Rising Fears That What We Do Know Can Hurt Us," *Los Angeles Times,* 18 November 2001, A1; Bob Egelko, "FBI Checking Out Americans' Reading Habits: Bookstores, Libraries Can't Do Much to Fend Off Search Warrants," *San Francisco Chronicle,* 23 June 2002, A5; Christopher Newton, "FBI Begins Visiting Libraries," *Washington Post.com,* 24 June 2002, distributed on plgnet-l@listproc.sjsu on 24 June 2002; Norman Oder, "Patriot Act and Privacy Concerns," *Library Journal,* 15 February 2002, 16; Norman Oder and Andrew Albanese, "Patriot Act Stats Won't Be Revealed," *Library Journal,* 15 September 2002, 17; "FBI's Interest in Library Records Piques Congressional Ire," *American Libraries,* 1 July 2002, <http://www.ala.org/alonline/news/2002/020701.html>; F. James Sensenbrenner, Jr., and John Conyers, Jr., letter to the Honorable John D. Ashcroft, 13 June 2002, <http://www.house.gov/judiciary/ashcroft061302.htm>; and Francis Buckley, Jr. (Superintendent of Documents), letter to Library Directors, 14 March 2002.

18. Leigh Estabrook, *Public Libraries' Responses to September 11, 2001* (Champaign, Ill.: Library Research Center, University of Illinois, 2002).

19. "ACLU, Judiciary Committee Seek Information on Use of Patriot Act Powers," *American Libraries,* 26 August 2002, <http://www.ala.org/alonline/news/2002/020826.html>.

20. Karen Schneider, "The Patriot Act: Last Refuge of a Scoundrel," *American Libraries,* March 2002, 86.

21. Laura Flanders, "Librarians Under Siege," *Nation,* 5–12 August 2002, 43.

22. American Association of Law Libraries, American Library Association, and the Association of Research Libraries, *Library Community Statement on Proposed Anti-Terrorism Measures,* 2 October 2001.

23. For example, on library services to the poor and ALA's long foot-dragging in carrying through on policy statements, see Sanford Berman, foreword to *Poor People and Library Services,* ed. Karen Venturella (Jefferson, N.C.: McFarland, 1998), 1–14.

24. Apple, 283, 286–87.

25. Mark Rosenzweig, "Many Voices, One Goal: Notes Towards a Critique of the 'One Voice' Policy for ALA," *SRRT Newsletter*, Spring 2001, 12–13.

26. A good summary can be found in Elaine Harger, "Editorial: Institutionalizing Silence Within ALA?" *Progressive Librarian* 14 (1998): 1–4.

27. Beverly Lynch and Mark Rosenzweig, "What's the Matter with Membership Meetings?" (interview and debate), *American Libraries,* December 1997, 41–44; Harger, "Editorial," 3; and S. Michael Malinconico, "[ALACOUN:5805] Re: Forum?" distributed on owner-alacoun@ala1.ala.org on 12 April 2001.

28. John Buschman, Mark Rosenzweig, and Elaine Harger, "The Clear Imperative for Involvement: Librarians Must Address Social Issues," *American Libraries,* June 1994, 575–76.

29. See Harger, "Editorial"; and Rosenzweig, "Many Voices."

30. Mark Rosenzweig, "ACTION REQUEST: re: Council listserv," distributed on plgnet-l@listproc.sjsu.edu on 9 April 2001 (with attached response to ALA Council); Mark Rosenzweig, "UPDATE: re: stifling dissent on Council," distributed on plgnet-l @listproc.sjsu.edu on 10 April 2001 (with previous attached responses from Karen Scheider, Larry Romans, and Mark Rosenzweig); S. Michael Malinconico, "Re: ACTION REQUEST: re: Council listserv," distributed on plgnet-l@listproc.sjsu.edu on 9 April 2001; and Mark Rosenzweig, "RE: Council listserv," distributed to the author 16 April 2001 (includes critiques of the listserv restriction proposals from Mark Scheu, John Buschman, and Rory Litwin).

31. John Buschman, "Editorial: Core Wars," *Progressive Librarian* 17 (2000): 1–2. Mark Rosenzweig collapsed during the Council debate (he was a passionate opponent of the statement) and only later found that the tide turned against what appeared to be a fait accompli.

32. In John Buschman and Mark Rosenzweig, "Intellectual Freedom Within the Library Workplace: An Exploratory Study in the U.S.," *Journal of Information Ethics* 8, no. 2 (1999): 37–39.

33. Buschman and Rosenzweig, 41.

34. Were not an important policy issue at stake, the repetitive obeisance in representative ALA publications and reports would be humorous: in Long, 130, "ALA's Office for Intellectual Freedom (OIF) and the Freedom to Read Foundation celebrated their 30th anniversaries [and] four First Amendment champions received special presidential awards: Judith Krug, OIF director since the office was founded . . . "; in Turock, 138, "Judith F. Krug, director of ALA's Office for Intellectual Freedom, who has served as the foundation's volunteer executive director since its establishment in 1969 . . . "; and in Beverly Goldberg, "On the Line for the First Amendment: An Interview with Judith Krug," *American Libraries,* September 1995, 774–75, "Krug was lauded for 26 years of distinguished service as the FTRF's executive director, an organization she was instrumental in launching two years after developing ALA's Office for Intellectual Freedom." I am not suggesting that these are not worthy achievements—or undeserved praise. Rather, I am suggesting that there is something of a monopoly in ALA on interpreting what intellectual freedom is for the association and the profession.

35. Buschman and Rosenzweig; and *Policy Documents and Reports.*

36. For example, the Office for Intellectual Freedom refused to comment on the Smithsonian's actions in the "Enola Gay" exhibition controversy. See Elaine Harger, "The 'Enola Gay' Controversy as a Library Issue," *Progressive Librarian* 10/11 (Winter

1995/96): 70–71. On the doctrinaire front, the South African Book Boycott was the subject of attack by Nat Hentoff at a talk given at "Intellectual Diversity and Political Correctness" (ACRL/NY Annual Symposium, New York, November 1992). Krug also spoke at the meeting and took Hentoff's position, invoking total claim on intellectual freedom principles and a simple application of them. The issue was a complicated one, coming down to disagreement over whether the donation of used books to schools for black South Africans represented the free flow of information—thus meriting intellectual freedom and its protections, or a propping up of an immoral apartheid educational system and a prolonging of those injustices by amelioration. In this rare instance, human rights and intellectual freedom were truly at odds, but Hentoff/Krug took an absolutist stand. They would not admit even the possibility that their position—no matter how well meant—might have helped prolong apartheid or indeed, that there was even another possible moral position at all. The ensuing discussion sparked by Hentoff's jeremiad was heated. When the author (who—along with other members of SRRT and the Progressive Librarians Guild present—disagreed with his position during the discussion) attempted to talk with Krug about the issue's relationship to intellectual freedom afterward, she flatly declared that there was no other interpretation of intellectual freedom than hers (and the conversation ended rather abruptly). For a little more thoughtful overview of this issue, the contending principles at stake, and the principals involved, see Latshaw, 71–72.

37. Buschman, "A House Divided." All subsequent listed examples for "Access to Electronic Information" are contained in this article.

38. Berman, Reid, and Willett.

39. Buschman, "A House Divided," 15–16.

40. Robert Moran, Jr., "The Campaign for America's Libraries: An Interview with Deborah Davis," *Library Administration & Management* 15, no. 2 (2001): 76–79; Kranich, "American Library Association," 117; and Berry, 125.

41. Harger, "Editorial," 2–3.

42. Berry, 125; and Elaine Harger, "Fw: Corporate Sponsorships," distributed on plgnet-l@listproc.sjsu.edu on 8 August 2001 (with attached responses to ALA Council from Elaine Harger, Mary Chelton, and Janet Swan Hill on committee responsibility for partnerships and public relations oversight/overlap).

43. See Harger, "Fw: Corporate Sponsorships," 8 August 2001 (with responses of Chelton and Hill); Mark Rosenzweig, "FWD: [Member-FORUM:2201] RE: Business Partnerships and ALA," distributed on plgnet-l@listproc.sjsu.edu on 20 April 2001 (with attached analysis by Mary Ann Meyers—including quotations of relevant ALA policy documents); Mark Rosenzweig, "Hucksterism @ your library: the 'branding' plan unveiled in action," distributed on plgnet-l@listproc.sjsu.edu on 2 February 2001 (with attached press release, "ALA NEWS 3M Library Systems joins @ your library, The Campaign for America's Libraries"); Mark Rosenzweig, "READ/FORWARD THIS VERSION!: (CORRECTED):Sleeping with the Enemy (for 'chump change')," distributed on plgnet-l@listproc.sjsu.edu on 2 August 2001 (attached reply to ALA Council list on ALA News Release, @ your library, vol. 7, no. 9); and "Concerns Arise Over Corporate Branding," *SRRT Newsletter,* Spring 2001, 4–5.

44. Moran, 76–78.

45. Rosenzweig, "Many Voices."

46. "Marketing and the Library Commitment," *Library Journal,* December 1989, 4; "Flexing the Library Muscle," *Library Journal,* January 1990, 4; "Flexing the Li-

brary Muscle, Part 2," *Library Journal,* 1 February 1990, 4; and "What's Going on Here?" *Library Journal,* 15 February 1990, 104.

47. Michael Harris, "Public Libraries and the Decline of the Democratic Dogma," *Library Journal,* 1 November 1976, 2225–2230; and Miriam Braverman, "From Adam Smith to Ronald Reagan: Public Libraries as a Public Good," *Library Journal,* 15 February 1982, 397–401.

48. Albert Henderson, "The Devil and Max Weber in the Research University," *Journal of Information Ethics,* Spring 1999, 25.

49. See Al Kagan, "IFLA and Human Rights," *Progressive Librarian* 10/11 (1995/ 1996): 79–82; and "Documents: Resolution on the Importance of Freedom of Expression and Free Access to Information, passed by IFLA, August 1995," *Progressive Librarian* 10/11 (1995/1996): 83–85.

50. Leslie Cambell, "Keeping Watch on the Waterfront: Social Responsibility in Legal and Library Professional Organizations," *Law Library Journal* 92, no. 3 (2000): 263–86. It is worth noting here that I served for three years on the National Council of the American Association of University Professors (with similar responsibilities to ALA's Council) and can attest to similar debates, tactics, and issues over professional principles in that organization as well.

51. Steven Joyce, "A Few Gates: An Examination of the Social Responsibilities Debate in the Early 1970s and 1990s," *Progressive Librarian* 15 (1998/1999): 1–13, documents the twisting of language and positions in the arguments against social responsibility in librarianship. In a similar observation George Bushnell, a former president of the American Bar Association, remarks that many in opposition to such a professional focus make a familiar argument that

> none of this is the business of a professional organization. [Yet] interestingly, when eight or nine past presidents of the Association wrote to the United States Senate condemning the appointment of Louis Brandeis to the Supreme Court, it *was* considered to be the ABA's business. Interestingly, when the Association, without exception, opposed every legislative recommendation of the Roosevelt Administration from 1932 to 1938, it *was* considered to be the business of the ABA (in Campbell, 284).

52. Charles Robinson, "The Public Library Vanishes," *Library Journal,* 15 March 1992, 53.

53. Blaise Cronin, "The Dean's List—The Digital Divide," *Library Journal,* 15 February 2002, 48.

54. Nancy Kranich, "Libraries Help to Build a Civil Society," *American Libraries,* June/July 2001, 7; Nancy Kranich, "Libraries: The Cornerstone of Democracy," *American Libraries,* August 2000, 5; and Nancy Kranich, "Libraries as Civic Spaces," *American Libraries,* November 2000, 7.

55. Bushnell in Campbell, 285–86.

# 8

---·••·---

# NOTES ON POSTMODERN
# TECHNOLOGY, TECHNOCRACY,
# AND LIBRARIES

## INTRODUCTION

To use a metaphor, the loudest guest who drinks and eats the most at librarianship's party (so to speak) must certainly be technology. Technology is a theme that has run through every chapter in this book and it is a factor influencing nearly every major decision in librarianship. Throughout the book I have often posed the funding, use, and preference for information technologies as being in opposition to print resources. That is not strictly true, however. Much of what I have previously written about technology and librarianship has focused a critique not on technology per se but on the *ways* in which we write and talk about technologies and the ways in which we don't.[1] We tend, in the main, to fall well within the boundaries of uncritical hype of technologies, and we do not exhibit a critical professional distance from the resources—tending to celebrate rather than evaluate. To give one instance, I have noticed that, when a print resource costing a good deal (say, a reference set at over $1,000) is being considered for purchase, librarians commonly pick through entries, check for bibliographies, pour through indexes, look for further reviews, evaluate the subject vs. patron need, and compare it to the quality of existing holdings. In other words, librarians will professionally and critically evaluate the resource against their needs and weigh costs. When an electronic resource costing multiples of that $1,000 is considered, our critical faculties seem to often go out the window. We concentrate on presentation style (screen design, color options), and the authority and efficacy of the product is often assumed[2]—and in fact must be disproved through software, coverage, and content problems. The thoroughness of indexes, content, and so on is not as critically examined and rarely compared to existing resources. It is not that good, professional reviews of such products don't exist (though they were very slow to make their appearance in the literature) but rather that a professionwide, common critical practice of skeptical evaluation of electronic resources (like those applied to expensive print resources) is taking a long time to take root in the field.

We remain largely unconnected to the ongoing scholarship that has raised critical questions about technologies. This is one of the primary reasons why our literature (which is so focused on the subject of technology) remains so theoretically and intellectually thin. To close the circle begun in the first chapter, I would suggest that this crucial thinness is part of our crisis culture in librarianship, is part of the faddishness and business bias of our management practices, is part of uncritical budgeting decisions, helps to move the profession (almost unwittingly) toward business models and the economic agenda of information capitalism, and can not form the basis of a positive reason *for* the field. The problem is that, in the way in which we've been situating librarianship, "there is no particular reason for all of these resources to be offered through libraries since libraries are putting themselves on an entrepreneurial/business footing. We will have become just another competitor in the information marketplace, not logically, socially, economically, or morally *any* better or more desirable than other information providers."[3] Defending librarianship and building the case for the field has been the purpose of this book, and any such project must deal with technology.

This chapter will not recount and summarize my own (or other's) previous critical work in this area (by this I am not suggesting that this line of scholarship is exhausted or completed). Instead, I will briefly review some of the more salient aspects of library technology as they apply to the themes of this book, and since my purpose here is to advance those themes, I must by necessity give an overview of technology issues. They fall into two broad categories: library technology and structures of social thinking and memory, and technocratic aspects of librarianship. I am situating both within a critique of postmodern trends, initially taken up in chapter 3, which will be extended incrementally here. Relying on an existing body of critical literature, it is my contention that the problems posed by postmodernism's relationship to media and technology characterize librarianship's relationship to it as well. I will begin with a brief review and a further critique of postmodernism (so intimately related to postindustrialism and the information society) before moving on to the overviews of the two broad areas identified.

## POSTMODERNISM AND TECHNOLOGY

To begin, there is a definite connection between postmodernist[4] trends and media/technology. As summed up by one scholar, we are facing "not one but two revolutions—an intellectual and a technological revolution which bear an uncanny resemblance to each other and have a symbiotic relationship to each other. . . . For the new technology is the perfect medium for the new ideology. Surfing through cyberspace is a truly postmodernist experience."[5] We are therefore not looking at merely an intellectual trend but a series of interconnected developments—economic, intellectual, cultural—that feed off and describe one another. Those interwoven postmodern characteristics relevant to librarianship—and the critique of them—can be summarized as follows:

## 1. Indeterminacy

Postmodernism broadly claims that language is only a signifier whose meaning shifts over time and is structured (even corrupted) by power. As Madan Sarup summarizes and explains it,

the structural relationship between the signifier and the signified constitutes a linguistic sign, and language is made up of these. . . . This means that there is no one-to-one correspondence between propositions and reality. [Others go] further; [language is] a system of floating signifiers pure and simple, with no determinable relation to any extra-linguistic referents at all. [This assumption] implies a shift [and] a perpetual detour on the way to a truth that has lost any status or finality, [or even of] concepts of causality, of identity, of the subject, and of truth.[6]

The problems with this were revealed in a celebrated hoax: a parody of a postmodern critique of "scientific" discourse was accepted for publication in a major cultural studies/postmodernist journal. As the authors note, postmodernists "exhibit a veritable intoxication with words, combined with a superb indifference to their meaning. [If such ] texts seem incomprehensible, it is for the excellent reason that they mean precisely nothing."[7] This humorous (but instructive) episode points to much deeper problems, illustrated by Jacques Derrida, a leading postmodernist/poststructuralist "trying to explain Nazi tendencies in his master Martin Heidegger and to explain them away in his colleague Paul De Man." Under such circumstances postmodern intellectual acrobatics pale, and "it becomes apparent that 'straight readings' are sometimes needed even by avant-garde interpreters."[8]

## 2. Fragmentation

Technology's increasing ability to store, sort, manipulate, and quickly process information (in its variety of forms) is an enabling tool for postmodern fragmentation. Rejecting the historical disasters of totalizing systems (Nazism, Communism, Capitalism), postmodernism blames these on unifying grand narratives (the heritage of the Enlightenment and Modernism and philosophy's search for truth). All have been attacked as a mask for the imposition of power. The only acceptable alternative is the individual and self-constructed "narrative"—everything else is an illegitimate, base corruption and represents domination.[9] Digital technologies—their capabilities and biases—encourage such technologically mediated "individualism." Bernd Frohmann has identified and outlined the networked technological characteristics of this fragmentation. He encapsulates it in a series of concepts and terms: disembodiment, techno-spirituality, technological metaphors of further human "evolution," virtual "community," participatory "democracy," and virtual subjectivity. He concludes that together they represent a "radicalism both compelling yet not so powerful as to destabilize highly concentrated forms of corporate control. [They are] the construction of meanings connected to familiar forms of domination, authority, and control," representing the dismantling of the public sphere in favor of the virtual.[10] On a social/economic level, this leads to the political isolationism of identity politics[11] and the technologically sorted, identified, and captured consumer identity, selling products that have themselves been stripped of real cultural connections to persons similarly conceived.[12] Frederic Jameson warned that if postmodern culture has robbed the society of the ability "to organize its past and future into coherent experience, it becomes difficult enough to see how the cultural productions of such [people] could result in anything but 'heaps of fragments.'"[13]

## 3. Discontinuity

There is within postmodernism an increasing emphasis on the receiving of, interpretation of, and manipulation of images (including self-image)—particularly as they are conveyed through technological media. In its more baroque forms, this has been theorized as a "hyperreality" that has become more real than the indeterminacy of reality: "nonlinear, multiperspecitival modes of space containing innumerable hyperreal constructs of unique, nonidentical realities."[14] The bias of such an environment is visual—using icons instead of language commands in computers for instance—and demonstrates a tendency to retreat from the "macroworld" to the "microworld of computer simulation, computer networks, and cyberspace." Its hallmarks are the lack of a fixed reference point, the lack of textual (or image or audio) finality as an authorial statement, and a parallel to "television's tendency towards discontinuity and incoherence." Despite its interactive and non-linear hype, computers are thoroughly based on a linear, literate, binary model and grammar, the difference being that this positivistic bias is much more deeply hidden.[15] Such an emphasis on media image reception and manipulation results in a culture of "pastiche . . . in which stylistic innovation is no longer possible [and] all that is left . . . is the imitation of dead styles, [an] inability to focus on our present [or] to locate ourselves historically."[16]

Clearly these are interrelated phenomena, and they are related to the characteristics of postmodernism previously outlined in chapter 3. Just as clearly, we should also remember that this intellectual trend came about in part as a theoretical response to the encroachments of late capitalism, as a protest to the philosophical quest for certainty—and some of its disastrous and bastardized intellectual results, and as a deep analysis of power relationships embedded in language construction. The consequent value placed on minority/marginalized groups (and their social perspective from the margin), on "multiple and contradictory forms of power, on nonreductive analysis, and on the local as an important site" are all valuable postmodern insights.[17] There is no attempt here to distance this project from those values—quite the contrary. However, as Andrew Feenberg points out, postmodernism

attacks all forms of totalizing discourse, including talk of potentiality, in the belief that totalization is the logic of technocracy. There is surely a moment of truth in the demand for dispersion and difference, but these purely negative qualifications are an insufficient basis for a critical theory of technology. Nuclear weapons, the systematic deskilling of the labor force, the exportation of pollution to the Third World are not the products of rigid bureaucracies whose authority is sapped by a new postmodern individualism, but of flexible centers of command that are well adapted to the new technologies they have designed and implemented.[18]

Michael Apple notes that much of what is called postmodern is familiar: its "high tech" image is shot through with the longstanding faith in the ability of technical rationality to solve economic and social problems; and while pluralism, individual difference, and the local are upheld in postmodern rhetoric (and to be realized through networked technology and media), information capitalism is leading a drive toward global cultural standardization and consumption. Postmodernism "may make it easier to see surface transformations (some of which are undoubtedly occurring) and yet at the same time may make it that much more difficult to recognize that these may be new ways of reorganizing and reproducing older hierarchies." Apple reminds us that we can not again be "economically reductive" in our explanations of society and culture. These were the ideas so rightfully criticized by postmodernism. On the other hand, as he states, "it seems a bit naïve to ignore" capitalism, particularly in light of the massive corporate, political, and think-tank push to make market practices our model of public reason.[19] In the end, I agree with Habermas's description of postmodernism as "neoconservative" in that "technical progress [is linked to] capitalist growth and rational administration [and] politics must be kept as far aloof as possible from the demands of moral-practical justification."[20] As such, I will argue that the problems identified in the critique of a postmodernist approach to technologies also characterize some of the problems in librarianship's approach to information technologies that have very troubling implications for the public sphere.

## LIBRARY TECHNOLOGY AND STRUCTURES OF SOCIAL THINKING AND MEMORY

Along with more prosaic versions of technological transformations of librarianship, there are "visions" that go much further, and they very much bear the hallmarks of postmodernism: networks as a "new means of controlling our personal locality," assembling one's coworkers, vendors, and friends in an electronic "neighborhood," the library role in construction of knowledge through collaboration and "freedom," and multimedia emulation of shared intellectual space.[21] Postmodern library descriptions tend to form an odd combination of authoritarianism and ecstatic technological highs:

We need to build libraries that are transformed into the networked information environment, and we need to propagate them with a variety of electronic data upon which systems can be designed and prototyped. . . . We need to play, to fulfill our drive to play [and] as we succeed we must prepare ourselves for a very different and exciting world where the social creation of knowledge is nurtured by the services of libraries and of multimedia.[22]

[Librarians] will need to act as guides through a technology which prides itself on being nonlinear. They will have to assist patrons in developing alternative strategies to negotiate hyperspace. . . . The ramifications of the introduction of multimedia technology in libraries will undoubtedly be at least as profound as those resulting from the incorporation of computers, [but] in the meantime, it is essential that we not allow ourselves to take the "band-aid" approach to integrating this new technology. Any integration must be on the theoretical, as well as applied, level.[23]

I would like to suggest that there are some serious problems with postmodernist visions of libraries—and they are very often blithely overlooked. In so doing, I am following the "media ecology" approach taken by Neil Postman, Marshall McLuhan, and others.[24] A commonsense summary of McLuhan's much-misused ideas provides the basis of my approach to postmodern, technological visions of libraries: "while we tend to pay attention to content and ignore the medium, it is actually the medium that has the more significant impact . . . the medium affects the kind of content that can be created and transmitted [, and] it affects the individual [and] society (e.g., political, economic, and social organization, institutions, roles, and values)."[25] What follows is a brief review of a number of very postmodernlike library problems as they relate to structures of social thinking and memory. So as not to repeat and summarize my earlier critiques of the relevant aspects of postmodernism each time, I will simply identify the particular issue (letting the reader make the connections to the problems of indeterminacy, fragmentation, and discontinuity) and turn to a discussion of them in terms of librarianship.

## 1. A Visual/Nonliterate Bias

There have long been questions about the relationship between technology (particularly visual and digital media) and literacy[26]—much of it suggesting (in the vein of media ecology analyses) that technology contains within itself an inherent bias for the visual as against print literacy.[27] Certainly librarianship's language reflects that bias when discussing the confluence between new "visual" learners (weaned on postmodern consumer culture), technologies, and how to teach one to the other.[28] But a number of the public sphere roles of librarianship become meaningless in this postmodern context. First, if we are—purposefully or not—moving away from print and print literacy, we are committing an act that furthers the bias that cuts society off from the vast majority of the information and value contained on the shelves in libraries. We know for a fact just how limited electronic resources (of whatever stripe, provenance, and veracity) are—especially when compared to the riches of a print collection.[29] But when books and print resources are conceptualized as a postmodernlike "prison,"[30] we are *not* expanding but rather *contracting* information freedom. Tom Mann has called this librarianship's inability to think outside the Internet box.[31] A nonprint, nonliterate bias in our resources and services is a limiting bias in our public sphere role of providing public information for a democratic culture.

Second, a visual bias strips our resources of any political meaning. As a colleague of mine puts it, you can't draw a picture explaining Thomas Jefferson's relationship to the founding ideas of American public education. If you somehow managed to do so, it could not be engaged, examined, identified, and debated in any real political, historical, or policy terms. Such an image could not be related to the present, because a postmodern visual bias treats both the present and the past as interchangeable, manipulable images—and calls to mind the critique of postmodern "pastiche" culture. Librarianship's public sphere role in sustained, rational public discourse connected to history and historical possibility vanishes. Postman has put it even more bluntly: "pictures ask to be recognized; words ask to be understood."[32] With a visual, nonliterate bias, librarianship's professional and public sphere emphasis on balanced points of view (how do you balance images?) and representation on our shelves is rendered meaningless. Remember the critique advanced in chapter 3: just as minority voices were gaining a foothold in print (and on library shelves), print has been declared a meaningless signifier, or worse, a form of domination.

The struggle for representative justice in catalog subject headings (long carried on by Sandy Berman) is rendered equally meaningless in this context. What visual image in a multimedia library is accurately described by his proposed subject headings like "corporate power," "classism in law," or "welfare consumers—rights"?[33] How are such topics to be researched or debated in visual terms? Accurately (and democratically) describing and balancing content when we're trying so hard to transform libraries into multimedia venues is surely a case in contradictory impulses. Postman again asks the most direct question: in this new postmodern, technological, nonprint library environment, does intellectual freedom (as we have historically conceived it) have any meaning?[34] At best, a visual bias represents a serious undermining of the rational, communicative, and democratic basis of the public sphere (historical memory, representing alternatives, enabling future possibility) that libraries have enacted. It is in the truest sense an apolitical, neoconservative bias. Or as noted in a nice parallel to Habermas's concept of the refeudalization of the public sphere, we are reviving a kind of "medievalism [in] lowered rates of literacy, reduced average levels of literacy, and a retreat from the goal of universal literacy to a state of craft literacy, i.e., literacy as a specialized skill employed by small segments of society."[35]

## 2. Authorless Authority

Digital, multimedia technology strip authorship, or at best obscure it. Indeed, this is—as has been noted—what is celebrated about the technology by postmodernists and postmodern visions of librarianship: information, words, and images "stored as random digital segments" do not have relationships or rational structures built in (and thus do not serve as instruments of language, perspective, and identity "domination"). But "what is now missing is the fixed structure of [a] composition that communicates a message to the viewer [or reader, leaving] elements unconnected and left for [people] to arrange . . . no longer need[ing] to understand the concept of point of view, as it is expressed by others."[36] Indeed, postmodernism rejects the fixed point of view—in a striking parallel to the multimedia, "hyperreal" library. The problem is the illusion that there is no authority or point of view built in, and so there is a strange kind of disembodied authority in such library resources. As Joseph Weizenbaum put it, when "I read what stood written, [I] imagine a human author, infer his values, and finally agree or disagree with him. Computer systems do not admit of exercises of imagination that may ultimately lead to authentic human judgment."[37]

We see this same phenomena all the time in our libraries. As previously noted, the Internet is an increasingly commercial site, with hidden, purchased access to our screens, our searches, and an authorless, invisible structuring and guiding of the content we see.[38] "People using these systems frequently do not know where they are, how they got there, and how to find the information they are looking for,"[39] and as a consequence librarians are struggling hard to teach distinctions between the legitimate resources we pay thousands of dollars per year for (online catalogs and electronic journals and indexes) and the random information, perspectives, and flotsam found out on the Internet. Those results are most often acquired with an indifferent, keyword search and represent the first ten to fifteen convenient hits. Academic libraries and higher education as a whole are very much struggling with random student citation of conveniently found "scholarly" sources of dubious provenance supporting specious academic claims—not to mention the ease of digital plagiarism.[40] However, the multimedia-driven library encourages such approaches in its postmodern authorless-but-with-the-authority-and-prestige-of-technology bias. After all, why worry about plagiarism when students are really engaging in postmodern, hypertextual "play" and "collaborative, hyperreal learning" when they capture—or buy—text off the Internet and put their names on it in an ironic play on "authorship"?

The postmodern multimedia library encourages the continued blurring of accuracy and authority that is taking place in the larger, media-driven culture. The appeal to a specious accuracy and authority in statements like "I got it off the Web" and "I heard it on TV" is more similar than we would care to admit. C. A. Bowers notes that technology "reinforces the view that the ideas, information, and data that are transmitted through language are objective. That is, the human authorship of knowledge is obscured. What moves through the conduit of language [in a technological context] takes on the appearance of objectivity."[41] In moving toward a postmodern, simulated library with our emphasis on all things technological, we undermine our public sphere role of collecting and preserving *identifiably human* cultural creation. In the process, we are blurring our traditional role of identifying and tracing the legitimacy and provenance of that cultural output and our role in verifying truth claims in the public sphere.

## 3. Ahistoricism

Postmodernist visions of librarianship are profoundly ahistorical. The primary postmodern cultural mode of interaction with information, text, and images is not one of analysis or situated context but of play and irony. Postmodern media "signs" and hyperreal messages "wink" at us, inviting a false skepticism. The "ironic detachment is not one of disengagement, but of unwitting collaboration with the corporate-sponsored . . . agenda."[42] Such a self-referential system is almost completely disconnected from the past, and any reading of the past must be (according to postmodernism) a form of domination—or at best a "playful" out-of-sequence appropriation and manipulation of its images (like those ads where George Washington flogs linens on President's Day White Sales).

Again, librarianship has played to this ahistorical bias. It is apparent, for instance, in the unwillingness to budget (or fight for the budgets) to stop the diminution of print collections while at the same time expanding electronic resources, and it is apparent in the massive "weeding" of collections without regard for historical or research value (the Ken Dowlin and Charles Robinson approaches). It is apparent in our acquiescence to here-today-gone-tomorrow electronic journal "collections" and the licenses that permit such practices.

We routinely ignore actual historical experience with technologies—in libraries and in society, and in both the distant and more recent past—and the possible insights to be gained from a historical perspective.[43] Librarianship demonstrates a preference for digital images vs. the "expense" of maintaining and preserving original documents. The fragility (read lack of historical longevity) of the resulting library digital preservation efforts[44] indicates an ahistorical bias—and reinforces the preference for the postmodern and manipulable digital vs. the stability print.

Over and over again, we are reminded that artifacts (real things, including printed books) contain information we have not yet discovered—or as yet have the means to discover. Committing to that future discovery means "taking history seriously [and] accepting some story as the means of knowing anything at all"—including placing an inherent value on the integrity and unchanged nature of the historical objects in our collections.[45] Librarianship's digitization of artifacts into unstable, manipulable, and highly impermanent "simulations" furthers the bias of ahistorical, ironic postmodern image "play" and endangers the historical record and its accuracy. Henry Giroux has again written of the connection of this idea to our public sphere role in democratic potential (or the diminution of it):

The present crisis in historical consciousness is linked to the American public's deepening commitment to an ever-expanding network of . . . systems and social . . . technologies. One consequence of this has been the removal of political decisions from public discourse by reducing the[m] to technical problems answerable to technical solutions. [H]istory has been stripped of its critical and transcendent content and can no longer provide society with . . . a collective critical consciousness. In this view, the critical sense is inextricably rooted in the historical sense. . . . To become aware of the processes of historical self-formation indicates an [understanding of] the taken-for-granted assumptions that legitimize existing institutional arrangements. [T]he capacity for a historically grounded critique is inseparable from those conditions that foster collective communication and critical dialogue.[46]

## POSTMODERN LIBRARIES AND TECHNOCRACY

The connection of postmodern multimedia libraries with technocracy begins with the important observation that sophisticated new technologies are not in fact fluid but rather quite structured and rule driven in their base mode of operation. Despite the fact that powerful computers and networked systems allow text and images to be randomly and incoherently accessed and recombined, "the bottom line is that the computer is a literate and linear machine. It employs binary mathematics and depends on grammar. When humans fail to follow the rules, the machine does not respond correctly."[47] There is a corollary observation that notes that social structures and institutions that incorporate and build around such technologies extend the basis and biases of the technical and economic rationality that are at the root of information technologies.[48] Again, these insights fit the media ecology analysis well, and they inform a less-casual look at the evolving postmodern nature of librarianship.

For instance, the widescale introduction of computers in education included—whether acknowledged or not—"agendas and curricula embedded in technologies influencing social relationships, and what constitutes knowledge, literacy, work and their related cultures."[49] Apple identifies an important extension of this insight: "vast areas of school life are now seen to be within the legitimate purview of technological restructuring [and there is a] linkage . . . between computers in schools and the needs of management for automated industries, electronic offices, and 'skilled' personnel."[50] Within this example of computers in schools lies the essence of technocracy: managed social and institutional organization of a public cultural institution around the needs, assumptions, and biases of a technical/technological system and its ideological/economic agendas. (This basic idea has been presented under a variety of names, most notably Jacques Ellul's term "technique" and Lewis Mumford's term "technics."[51]) While technology is a focal point and a significant tool (and embodiment) of technocracy, it is not the whole of it. C. A. Bowers writes that it "should be understood to mean the complex interlocking set of social and economic activities that sustains our current fever-pitch level of consumerism [with] techniques of production, techniques of distribution; techniques for creating the need for a certain product or service; [and] techniques for storing and retrieving information on the whereabouts of people and products."[52] Briefly defined, the hallmarks of technocracy are a perception of the world as a set of problems to be rationally solved through expertise; the interconnection of science, technology, and modernization; a rationalized human social order with technical expertise (and its tools and purposes) at its center; and centralized managerial control.[53] For instance, the technocratic organization of schools can be seen in technological and standardized curriculum packages that represent central management control of content, the school year, and teachers' professional work.[54]

Postmodernist visions of librarianship show these basic hallmarks of technocracy, and they tend to be most clearly revealed when one looks at technologies from the media ecology perspective. For instance, the review of management practices and models in chapter 5 clearly linked those developments with the pursuit of the role of Daniel Bell's technocratic knowledge manager in an information society. The theme that librarians and libraries must be transformed and organized around the "new" information economy and technology is one that has run throughout this book. This clearly represents the technocratic reorganization of a public, social institution around rationalized, instrumental, and economic purposes. This takes place at the highest organizational level in the form of more centralized management control of content. Most library decisions to purchase and make electronic content (journals, indexes, ebooks, etc.) available tend to be centrally made by library administrators and technical personnel[55]—paralleling the technocratic and centralizing trends of outsourcing noted earlier. We now see technocratic library management strategies to identify noninnovative personnel (with psychometric instruments) and structures (like standing committees) that "stifle" digital innovation.[56] It is not enough to merely integrate and organize libraries around technologies; we are now urged to take the next technocratic step in planning and control and use our collective purchasing power to help design the initial products around which librarians are then to organize themselves and their institutions.[57]

As a final case in point, academic libraries' role in distance learning is most certainly linked to the issues of management control in the capturing and distribution of intellectual content in higher education. It is not merely the for-profits (like the "University" of Phoenix) who demonstrate this technocratic bent—prestigious universities are doing so and also aiming for profit.[58] It is notable that such schemes often focus on library resources as one of the few real areas of centralized knowledge distribution—and library administrators and for-profit companies alike flog the distance education model frequently in the library literature.[59] Library technocracy absolutely reflects the rationalized purposes of institutions and people and centralized control, and as such, the postmodern multimedia library is a site of far less freedom, play, and fluidity than its image and pop analysts would suggest. It instead reflects the deeper grammar of technology: rational—and rationalizing—centralized planning and control in content and the social organization of libraries and librarians toward economic (vs. social or democratic) ends.[60]

## CONCLUSION

The historian of technology Leo Marx offers two helpful analyses that sum up a good deal of librarianship's relationship to technologies. In adapting an analysis of the concept of culture, Marx argues in parallel that technology as a concept

acquired its meanings in response to the very changes [it was being used to] analyze. It was not simply that the word . . . had been influenced by those changes, but that its meaning had in large measure been entangled with—and in some degree generated by them. A recognition of this circular process helps to account for . . . the significance of technology. [T]he concept itself—especially when the singular noun . . . is the subject of an active verb, and thus by implication an autonomous agent capable of determining the course of events.[61]

I would suggest that Marx is also correct in our case. We too are caught in a loop of seemingly autonomous technological forces that are described and thought about using the same term, on its own terms. Librarians consistently speak and write about technology as cause, effect, reason for, reason against, source, subject, and object in a logically closed circle.

This leads to Marx's second insight. He has concluded that our technologies so conceived are "hazardous," contributing to a masking of human actors, feelings of political impotence in the face of autonomous systems, and that "collective life is uncontrollable."[62] Elsewhere he labeled this a form of postmodern pessimism:

There are striking affinities between the bold new conceptions of power favored by influential postmodern theorists . . . and the functioning of large technological systems. [But] in rejecting the old illusion of historical progress [they propose] a redescription of social reality that proves to be even more technocratic than the distorted Enlightenment ideology they reject. . . . In their hostility to . . . collective belief systems, moreover, many postmodernist thinkers relinquish all old-fashioned notions of putting the new systems into the service of a larger political vision of human possibilities. . . . This pessimistic tenor of postmodernism follows from this inevitably diminished sense of human agency [in] the vision of a postmodern society dominated by immense, overlapping, quasi-autonomous technological systems.[63]

Again, I would suggest that Marx's analysis fits librarianship well. Though most of us are far from dour fatalists in our professional outlook and our uncritical celebration of technology, we still manage to demonstrate the characteristics of much of what he describes. Technologies, their budgets, information capitalism, technologically transformed libraries, redefined public purposes, and whatever else washes up on library shores from the "new" economy all seem to be uncontrollable (in Marx's sense) by library professionals. We only react in our crisis culture. These tend to be accepted without much protest—a kinder and gentler version of what Marx described—and taken as autonomous, neutral facts in and of themselves. Librarians generally don't consider that we can—or should—do much about them. The consequence of this congenial kind of fatalism has been the diminution (without much discussion or protest) of our public sphere role in a democratic society and steady movement toward centralized technocratic control of librarianship in line with information economy trends. We have adopted a postmodern approach to our technologies (whether consciously or not) and in so doing, helped along the process of dismantling the public sphere in our institutions. In the end, I come back full circle. Technologies are not "evil," but the media ecology perspective helps us to look at their biases. Evaluated critically, budgeted fairly and carefully (in proportion to their real value vs. hype), taught effectively (including some balanced skepticism, as we do with print sources) to our patrons, technologies have every potential to further the *public* mission of libraries. The problem is in the postmodern way in which we have adopted them—and their biases—without examining those biases and proclivities as independent, public professionals with a social purpose.

## NOTES

1. See John Buschman, ed., *Critical Approaches to Information Technology in Librarianship: Foundations and Applications* (Westport, Conn.: Greenwood, 1993); John Buschman, "Information Technology, Power Structures, and the Fate of Librarianship," *Progressive Librarian* 6/7 (1993): 15–29; and John Buschman and Michael Carbone, "A Critical Inquiry into Librarianship: Applications of the 'New Sociology of Education'," *Library Quarterly* 61, no. 1 (1991): 15–40.

2. See, for example, Joseph Weizenbaum, *Computer Power and Human Reason: From Judgment to Calculation* (San Francisco: W. H. Freeman, 1976); and C. A. Bowers, *The Cultural Dimensions of Educational Computing: Understanding the Non-Neutrality of Technology* (New York: Teachers College Press, 1988). For an example of librarianship's concentration on style with information technology, see Nathan Smith, Mary Piette, and Betty Dance, "Effective Computer-Based/Hypermedia Instruction for Libraries: The Design, Evaluation, Implementation and Challenge!" in *Working with Faculty in the New Electronic Library*, ed. Linda Shirato (Ann Arbor, Mich.: Pierian Press, 1992), 25–40. For a critique of this tendency in a service area, see John Buschman and Dorothy Warner, "A Slip Between the Cup and the Lip: Practical and Intellectual Problems of Marketing U.S. Academic Libraries," in *Education and Research for Marketing and Quality Management in Libraries*, ed. Rejean Savard (Munich: K. G. Saur, 2002), 267–78.

3. Buschman, "Information Technology, Power Structures," 24.

4. I am again using the term "postmodernism," following Madan Sarup, *An Introductory Guide to Post-Structuralism and Postmodernism* (Athens: University of Georgia Press, 1989).

5. Gertrude Himmelfarb, "Revolution in the Library," *American Scholar* 6, no. 2 (1997): 202. Though I do not share her political perspective, this is a very clear and concise explication of the issue. The same point is made more generally in C. A. Bowers, *Let Them Eat Data: How Computers Affect Education, Cultural Diversity, and the Prospects of Ecological Sustainability* (Athens: University of Georgia Press, 2000), 18–22; Leo Marx, "The Idea of 'Technology' and Postmodern Pessimism," in *Does Technology Drive History? The Dilemma of Technological Determinism*, ed. Merritt Smith and Leo Marx (Cambridge, Mass.: MIT Press, 1994), 237–57; and Richard Brosio, *A Radical Democratic Critique of Capitalist Education* (New York: Peter Lang, 1994).

6. Sarup, 3–4. Sarup frequently notes throughout this volume that much postmodernist/poststructuralist thought was in direct opposition to Habermas's ideas, as does Douglas Kellner, "Habermas, the Public Sphere, and Democracy: A Critical Intervention." 12 October 2002, <http://www.gseis.ucla.edu/faculty/kellner/papers/habermas.htm>. Finally Marx, "The Idea of 'Technology'," 255, and Peter Hohendahl, "Jürgen Habermas: 'The Public Sphere' (1964)," *New German Critique* 4 (Fall 1974): 45–48, both locate the time when much of the disagreement between the two camps developed in the differing theoretical reactions to the student uprisings and the New Left in the late 1960s.

7. Alan Sokal and Jean Bricmont, *Fashionable Nonsense: Postmodern Intellectuals' Abuse of Science* (New York: Picador, 1998), 5. The hoax article, called "Transgressing the Boundaries: Toward a Transformative Hermeneutics of Quantum Gravity" was published in the journal *Social Text* in 1996 while under the editorship of Andrew Ross for that particular issue. It is reprinted in the Sokal and Bricmont volume on

pp. 212–58. They note that when major postmodernist thinkers claim to be using the most recent developments in an area of science or raise the question of what they have to teach Einstein (p. 5), then they probably deserve parody.

8. Howard Gardner, *The Unschooled Mind* (New York: Basic Books, 1991), 178–79.

9. Sarup, 138–40, 132–33.

10. Bernd Frohmann, "The Social and Discursive Construction of New Information Technologies" (Internationales Symposium fur Informationswissenschaft, Graz, Austria, 2–4 November 1994).

11. Carl Boggs, *The End of Politics: Corporate Power and the Decline of the Public Sphere* (New York: Guilford Press, 2000), 208–41.

12. Bernd Frohmann, "Communication Technologies and Human Subjectivity: The Politics of Postmodern Information Science," *Canadian Journal of Information and Library Science* 19, no. 2 (1993): 1–22. He notes the particularly egregious case of Pepsico's full media blitz in its plans to sell Mexican food from Taco Bell outlets to Mexicans in Mexico.

13. Jameson in Brosio, *Radical Democratic,* 607.

14. Timothy Luke, *Screens of Power: Ideology, Domination, and Resistance in Informational Society* (Urbana: University of Illinois Press, 1989), 48. He reviews the work of Jean Baudrillard (30–54), the primary proponent of this postmodern approach.

15. Sue Barnes and Lance Strate, "The Educational Implications of the Computer: A Media Ecology Critique," *New Jersey Journal of Communication* 4, no. 2 (1996): 196–98, 202–4.

16. Sarup, 133 (summarizing Frederic Jameson).

17. Michael Apple, *Cultural Politics & Education* (New York: Teachers College Press, 1996), x.

18. Andrew Feenberg, *Critical Theory of Technology* (New York: Oxford University Press, 1991), 18–19.

19. Apple, *Cultural Politics,* xi–xii.

20. Jürgen Habermas, "Modernity Versus Postmodernity," *New German Critique* 22 (1981): 13–14.

21. Gregory Anderson, "Dimensions, Context, and Freedom: The Library in the Social Creation of Knowledge," in *Sociomedia: Multimedia, Hypermedia, and the Social Construction of Knowledge,* ed. Edward Barrett (Cambridge, Mass.: MIT Press, 1992), 107–8.

22. Anderson, 127.

23. Kathleen Burnett, "Multimedia and the Library and Information Studies Curriculum," in *Sociomedia,* ed. Barrett, 138–39. See also Gloria Rohmann, "Media on Demand: Approaches to Web-Based Media Services in Libraries," *Advances in Librarianship* 23 (2002): 39–61, which is a more straightforward, technical description of such library operations but is still largely based on the same epistemological and professional assumptions (as Anderson and Burnett).

24. Summarized in Barnes and Strate.

25. Barnes and Strate, 181–82.

26. Some of the basics of this issue are summarized in John Buschman, "Issues in Censorship and Information Technology," in *Critical Approaches to Information Tech-*

*nology in Librarianship: Foundations and Applications,* ed. John Buschman (Westport, Conn.: Greenwood Press, 1993), 136–39.

27. For a good summary of some of the relevant research see Barnes and Strate; see also Neil Postman, *Teaching as a Conserving Activity* (New York: Delta, 1979), 29–106; Neil Postman, "The Contradictions of Freedom of Information," *WLA Journal,* June 1985, 4–19; Jay Rosen, "Playing the Primary Chords," *Harper's,* March 1992, 22–26; Sven Birkerts, *Gutenberg Elegies: The Fate of Reading in an Electronic Age* (New York: Fawcett Columbine, 1994); and Alexander Stille, *The Future of the Past* (New York: Farrar, Straus and Giroux, 2002), 311–39. A series of articles on the theme of "Terminal Reading" also provides good summary analyses: Sven Birkerts, "Into the Electronic Millennium," *Boston Review,* October 1991, 15–19; Roger Shattuck, "From the Swiss Family Robinson to Narratus Interruptus," *Boston Review,* May–July 1992, 22–24; Jascha Kessler, "Epimetheus—or, A Reflection on the 'Box'," *Boston Review,* February 1992, 13–14; and Ella Taylor, "Virtual Reality," *Boston Review,* December 1991, 18–19.

28. See, for example, Dees Stallings, "The Virtual University: Organizing to Survive in the 21st Century," *Journal of Academic Librarianship* 27, no. 1 (2001): 3–14; Gary Marchionini, *Information Seeking in Electronic Environments* (Cambridge: Cambridge University Press, 1995), 14–17, 11–26 generally; Bruce Flanders, "Multimedia Programs to Reach an MTV Generation," *American Libraries,* February 1992, 135–36; and Anderson. For skeptical views of the same issue, see Thomas Mann, "The Importance of Books, Free Access, and Libraries as Places—and the Dangerous Inadequacy of the Information Science Paradigm," *Journal of Academic Librarianship* 27, no. 4 (2001): 270–71; and Michael Harris, Stan Hannah, and Pamela Harris, *Into the Future: The Foundation of Library and Information Services in the Post-Industrial Era,* 2nd ed. (Greenwich, Conn.: Ablex, 1998), 22–23.

29. Mark Herring, "10 Reasons Why the Internet is No Substitute for a Library," *American Libraries,* April 2001, 76–78; Mann, "Importance of Books"; and Thomas Mann, *The Oxford Guide to Library Research* (New York: Oxford University Press, 1998).

30. Eldred Smith, "The Print Prison," *Library Journal,* 1 February 1992, 48–51.

31. Mann, "Importance of Books," 274–75.

32. Postman, "The Contradictions of Freedom of Information."

33. Sanford Berman, foreword to *Poor People and Library Services,* ed. Karen Venturella (Jefferson, N.C.: McFarland, 1998), 1–14.

34. Postman, "The Contradictions of Freedom of Information."

35. Barnes and Strate, 203.

36. Barnes and Strate, 194–95, 200.

37. Weizenbaum, 240.

38. Juris Dilevko, "Why Sally Tisdale is *Really* Upset About the State of Libraries: Socio-Political Implications of Internet Information Sources," *Journal of Information Ethics,* Spring 1999, 40–56; and David Corn, "Anatomy of a Netscam," *Washington Post,* 7 July 1996, C5. On a more prosaic note, one author examined how a simple technology, in this case *PowerPoint* software, structures how we communicate and what is considered *worth* communicating; see Ian Parker, "Absolute Powerpoint," *New Yorker,* 28 May 2001, 76, 78–80, 85–87. On a more humorous note, Michael Gorman, "Human Values in a Technological Age," *Information Technology and Libraries,* March 2001, 8, quotes Dave Barry as observing that the "Internet is the most im-

portant single development in the history of human communications since 'call waiting,'" and Brian Winston, who notes that "the only effective marketers on the vaunted
Information Highway [are] pornographers."

39. Barnes and Strate, 203.

40. Ann Lathrop and Kathleen Foss, *Student Cheating and Plagiarism in the In-
ternet Era: A Wake-Up Call* (Englewood, Colo.: Libraries Unlimited, 2000); Jeffrey
Young, "The Cat-and-Mouse Game of Plagiarism Detection," *Chronicle of Higher
Education,* 6 July 2001, A26; Julianne Basinger and Kelly McCollum, "Boston U.
Sues Companies for Selling Term Papers Over the Internet," *Chronicle of Higher Edu-
cation,* 31 October 1997, A34; Ellen Laird, "Internet Plagiarism: We All Pay the
Price," *Chronicle of Higher Education,* 13 July 2001, B5; Mark Fritz, "Redefining
Research, Plagiarism," *Los Angeles Times,* 25 February 1999, A1; David Isaacson,
"Instant Information Gratification," *American Libraries,* February 2002, 39; and An-
drew Carnie, "How to Handle Cyber-Sloth in Academe," *Chronicle of Higher Edu-
cation,* 5 January 2001, B14.

41. Bowers, *Cultural Dimensions,* 42.

42. Richard Brosio, review of *Boxed In: The Culture of TV,* by Mark Crispin Miller,
*Educational Studies* 21, no. 1 (1990): 55.

43. See, for example, David Staley, "Digital Technologies and the Mythologies of
Globalization," *Bulletin of Science, Technology & Society* 18, no. 6 (1998): 421–25;
Neal Postman, *Technopoly: The Surrender of Culture to Technology* (New York: Vintage,
1993); John Durham Peters, "Information: Notes Toward a Critical History," *Journal
of Communication Inquiry* 12, no. 2 (1988): 9–23; James Beniger, "Origins of the
Information Society," *Wilson Library Bulletin,* November 1986, 12–19; Gorman; and
Mann, "Importance of Books," 268–69. On electronic subscription impermanence
see Francine Fialkoff, "Inside Track: The Hidden Costs of Online," *Library Journal,*
1 December 2001, 97.

44. In addition to those sources previously cited on this topic, see Alison Mitchell,
"Ingenuity's Blueprints, into History's Dustbin," *New York Times,* 30 December
2001, A1, A22; and Dennis O'Mahoney, "Here Today, Gone Tomorrow: What Can
Be Done to Assure Permanent Public Access to Electronic Information?" *Advances in
Librarianship* 22 (1998): 107–21.

45. Sarup, 143. See also note 66 in chapter 6 for examples of the value of preservation.

46. Henry Giroux, "Schooling and the Culture of Positivism: Notes on the Death
of History," *Educational Theory* 29, no. 4 (1979): 265, 270, 282.

47. G. Phillips in Barnes and Strate, 203–4, 202; see also Bowers, *Cultural Dimensions;* and C. A. Bowers, "The Reproduction of Technological Consciousness: Locating the Ideological Foundations of a Radical Pedagogy," *Teachers College Record*
83 (1982): 529–88 on this point. Stuart Hall, "On Postmodernism and Articulation,"
*Journal of Communication Inquiry* 10 (1986): 49–50, makes a very interesting point:
the technology postmodernists celebrate "does not destroy the process of encoding,
which always entails the imposition of an arbitrary 'closure.' Indeed, it actually enriches
it. . . . "

48. See Michael Carbone, "Are Educational Technology and School Restructuring
Appropriate Partners?" *Teacher Education Quarterly* 22 (Spring 1995): 4–17; Post-
man, *Technopoly;* Postman, "The Contradictions of Freedom of Information"; Bowers,
"Reproduction"; and Peters.

49. Carbone, "Are Educational Technology?" 13.

50. Michael Apple, "A Critical Analysis of Three Approaches to the Use of Computers in Education," in *The Curriculum: Problems, Politics, and Possibilities,* ed. Landon Beyer and Michael Apple (Albany: State University of New York Press, 1988), 291.

51. See the summary in John Buschman and Michael Carbone, "Technocracy, Educational Structures and Libraries: Historical Notes from the United States," *Journal of Education Policy* 11, no. 5 (1996): 562–63. Basic, short works by Mumford, Ellul, and others can be found in John Zerzan and Alice Carnes, eds., *Questioning Technology: Tool, Toy, or Tyrant?* (Philadelphia: New Society Publishers, 1991).

52. C. A. Bowers, "Curriculum and Our Technocracy Culture: The Problem of Reform," *Teachers College Record* 78, no. 1 (1976): 54.

53. Adapted from Buschman and Carbone.

54. Michael Carbone, "Critical Scholarship on Computers in Education: A Summary Review," in *Critical Approaches to Information Technology in Librarianship: Foundations and Applications,* ed. John Buschman (Westport, Conn.: Greenwood, 1993), 41–57; and Michael Apple and Susan Jungck, "You Don't Have to Be a Teacher to Teach This Unit: Teaching, Technology, and Gender in the Classroom," *American Educational Research Journal* 27 (1990): 223–51.

55. Kenneth Frazier, "The Librarians' Dilemma: Contemplating the Costs of the 'Big Deal'," *D-Lib Magazine* 7, no. 3 (March 2001), <www.dlib.org/dlib/march01/frazier/03frazier.html>; and Andrew Albanese, "An LJ Round Table with the Aggregators," *Library Journal,* 15 March 2002, 34–38; see also Harris, Hannah, and Harris, 40–43.

56. Roy Tennant, "Digital Libraries—The Engines of Innovation," *Library Journal,* 15 June 2002, 28–29.

57. Joe Janes, "How to Think About Technology," *Library Journal,* 1 February 2002, 50–51.

58. See Stanley Katz, "In Information Technology, Don't Mistake a Tool for a Goal," *Chronicle of Higher Education,* 15 June 2001, B7; the David Noble series, "Digital Diploma Mills," Part I, 1998, Part II, 1998, Part III, November 1998—all available at <http://www.ucsd.edu/dl.htm>, Part IV, November 1999 distributed on e-mail by pagre@alpha.oac.ucla.edu on 26 November 1999, Part V, June 2001 at <http://www.ucsd.edu/dl/ddm5.htm.>; John Palatella, "Ivory Towers in the Marketplace," *Dissent,* Summer 2001, 70–73; Jeffrey Selingo, "Aiming for a New Audience, U. of Phoenix Tries Again in New Jersey," *Chronicle of Higher Education,* 21 September 2001, A23; and James Traub, "Drive-Thru U," *New Yorker,* 20 & 27 October 1997, 114, 116–18, 120–22.

59. Buschman and Carbone; John Buschman and Dorothy A. Warner, "Wider Access to Higher Education in the United States: An Evaluative Case Study of the Library," in *Researching Widening Access: International Perspectives,* ed. Mike Osborne and Jim Gallacher (Glasgow, Scotland: Center for Research in Lifelong Learning, Glasgow Caledonian University, 2001), 60–61; and Ron Chepesiuk, "Internet College: The Virtual Classroom Challenge," *American Libraries,* March 1998, 52–55. "Articles" on distance learning in the library literature, written by representatives of the companies marketing such approaches, can be found in Stallings (of VCampus Corporation); and Robert Antonucci and Joseph Cronin, "Creating an Online University, "*Journal of Academic Librarianship* 27, no. 1 (2001): 20–23 (of Harcourt Higher

Education). In a close parallel, Richard Dougherty, "Reference Around the Clock: Is It in Your Future?" *American Libraries,* May 2002, 44, 46, is a former academic library administrator who has begun a consulting firm (Dougherty and Associates) "that offers workshops on the creation of new reference-service environments" based on the distance learning model.

60. The seminal article on this concept is Lewis Mumford, "Authoritarian and Democratic Technics," in *Questioning Technology,* ed. Zerzan and Carnes, 13–21.

61. Leo Marx, "Technology: The Emergence of a Hazardous Concept," *Social Research* 64, no. 3 (1997): 967–68. Marx borrowed the concept from the work of Raymond Williams.

62. Marx, "Technology: The Emergence," 984.

63. Marx, "The Idea of 'Technology'," 256–57.

# 9

## CONCLUSION: TOWARD A SUSTAINABLE CASE FOR LIBRARIANSHIP: THE PUBLIC SPHERE AND DEMOCRATIC POSSIBILITY

### INTRODUCTION

There is some need of summary of the last five chapters prior to moving on to the task of constructing a sustainable case for librarianship. So as not to continually repeat large parts of the critical context of the new public philosophy and the diminution of librarianship's enacting of the public sphere idea in each chapter, I made only brief references throughout to connect each area reviewed to the theses put forward in chapters 2 and 3. I believe the argument for situating librarianship in this context is a compelling one. My chosen frame of reference—education—has proven fruitful (and it will be an important source for a sustainable case for librarianship). Like education, librarianship has been the subject of government and foundation review and reporting that, in their sum, recast the field's purpose in economic terms. Like education, the model of the market, business management, and entrepreneurial practices have all been ascendant in the field—and the specific context is librarianship's new role in support of the "new" economy and information capitalism. Like education, our field has been called upon to play a "crucial" role in bringing the information society and the "new" economy about, but without the public funding support for that expanded (and essentially economic) mission. Therefore, libraries have closely paralleled the problems and biases of education's public funding patterns and, like education, carefully imitated the business management fashions, fads, and tactics appropriate to adapting to information capitalism. In the process, we have transformed library users into "customers" and then adopted the corollary business practices of marketing and public relations, measuring "quality" as defined by "customer satisfaction," and adopted the market model of "competition" and an entrepreneurial approach to funding shortages and library practices. This economic model and purpose has had its effect on our overall professional directions, as evinced by the corporate drift of ALA. Finally, our relationships to technology bear many of the intellectual and epistemological problems of an apolitical postmodern accommodation to the antidemocratic cultural and economic biases of networked resources and information capitalism. In sum, these trends represent a change in the purpose of librarianship—one that has come about almost "naturally" and without much debate as part of the general trend of the new public philosophy for public cultural institutions.

Implicit in the educational critique of the new public philosophy is the notion of disabling the democratic public sphere. (The idea of the democratic purposes and bases of education is one to which I will return.) This idea formed the second basic part of the context of librarianship, and it is grounded in the ideas of Jürgen Habermas. Essentially, my argument is that the specific trends identified in librarianship that accommodate the new public philosophy of casting public cultural institutions in economic terms represent a further diminution of the democratic public sphere. While Habermas's analyses of the structural transformation and the refeudalization of the public sphere formed the theoretical backdrop for this analysis, I have proposed an important variation appropriate to librarianship. As noted, Habermas's identification of the public sphere—its role in creating democratic institutions and processes—and its destruction is based on his theory of a rational communicative process that has been corrupted within mass society and advanced capitalism. In adapting Habermas's ideas, I have proposed that librarianship, in many important, thorough, latent, and concrete ways *embodies* and *enacts* the public sphere idea in the form of rational organization of human discourse, a resource to check validity claims, and so forth. Therefore, library collections, services, values, and traditions—probably because of their sheer bulk and some residual professional conservatism in the field— still contain within them many of the characteristics—and possibilities—of the public sphere. The new public philosophy trends and practices in librarianship represent not merely another variation on the corruption of the communicative processes that make the democratic public sphere but also its *dismantling* in the ways it has been enacted and embodied in the field. Our acceding to the new public philosophy model is, in many ways, an active deconstructing of the democratic public sphere discourse that libraries represent.

To bring this back full circle, it is the lack of debate or consensus on the reconstructed economic purposes of librarianship in information capitalism that is the source of much of our crisis culture. We continue to be incompletely transformed as technocratic agents of the information society (knowledge managers), and in the absence of open proposals and debate over such a change of purpose, the new public philosophy assumptions tend to fill the vacuum. The combination of ambitious, aggressive library administrators and information scientists who wish to "adapt" rather than "die" and residual (democratic) habits, practices, and discourses embodied within librarianship make for an overheated and simplistic rhetoric that continually declares a crisis in the field. To be certain, the lack of consensus on the philosophical purpose and epistemology of librarianship has been a longstanding cri de coeur in the field,[1] and I do not wish to minimize the considerable efforts of those who have tried to push and pull these questions into a sensible and defensible framework. I propose to take this discussion in a different direction toward a democratic theory of the social purposes of librarianship. It is not surprisingly grounded in theories of democratic education and Habermas's public sphere and epistemology.

## CONTEXT, ONE LAST TIME

The search for purpose and meaning in secular societies under capitalism is a general question, and so our questions are not at all limited to librarianship—or even the much broader context of education. Declaring the "end of ideology"—as Daniel Bell[2] did—has not brought consensus or purpose, nor has the declaration of the "end of history" with the end of the cold war and the "finality" of the triumph of the combination of market economies and democratic pluralism.[3] However, "in the current context of late capitalism, with an interventionist state attempting to manage the social environment and cope with political and economic crises, democratic ideals are on the defensive."[4] Intellectually, crucial "doubts have been raised about the conceptual foundations of Western modernity. Hard questions have emerged about the predominant modern understandings of reason, subjectivity, nature, progress, and gender [and] that the systematic pursuit of enlightened reason and freedom had the ironic long-term effect of engendering new forms of irrationality and repression."[5] These issues have been raised from the left, the right, and a variety of positions in between, noting widespread social dysfunction in the face of peace and prosperity, political apathy and disempowerment, cultural diminution and enervation, and a desperate search for social, national, and personal purpose in a secular world.[6] Habermas notes that

the neoconservative doctrine blurs the relationship between the welcomed process of societal modernization on the one hand, and the lamented cultural development on the other [like] hedonism, the lack of social identification, the lack of obedience, narcissism, the withdrawal from status and achievement competition. [T]hose intellectuals who still feel themselves committed to the project of modernity are then presented as taking the place of . . . unanalyzed causes [but these problems] have not been called into life by modernist intellectuals. They are rooted in deep seated reactions against the process of societal modernization. Under the pressures of the dynamics of economic growth and the organizational accomplishments of the state, this social modernization penetrates deeper and deeper into previous forms of human existence.[7]

On a personal and professional level, relentless economic and cultural modernization has extracted a price. The demands for an ever-flexible, ever-adapting workforce, combined with our cultural bias toward independence, have stripped much of the meaning we can derive from work (while work ironically is held as the highest of personal priorities), de-coupled sociability and social integration, and led to a pathology of personal responsibility (or failure) to individually keep up with the demands of relentless adaptation and retraining.[8] Social, cultural, and political issues are thus recast as individual problems in adapting to the demands of an "objective reality": the "new" economy. This is not a hard theme to identify in librarianship. In response to the question of "how can librarians cope with continuing changes and the other stresses associated with digital reference," a prominent library educator admonished librarians to "get over it . . . and no more whining."[9] Another article suggested that the stresses and anxieties of adjusting to the demands of an "era of information technology" had to be met with a change in librarian attitudes and skills to accommodate it.[10] Finally, librarianship has faced its own "end of history" ramifications: there is little point in debating first principles (like the meanings of intellectual freedom or library social responsibility) if we are firmly settled in the best of all possible worlds—a democratic, market society without need of ideology.[11] Needless to say, I agree with Habermas when he asserts that we should "hold on to the *intentions* of the Enlightenment . . . learn from the mistakes of those extravagant programs which have tried to negate modernity, [and not] declare the entire project . . . a lost cause."[12] Declaring the triumph of market capitalism and neoconservative democracy has not solved entrenched social problems (or even explained them well), and it has not provided a public purpose for those societies or their institutions—libraries among them. Our search for purpose—both institutionally and as a profession—is very much in the mainstream of a more general struggle.

## THE CASE FOR LIBRARIANSHIP AND ITS ROLE IN THE DEMOCRATIC PUBLIC SPHERE

In laying out the basis for a sustainable defense of librarianship—a reason *for* the field and its institutions—I am adapting the work of the philosopher Amy Gutmann, who has written on a philosophy of democratic education. In utilizing her analysis, I take some issue with her categorization of libraries in the role of "extramural education" (along with television), noting their supplemental role in helping to equalize educational opportunity.[13] While I do not want to be guilty of overstating librarianship's role or potential, nor the scale of our possible positive contribution to society,[14] I would suggest that the field occupies a larger cultural and educational role than this—particularly in light of the cultural drift toward infotainment and the ahistorical nature of public and political questions. Having said that, Gutmann does firmly link librarianship to the public purposes of education, and her framework is an instructive one for our field. She begins by noting that a democracy entails a decision on "how future citizens will be educated. Democratic education is therefore a political as well as an educational ideal. . . . Education not only sets the stage for democratic politics, it plays a central role in it."[15] As a colleague has put it, when we discuss our institutions, we are talking (whether we know it or not) about the meaning of what constitutes the "good society" and the "good life." In this case I am suggesting that librarianship's role is, at its core, a public one in support of the democratic public sphere.

Gutmann notes that when we look at our institutions and propose reforming them, we often identify a number of problems and issues. However, we only pursue the solutions to *some* of them purposefully and systematically: "all significant policy prescriptions presuppose a theory [and] when it remains implicit, we cannot adequately judge its principles or the polic[ies] that flow from them."[16] Undiscussed, they generally follow what Neil Postman called the unchecked biases of the culture.[17] The issue is not that recommendations and analyses of libraries and other public institutions are necessarily wrong, "but that we cannot judge them without a more principled understanding of our . . . purposes." Avoiding the question of purposes extracts a high price: "we neglect . . . alternatives that may be better than those to which we have become accustomed or that may aid us in understanding how to improve . . . before we reach the point of crisis, when our reactions are likely to be less reflective because we have so little time to deliberate."[18] I would strongly argue that this analysis characterizes the field of librarianship and describes our need of a public purpose. But, like Gutmann, it is appropriate to ask why base such a purpose on a democratic theory? First, she reviews other theoretical approaches, as I will here. An economistic view of public institutions (including libraries) fails to give a reason *why* any individual should fiscally support a social goal that does not maximize their own utility. As John Kenneth Galbraith characterizes it, the objection to paying taxes that support others "is an honest and unsurprising statement of a very common preference, [but the] practice [of] pecuniary self-interest [now has] a rewarding moral tone." The inherent argument is "that public services are relentlessly in conflict with human liberty."[19] The result of this view of public institutions, as Michael Walzer notes, is that "citizens are transformed into autonomous consumers, looking for [that which] most persuasively promises to strengthen their market positions. [T]he profit motive brings them into conflict with democratic regulations" and there is no inherent concept of mutual assistance, or social solidarity, let alone equity or justice in this form of public reasoning.[20] This theory of public institutions can not generate a public justification for public support, because only the private good is a consideration.

Conservative and liberal theories do not effectively draw lines on when and where a democratic society should—and should not—support public institutions and determine the boundaries of their purposes and actions. Adapting Gutmann's example, conservative theory would hold that libraries must stay out of the family decision on when, how, or whether to introduce information on sex and reproduction (an essentially democratic position). That same conservative theory would *also* seek to deny the availability of such materials to those who *would* choose to allow their children access to them on a moral basis—holding an undemocratic position in the imposition of that value on the community as a whole. Gutmann concludes that conservative theory is unable to negotiate between these boundaries. Liberal theories of individual autonomy would avoid the issue of the limits of democratic and parental authority altogether in the mandating of rights. As she puts it, "the more philosophical liberal theories become, the less they face up to the facts of life in our society: that reasonable people disagree over what forms of freedom are worth cultivating."[21] Further, the liberal model of proscribing institutional solutions to social issues is inherently undemocratic toward those "misguided" enough to oppose the policies and the good they attempt to enforce.[22] Finally, postmodernist notions have no ethical or epistemological basis on which to justify (or coherently argue for or against) the public institution or purpose of libraries. I will not review that critique again, but rather note with Linda Benn that a theory "that equates TV with cultural liberation is woefully inadequate to the task of addressing the politics of spectacle." The meanings of the Gulf War, the Hill/Thomas hearings, the 2000 presidential elections, and September 11th for a democracy cannot be parsed in the same ways as game shows, weather channels, *Twin Peaks,* and *Star Trek.*[23] Such a framework has no compelling statement to make at all in the context of information equity or public funding of libraries.

The democratic basis of librarianship cannot be proven in the negative, however, and it is here that Gutmann places the role of public institutions like libraries in the Habermasian public sphere: "the most distinctive feature of a democratic theory . . . is that it makes a democratic virtue out of our inevitable disagreement. [W]e can publicly debate . . . problems in a way much more likely to increase our understanding of . . . each other than if we were to leave the management of [public institutions], as Kant suggests, 'to depend entirely upon the judgment of the most enlightened experts.'" The results—in terms of decisions and institutional structures—"will not always be the right ones, but they will be more enlightened—by the values and concerns of the many communities that constitute a democracy."[24] It is in the *process* of debating and deciding on the purpose, boundaries, and support of public institutions—the democratic process—that both defines their purpose and the reason for continuing them as a democratic public good, and at its core lies the irreducible value placed on enacting democracy:

[We] can use democratic processes to destroy democracy [and] undermine the intellectual foundations of future democratic deliberations by implementing . . . policies that either repress unpopular (but rational) ways of thinking or exclude some future citizens from [the resources] adequate for participating in democratic politics. . . . A democratic theory of [public institutions] recognizes the importance of empowering citizens to make . . . policy and also of constraining their choices among policies in accordance with those principles—of non-repression and nondiscrimination—that preserve the intellectual and social foundations of democratic deliberations.[25]

When public monies are involved, there must be policies—the public purposes and reasons for which must be manifest. When the state is involved (in whatever form and level), its influence and limits are also at issue. The basis and process of deliberation (and its limits) become central, as are limits on the imposition of the majority view and the protection of minority expression within a public purpose. All such questions assume not the atomized consumer or viewer or Web surfer, but the citizen and the polity in a democracy. Within this framework, Gutmann envisions democratic debate—the thrashing out of social and public values and purposes for such institutions—and the results will reflect the irreducible value and purposes of democracy: "without the tumult of democratic politics, our . . . institutions would not be governed by common values."[26] Under such circumstances, equity in the policies of our public institutions becomes paramount: "democratic politics puts a high premium on citizens being both knowledgeable and articulate" and the key question is access to the ability to effectively participate in democratic decision making.[27] She concludes that political (that is, democratic) purposes have "causal primacy" in public institutions like libraries, and "the cultivation of the virtues, knowledge, and skills necessary for political participation has moral primacy over other purposes of public [institutions] in a democratic society. Political education prepares citizens to participate in consciously reproducing their society, and conscious social reproduction is the ideal not only of democratic [public institutions] but also of democratic politics."[28]

The compelling case for the democratic purposes of librarianship is the same as for public educative projects: in a democracy, producing and reproducing the circumstances that enable democratic processes is the fundamental, core value. Librarianship enacts its democratic purpose through democratic processes—its fundamental basis (fiscally and socially) is in the public realm—not the private good. Gutmann thus suggests answers to two of the crucial questions at the core of this book: can librarianship sustain itself in society through recourse to justifications based on individual/consumer (economistic) models of value? And, do such justifications and practices fundamentally damage the democratic potential of the institutions? The answer to the first is no—without a public, democratic purpose for librarianship there is no compelling reason/argument in the long run to continue libraries. This would amount to a public subsidy for a private good, and while multinational corporations can pull off such a trick (broadcasting comes first to mind), librarianship would not fair as well as part of the "fat" in public expenditures (in the form of direct funding, tax-free subsidies, government grants, preferred mail and E-rates, etc.). The answer to the second question is yes. Beyond the dismantling of the public sphere (which I have already outlined), the policy decisions emanating from private justifications will continue to undermine democratic principles like equal access (with practices like fees and targeted services) and will further morph the citizen and the student into the customer. It will further the consumer model of education and learning—where notions of ease and convenience replace democratic notions of inquiry, knowledge, and informed decisions.

In addition to Gutmann's important framework, the ideas of two other theorists supplement her argument (as I have adapted it) for our purposes here. The first of these ideas has been put forward by Michael Katz. He asks the questions (again, adapted for our purposes here), what are our rights to education and educational resources, and what are the implications of governmental involvement (control and funding) in those activities in a democracy? He begins his answer to those questions by suggesting that, if these are "to be conceived of as a right in a democracy, [they] should be conceived of as the right to those . . . opportunities necessary to develop critical literacy." Here he comes in close contact with Gutmann's (and Habermas's) democratic ideas of informed participation as the purpose for public, cultural institutions, similarly linking them to notions of the good society. Critical literacy means that "a democratic society is committed, in theory, to enabling people to achieve the kind of intellectual self-sufficiency necessary to experience a fulfilling sense of personal and political liberty. This theoretical commitment gives meaning to the ideal of universal education."[29]

This does not mean a rulelike entitlement to libraries of a certain size, staffing, and so forth, nor does it posit a direct relationship between the availability of such resources and their translation into knowledgeable, participatory citizens, and students. There is no one-to-one correspondence (nor in the relationship between schooling and acquiring an education, as Katz acknowledges). Rather, if this is to be a meaningful concept, he proposes that it "must be conceived of as the entitlement to those opportunities that would enable a person" to be critically literate.[30] In making this argument, he cites Justice Thurgood Marshall's dissent in a landmark case in which the Supreme Court held that a right to an education was equivalent to the right to schooling, not equal education. Marshall's dissenting opinion held that there are recognized explicit and implicit rights in the Constitution that are not specifically spelled out, like procreation or privacy. Further, society's overriding interest in the issue of education in a democracy makes it similarly "funda-mental." Therefore, the right to equal educational opportunity is a societal/Constitutional *principle*—not a mechanical entitlement.[31] "Principles func-tion as important considerations to be taken into account in arriving at a decision, but they do not by themselves prescribe the decision to be reached."[32] In other words, equal access to information and the resources of self-directed inquiry (and leisure for that matter) in libraries is not a strict entitlement but rather a principle on which library decisions/policies/funding should be made for the public purposes of citizens in a democracy:

Access to information and divergent, critical views in the press and in the street be-comes essential in enabling one to interpret the world in an intelligent fashion and to think critically about what is happening and why it is happening. [This is] influenced, for example, by all of the following: the nature of newspaper and television reporting, the tolerance of dissenting views in society, the access of people to libraries, the absence of unreasonable censorship . . . and the nature of the political process. The develop-ment of critical thought is not something that can simply be assigned to the schools; rather it must be encouraged throughout the cultural life of a democratic society.[33]

In essence, Katz makes the argument for funding libraries in the dual reason-ing of equality of opportunity and access and the development of critical literacy in a democracy, and he situates both in terms of a social/legal dem-ocratic principle.

The second extension of Gutmann's framework is provided by Postman's thermostatic view of public institutions.[34] As noted, Postman argued that such institutions best fulfill their role in a democracy when they provide a space apart from—and sometimes in opposition to—dominant cultural bi-ases. If unchecked, those biases damage society (an excess of freedom is an-archy, etc.). The answer to the question "why shouldn't libraries be more like bookstore superchains"—or other economic/business models—is the ques-tion of who will provide the alternative. What *public* purpose is served by public funding of a project imitative of the private sector? What right do we have to public funding to compete with businesses? Perhaps more impor-tantly, does society *need* another model of media-dominated, entertainment-oriented consumerism in its public institutions? If we (libraries, schools, museums) do not hold out the possibility of alternatives and enact them, who will? To argue that libraries must follow the privatized model is to argue (contra our professional intellectual freedom principles) that there *should be no alternative*. To claim it is not librarianship's responsibility is to break the *public* contract on which we are based—if we will not take a public respon-sibility, the public has no responsibility to fund us. Finally, I return to the idea of balance. In providing alternative public spaces, we provide a socially healthy balance. As Postman wrote of the introduction of computers, we may be "breaking a four-hundred-year-old truce between the gregariousness and openness fostered by orality and the introspection and isolation fostered by the printed word."[35] Society, culture, education, and learning benefited from the balance between the two, as Postman argues, but the computer may allow one to dominate thoroughly—and we're not sure which. The social, democratic—in short, public—role and purpose of libraries is one of providing alternatives (possibility and balance) in a society dominated by the ethic of the private and the consumer. No other types of institutions will be able to do so; certainly none have a compelling reason to.

## BACK TO HABERMAS AND THE PUBLIC SPHERE

These ideas in combination—the reasons *for* libraries—clearly bear the hall-marks of Habermasian concepts of "an institutional location for practical reason in public affairs and for the accompanying valid, if often deceptive, claims of formal democracy. [A] public sphere adequate to a democratic polity depends upon both quality of discourse and quantity of participation."[36] In so doing, libraries overcome many of the problems and criticisms Habermas has encountered in his self-described "stylized"[37] account of the public sphere: the fact of a plurality of publics and public spheres, the patriarchal and exclusionary nature of his historically grounded example of the public sphere, the problems of rational public discourse in the forming of a public sphere (when communication is systematically distorted), and the problems of the relationship between information and entertainment.[38] Each of the ways in which librarianship enacts and embodies it (as outlined at the end of chapter 3) takes an important step in a fuller—and fairer—realization of the democratic public sphere. Libraries have no theoretical problems—it is in fact one of their strengths—in accommodating multiple publics, multiple perspectives, and multiple discourses. Our basic professional credo is to include the excluded from the discourses organized in our resources. And, as has been noted, the existence of those resources, preserved and organized over time (as libraries do), tends to connect separate discourses and allow for a cross checking of validity claims both currently and in the future.

Most importantly, the model of librarianship-as-enacting-the-public-sphere is the essence of the democratic potential—the reason *for* libraries: "radical democratization now aims for a shifting of forces within a 'separation of powers' that itself is to be maintained in principle. The new equilibrium to be attained is not one between state powers but between different resources for social integration. The goal is . . . to erect a democratic dam against the colonializing *encroachment* of system imperatives" on social and personal life.[39] The key to attaining this equilibrium is in finding communicative processes and spaces not guided by the "steering mechanisms" of money and power (i.e., corporate-dominated mass media) and "discovery and problem resolution . . . that in this sense is *nonorganized*."[40] These two statements contain the essence of the role of librarianship in the public sphere, and Habermas takes this notion one step further: we must reform "those institutions that we have already established in Western countries, to direct them toward a form of radical democracy that makes it possible . . . to change or at least to affect [their] administration."[41]

In Habermas's high-theory terms, he has articulated the concept of libraries as democratic public spheres, holding out the possibility of communicative reason, truth verification, rational argumentation, and the providing of alternatives and alternative public spaces—all essential to a democratic culture. For librarianship, this model avoids the public dead end of economistic models. It further solves many of the problems of a positivistic approach and epistemology that have been so thoroughly critiqued in librarianship and elsewhere.[42] The democratic possibility of rational communication also gives a way out of the radical pessimism that the critique of positivism and instrumental rationality has sometimes engendered in librarianship[43]—in parallel to the dead end that the work of Critical Theory and its educational scholarship offshoot found itself in. At the same time, it does not disallow seeing the important role that economics and economic reasoning play in the problems librarianship faces. It provides a way to define and defend the value and potential of both entertainment and higher culture sources on our shelves and in our resources.[44] Libraries embody "the Deweyan idea that democracy means a community-in-the-making . . . an articulate public empowered and encouraged to speak for itself, perhaps in many voices."[45] Finally, this conception of libraries avoids the postmodern morass of a contextless, meaningless jumble of media signifiers—with all its apolitical, antipolitical, and ahistorical consequences—and the conclusion "that there is nothing else of any significance—no contradictory forces, and no counter-tendencies; and . . . these changes are terrific, and all we have to do is reconcile ourselves to them."[46] This issue is closely related to the question of whether or not the Internet and the media can be cultivated or captured to embody a new public sphere.[47] While the impulse behind this idea is fundamentally a democratic one, Habermas poses the salient question: "whether, and to what extent, a public sphere dominated by mass media provides a realistic chance for the members of civil society, in their competition with the political and economic invader's media power, to bring about changes in the spectrum of values, topics, and reasons channeled by external influences to open it up in an innovative way, and to screen it critically."[48] The Internet, in my view, will not be that panacea. It will—like the various forms of publishing—remain an undifferentiated resource that we must critically evaluate and from which we will select. In so doing and in so organizing, it will be libraries that will enact the public sphere potential of such resources, not the other way around.

## CONCLUSION

Am I suggesting that librarianship will lead the West out of the wilderness of a soulless capitalism, dominated by media spectacle? No. I am suggesting that what libraries can embody in terms of the potential of the democratic public sphere is very important. Like the public sphere ideal type, this is a somewhat stylized model of librarianship. It will not—can not—be realized perfectly, but it is not a dead concept in libraries or in society.[49] We will never achieve the perfect balance of voices and perspectives on our shelves, we will never be the perfect democratic, communicative mirror for the society we serve, and we will never perfectly handle our choices of resources. That is not the point. A democratic public sphere theory of librarianship posits not only the prime purpose of the field but also its process of grappling with such questions. What is the proper balance to budget between print and electronic resources? What is the proper division between resources and services for different constituencies (children, people of color, adolescents, the elderly, the poor, women's needs, etc.)? What is the dividing line in emphasis between entertainment and more serious materials in the library? When is it still a good purchase of an electronic resource if there is the real prospect that it will not be permanently available? How much in the way of staff resources should go toward reaching out to constituencies who might benefit from, but do not use, library resources? How far does/should one anticipate curricular-related inquiry to be stretched? How far should we guide students toward quality in online vs. print resources? Do we have an adequate idea of the relevant quality of each?

As Amy Gutmann and others note, the answers to such questions will not be perfect or permanent solutions. That is again not the point. The fact that they are democratically debated (both within the institution and in the form of institutional oversight) in light of public, democratic purposes represents a radical departure from our current trajectory. The questions themselves represent this perspective: entrepreneurial hustling and "customer" surveying are inappropriate and unnecessary. This is not a vision of an imperial librarianship with an unassailable "higher purpose." Rather it is the vision of a library democratically connected to its community (be it a university, school, or town/city), engaging it in a rational dialogue about what it should be in light of democratic public purposes, and the need to provide alternatives and alternative spaces in a culture dominated by information capitalism and media image and spectacle. It is the core responsibility of librarianship in a democracy. Such a theory is broadly suggestive of the internal and external means to be utilized to connect to our communities, carry on the discussion of purposes, and carry through the agreed-upon goals and policies. Our boards and our sponsoring institutions need to be reminded that the value of and effects of a library—like good teaching—are extraordinarily difficult to quantify (monetarily or in terms of quality). Their effects may be profound but latent for many years. Despite our best efforts to crack both their secrets, this remains true. And it remains true that informed deliberation and communication remain the essence of both education and democracy, and librarianship plays a pivotal—if undervalued—role in both. This vision and purpose for librarianship stands in stark contrast to the banal, economic purposes of a "transformed" field in obeisance to the new public philosophy climate. Maxine Greene reminds us that "nowhere is it written" that we are required to organize ourselves "in response to the demands of the Pentagon or to those obsessed with exploiting markets overseas."[50] To accede to that purpose robs us—both librarianship and the society we serve—of an important, if ineffable, resource. As she writes:

Who knows better how important it is to look at things, whenever possible, as if they could be otherwise? To speak that way is to summon up the idea of imagination. Imagination is, in part, the capacity to apply concepts to things, to recognize the range of applications, and to invent new concepts. It is the possibility to move between . . . "spontaneous concepts" and more formal or schematic ones. It is the capacity to make metaphors, to create new orders in experience and to realize that there is always more in experience than anyone can predict. It is, also, the power to perceive unexpected relationships, to envisage alternative realities, and to reach beyond the taken-for-granted towards possibility.[51]

If Karl Marx told us that economic power was an important factor in our understanding of society, Max Weber told us that ideas are as well. Our ideas—of becoming professional knowledge managers and information entrepreneurs—should not be so limited, so economically driven. Such visions pale in comparison to the deeper, more sustainable and democratic purposes of librarianship.

## NOTES

1. For example, see Barbara McCrimmon, ed., *American Library Philosophy: An Anthology* (Hamden, Conn.: Shoe String Press, 1975); Jesse Shera, "Failure and Success: Assessing a Century," *Library Journal*, 1 January 1976, 281–87; Archie Dick, "Epistemological Positions and Library and Information Science," *Library Quarterly* 69, no. 3 (1999): 305–20; John Budd, "An Epistemological Foundation for Library and Information Science," *Library Quarterly* 65, no. 3 (1995): 295–318; Gary Radford and Marie Radford, "Libraries, Librarians, and the Discourse of Fear," *Library Quarterly* 71, no. 3 (2001): 299–329; Gary Radford, "Flaubert, Foucault, and the Biblioteque Fantastique: Toward a Postmodern Epistemology for Librarianship," *Library Trends* 46, no. 4 (1998): 616–34; Michael Harris, "The Dialectic of Defeat: Antimonies in Research in Library and Information Science," *Library Trends* 34, no. 3 (1986): 515–31; Michael Harris and Masaru Itoga, "Becoming Critical: For a Theory of Purpose and Necessity in American Librarianship," in *Library and Information Science Research: Perspectives and Strategies for Improvement*, Information Management, Policy, and Services Series (Norwood, N.J.: Ablex, 1991), 347–57; and Michael Harris, "State, Class, and Cultural Reproduction: Toward a Theory of Library Service in the United States," *Advances in Librarianship* 14 (1986): 211–53.

2. Daniel Bell, *The End of Ideology: On the Exhaustion of Political Ideas in the Fifties* (Glencoe, Ill.: Free Press, 1960); Daniel Bell, *The Coming of Post-Industrial Society*

(New York: Basic Books, 1973); and Daniel Bell, *The Cultural Contradictions of Capitalism* (New York, Basic Books, 1976).

3. Francis Fukuyama, *The End of History and the Last Man* (New York: Free Press, 1992).

4. Peter Dahlgren, "Ideology and Information in the Public Sphere," in *The Ideology of the Information Age,* ed. Jennifer Slack and Fred Fejes (Norwood, N.J.: Ablex, 1987), 26.

5. Stephen White, "Reason, Modernity, and Democracy," in *The Cambridge Companion to Habermas,* ed. Stephen White (Cambridge: Cambridge University Press, 1995), 3.

6. Michael Harrington, *The Politics at God's Funeral: The Spiritual Crisis of Western Civilization* (New York: Holt, Rinehart, and Winston, 1983); Francis Fukuyama, *The Great Disruption: Human Nature and the Reconstitution of Social Order* (New York: Free Press, 1999); Christopher Lasch, *The Revolt of the Elites and the Betrayal of Democracy* (New York: W. W. Norton, 1995); Carl Boggs, *The End of Politics: Corporate Power and the Decline of the Public Sphere* (New York: Guilford Press, 2000); Carl Boggs, "Social Crisis and Political Decay: The Contemporary American Malaise," *New Political Science* 20, no. 3 (1998): 301–22; Frank Webster, "Information, Capitalism, and Uncertainty," *Information, Communication & Society* 3, no. 1 (2000): 69–90; Kevin Robins, "Forces of Consumption: From the Symbolic to the Psychotic," *Media, Culture & Society* 16 (1994): 449–68; Henry Giroux, "Pedagogy of the Depressed: Beyond the Politics of Cynicism," *College Literature* 28, no. 3 (2001): 1–31; Richard Sennett, "The New Capitalism," *Social Research* 64, no. 2 (1997): 161–80; Richard Sennett, "How Work Destroys Social Inclusion," *New Statesman,* 31 May 1999, 25–27; and Allan Bloom, *The Closing of the American Mind* (New York: Simon & Schuster, 1987).

7. Jürgen Habermas, "Modernity Versus Postmodernity," *New German Critique* 22 (1981): 7.

8. Sennett, "New Capitalism"; Sennett, "How Work Destroys"; Richard Sennett, "Cities Without Care or Connection," *New Statesman,* 5 June 2000, 25–27; Michael Apple, "How the Conservative Restoration is Justified: Leadership and Subordination in Educational Policy," *International Journal of Leadership in Education* 1, no. 1 (1998): 12; and Christopher Lasch, "After the Foundations Have Crumbled," review of *Crossing the Postmodern Divide,* by Albert Borgmann, *Commonweal,* 20 November 1992, 22–23.

9. Jennifer Pierce, "Digital Discomfort? 'Get Over It,' Says McClure," *American Libraries,* May 2002, 45.

10. Mary Rice-Lively and J. D. Racine, "The Role of Academic Librarians in the Era of Information Technology," *Journal of Academic Librarianship* 23, no. 1 (1997): 31–37.

11. Mark Rosenzweig, "Libraries at the End of History?" *Progressive Librarian* 2 (1990/91): 2–8.

12. Habermas, "Modernity vs. Postmodernity," 9, 11.

13. Amy Gutmann, *Democratic Education* (Princeton, N.J.: Princeton University Press, 1987), 232–55.

14. Henry Perkinson, *The Imperfect Panacea: American Faith in Education, 1865–1965* (New York: Random House, 1968), has admirably traced the disastrous results of overexpectation concerning what schooling can and should do and the consequent

loss of public faith. Michael Harris, "Public Libraries and the Decline of the Demo-cratic Dogma," *Library Journal,* 1 November 1976, 2225–2230, has linked this no-tion to the limits of librarianship, which he thoroughly outlined in Harris, "State, Class."

15. Gutmann, 3.

16. Gutmann, 4, 6.

17. Neil Postman, *Teaching as a Conserving Activity* (New York: Delta, 1979).

18. Gutmann, 4–5.

19. John Kenneth Galbraith, "Are Public Libraries Against Liberty?" *American Li-braries,* September 1979, 483. See also the arguments of Wolin, Giroux, and Apple in chapter 2.

20. Michael Walzer, "The Idea of Civil Society," *Dissent* 38 (1991): 296–97.

21. Gutmann, 8–9.

22. Gutmann, 11.

23. Linda Benn, "The Unbearable Lightness of Theory," *Boston Review,* February 1992, 19; see also Stuart Hall, "On Postmodernism and Articulation," *Journal of Communication Inquiry* 10 (1986): 45–60.

24. Gutmann, 11.

25. Gutmann, 14.

26. Gutmann, 287.

27. Gutmann, 285.

28. Gutmann, 287. I see this as a form of "democratic hegemony"—a reverse of Gramsci's notion of the hegemony of capitalism, which reproduces its necessary con-ditions through everyday culture. For a brief introduction to Gramsci, see Michael Walzer, *The Company of Critics: Social Criticism and Political Commitment in the Twentieth Century* (New York: Basic Books, 1988), 80–100.

29. Michael Katz, "Critical Literacy: A Conception of Education as a Moral Right and a Social Ideal," in *The Public School Monopoly: A Critical Analysis of Education and the State in American Society,* ed. Robert Everhart (Cambridge, Mass.: Ballinger, 1982), 193–94.

30. Katz, 205, see generally 195–205.

31. Katz, 211–13.

32. Katz, 207.

33. Katz, 210–11.

34. Postman, *Teaching as a Conserving.*

35. Neil Postman, *Technopoly: The Surrender of Culture to Technology* (New York: Vintage, 1993), 17; on the need for balance, see also Henry Mintzberg, "Managing Government, Governing Management," *Harvard Business Review,* May–June 1996, 75–83.

36. Craig Calhoun, "Introduction: Habermas and the Public Sphere," in *Habermas and the Public Sphere,* ed. Craig Calhoun (Cambridge, Mass.: MIT Press, 1992), 1–2.

37. Jürgen Habermas, "Further Reflections on the Public Sphere," in *Habermas and the Public Sphere,* ed. Calhoun, 421–61.

38. Adapted from Nicholas Garnham, "The Media and the Public Sphere," in *Ha-bermas and the Public Sphere,* ed. Calhoun, 359–60; see also William Outhwaite, *Ha-bermas: A Critical Introduction* (Cambridge: Polity Press, 1994), 7–13. Habermas responded to these issues raised over the years in the second German edition of *Struc-tural Transformation of the Public Sphere* (Outhwaite) and in Habermas, "Further

Reflections"; Jürgen Habermas et. al., "Concluding Remarks," in *Habermas and the Public Sphere,* ed. Calhoun, 462–79; and Jürgen Habermas, "A Reply to My Critics," in *Habermas: Critical Debates,* ed. John Thompson and David Held (London: MacMillan, 1982), 219–83.

39. Habermas, "Further Reflections," 444.

40. Habermas, "Further Reflections," 451 (emphasis in original).

41. Habermas et. al., "Concluding Remarks," 470.

42. See, for example, Harris, "State, Class"; Harris, "The Dialectic of Defeat"; Budd, "An Epistemological Foundation"; and Radford, "Flaubert, Foucault."

43. For example, Michael Harris, "The Fall of the Grand Hotel: Class, Canon, and the Coming Crisis of Western Librarianship," *Libri* 45 (1995): 231–35; and Michael Harris, "Portrait in Paradox: Commitment and Ambivalence in American Librarianship, 1876–1976," *Libri* 26, no. 4 (1976): 281–301. In general, I have found Harris's work to be very admirable and useful, but he has occasionally worked his way into the dead end of economic determinism in his critiques.

44. Michael Apple, "Standards, Subject Matter, and a Romantic Past," *Educational Policy* 15, no. 2 (2001): 331; and Wayne Wiegand, "The Politics of Cultural Authority," *American Libraries,* January 1998, 80–82.

45. Maxine Green, "Imagining Futures: The Public School and Possibility," *Journal of Curriculum Studies* 32, no. 2 (2000): 274.

46. Hall, 46.

47. Douglas Kellner, "Habermas, the Public Sphere, and Democracy: A Critical Intervention," 12 October 2002, <http://www.gseis.ucla.edu/faculty/kellner/papers/habermas.htm>, holds out this hope. See also David Brin, "The Internet as Commons," *Information Technology and Libraries,* December 1995, 240–42; and Mark Poster, *What's the Matter with the Internet?* (Minneapolis: University of Minnesota Press, 2001). The degree to which the left is struggling with this very issue is reflected in the call for papers for "Dark Markets: A Two Day Strategic Conference That Will Look into the State of the Art of Media Politics, Information Technologies, and Theories of Democracy," sponsored by Public Netbase/t0, Museumplatz, Vienna, 3–4 October 2002.

48. Habermas, "Further Reflections," 455.

49. There has been a spate of commentary and response on civil society, greed culture, and cultural/political introspection after the September 11th attacks. See, for example, Paul Auster, "The City and the Country," *New York Times,* 9 September 2002, A23; William Safire, "A Spirit Reborn: How to Listen to Lincoln," *New York Times,* 9 September 2002, A23; "New York, a Year Later," *New York Times,* 9 September 2002, A22; Simon Schama, "A Whiff of Dread for the Land of Hope," *New York Times,* 15 September 2002, sec. 4, 1, 6; Bruce Schulman, "Building National Resolve by Talking About It, *New York Times,* 15 September 2002, sec. 4, 5; Thomas Friedman, "Going Our Way," *New York Times,* 15 September 2002, sec. 4, 15; Rachel Lehmann-Haupt and Warren St. John, "Corporate Bad Guys Make Many Seek the Road Less Traveled," *New York Times,* 21 July 2002, sec. 9, 1, 5; and "When Greed Was a Virtue and Regulation the Enemy (Word for Word: Alan Greenspan)," *New York Times,* 21 July 2002, sec. 4, 7.

50. Maxine Greene, foreword to *The New Servants of Power: A Critique of the 1980s*

*School Reform Movement,* ed. Christine Shea, Ernest Kahane, and Peter Sola (New York: Greenwood Press, 1989), ix–x.

51. Maxine Greene, "Liberal Learning and Teacher Education," in *Excellence in Teacher Education Through the Liberal Arts: Proceedings of the Conference,* ed. Michael Carbone and Ann Wonsiewicz (Allentown, Penn.: Education Department, Muhlenberg College, 1986), 26–27.

# SELECTED BIBLIOGRAPHY

Author's Note: This listing represents a selected bibliography of the works consulted. A full listing of the sources noted in the chapters would be unwieldy and less than useful since it would contain so many items of news, reports, and statistics. I have also been quite critical of much of the library literature I have cited. Therefore, I chose to focus this selected bibliography primarily on those sources from which I have drawn critical and historical perspectives—both within librarianship and without. Some of the more important representative samples of the literature of librarianship in, for instance, library management or discussions of the future of technologies are also included.

Agre, Phil. "The End of Information & the Future of Libraries." *Progressive Librarian* 12/13 (1997): 1–6.

Allen, Bryce. "The Benton Report as Research." *Library Trends* 46, no. 1 (1997): 5–18.

Altman, Ellen, and Peter Hernon. "Service Quality and Customer Satisfaction Do Matter." *American Libraries,* August 1998, 53–54.

American Association of School Librarians and the Association for Educational Communications and Technology. *Information Power: Guidelines for School Library Media Programs.* Chicago: American Library Association, 1988.

American Association of University Professors. *Policy Documents and Reports.* Washington, D.C.: American Association of University Professors, 1990.

American Library Association. *Access to Electronic Information, Services, and Networks: An Interpretation of the Library Bill of Rights.* Chicago: American Library Association, 24 January 1996.

———. *Libraries: An American Value.* Reprinted in Berman, Sanford, Carol Reid, and Charles Willett. "The American Library Association, Intellectual Freedom, the Alternative Press, and 'Libraries: An American Value'." *Counterpoise* 2, no. 4 (1998): 28.

———. "12 Ways Libraries Are Good for the Country." *American Libraries* online ed. (2000 rev. orig. pub. in 1995). 26 August 2002. <http://www.ala.org/alonline/news/12wayshtml>.

Anderson, Gregory. "Dimensions, Context, and Freedom: The Library in the Social Creation of Knowledge." In *Sociomedia: Multimedia, Hypermedia, and the Social Construction of Knowledge,* edited by Edward Barrett, 107–24. Cambridge, Mass.: MIT Press, 1992.

Apostle, Richard, and Boris Raymond. "Librarianship and the Information Paradigm." *Canadian Library Journal* 43 (December 1986): 377–86.

———. *Librarianship and the Information Paradigm.* Lanham, Md.: Scarecrow, 1997.

Apple, Michael. "Comparing Neo-Liberal Projects and Inequality in Education." *Comparative Education* 37, no. 4 (2001): 409–23.

———. "Conservative Agendas and Progressive Possibilities: Understanding the Wider Politics of Curriculum and Teaching." *Education and Urban* Society 23, no. 3 (1991): 279–91.

———. "A Critical Analysis of Three Approaches to the Use of Computers in Education." In *The Curriculum: Problems, Politics, and Possibilities,* edited by Landon Beyer and Michael Apple, 289–311. Albany: State University of New York Press, 1988.

———. *Cultural Politics & Education.* New York: Teachers College Press, 1996.

———. *Education and Power.* Boston: Routledge & Kegan Paul, 1982.

———. "How the Conservative Restoration Is Justified: Leadership and Subordination in Educational Policy." *International Journal of Leadership in Education* 1, no. 1 (1998): 3–17.

———. "Knowledge, Pedagogy, and the Conservative Alliance." *Studies in the Literary Imagination* 31, no. 1 (1998): 5–23.

———. "Markets and the Production of Inequality in Education." *Educational Policy* 20 (2000): 315–18.

———. "Markets, Standards, Teaching, and Teacher Education." *Journal of Teacher Education* 52, no. 3 (2001): 182–96.

———. "National Reports and the Construction of Inequality." *British Journal of Sociology of Education* 7, no. 2 (1986): 171–90.

———. *Official Knowledge: Democratic Education in a Conservative Age.* New York: Routledge, 1993.

———. "Producing Inequality: Ideology and Economy in the National Reports on Education (AESA R. Freeman Butts Lecture—1986)." *Educational Studies* 18, no. 2 (1987): 195–220.

———. "Redefining Equality: Authoritarian Populism and the Conservative Restoration." *Teachers College Record* 90, no. 2 (1988): 167–84.

———. "Review Article—Bringing the Economy Back into Educational Theory." *Educational Theory* 36, no. 4 (1986): 403–15.

———. "Standards, Subject Matter, and a Romantic Past." *Educational Policy* 15, no. 2 (2001): 323–34.

———. *Teachers and Texts: A Political Economy of Class & Gender Relations in Education.* New York: Routledge, 1986.

———. "Textbook Publishing: The Political and Economic Influences." *Theory into Practice* 28, no. 4 (1989): 282–87.

Apple, Michael, and Susan Jungck. "You Don't Have to Be a Teacher to Teach This Unit: Teaching, Technology, and Gender in the Classroom." *American Educational Research Journal* 27 (1990): 223–51.

Apple, Michael, and James Beane, eds. *Democratic Schools.* Alexandria, Va.: Association for Supervision and Curriculum Development, 1995.

Arato, Andrew, and Eike Gebhardt, eds. *The Essential Frankfurt School Reader.* New York: Continuum, 1982.

Aronowitz, Stanley, and Henry Giroux. *Education Still Under Siege.* 2nd ed. Westport, Conn.: Bergin & Garvey, 1993.

Baker, Nicholson. "The Author vs. the Library." *New Yorker,* 14 October 1996, 50–62.

———. "The Collector." Interview with Dwight Garner. *New York Times Book Review,* 15 April 2001, 9.

———. "A Couple of Codicils About San Francisco." *American Libraries,* March 1999, 35.

———. "Discards." *New Yorker,* 4 April 1994, 64–86.

———. *Double Fold: Libraries and the Assault on Paper.* New York: Random House, 2001.

Balint, Kathryn. "Public Laws Owned by the Public? Think Again, Copyright Rulings Show." *San Diego Union-Tribune,* 13 May 2001, A1.

Barnes, Sue, and Lance Strate. "The Educational Implications of the Computer: A Media Ecology Critique." *New Jersey Journal of Communication* 4, no. 2 (1996): 180–208.

Barrett, Edward, ed. *Sociomedia: Multimedia, Hypermedia, and the Social Construction of Knowledge.* Cambridge, Mass.: MIT Press, 1992.

Basbanes, Nicholas. "Controversy Redux." *Biblio,* August 1998, 8–11.

Bayer, Arthur. "What Is Wrong with Customer?" *College Teaching* 44, no. 3 (1996): 82.

Baynes, Kenneth. "Democracy and the *Rechtsstaat:* Habermas's *Faktizitat un Geltung.*" In *The Cambridge Companion to Habermas,* edited by Stephen White, 201–32. Cambridge: Cambridge University Press, 1995.

Bell, Daniel. *The Coming of Post-Industrial Society.* New York: Basic Books, 1973.

———. *The Cultural Contradictions of Capitalism.* New York: Basic Books, 1976.

———. *The End of Ideology: On the Exhaustion of Political Ideas in the Fifties.* Glencoe, Ill.: Free Press, 1960.

———. "The Third Technological Revolution." *Dissent* 36, no. 2 (1989): 164–76.

———. "Welcome to the Post-Industrial Society." In *Libraries in Post-Industrial Society,* edited by Leigh Estabrook, 3–7. Phoenix, Ariz.: Oryx, 1977.

Beniger, James. "Origins of the Information Society." *Wilson Library Bulletin,* November 1986, 12–19.

Benn, Linda. "The Unbearable Lightness of Theory." *Boston Review,* February 1992, 1–2.

Bennett, Scott. "The Golden Age of Libraries." *Journal of Academic Librarianship* 27, no. 4 (2001): 256–59.

Benton Foundation. *Buildings, Books, and Bytes: Libraries and Communities in the Digital Age.* Washington, D.C.: Benton Foundation, 1996.

Berman, Sanford. Foreword to *Poor People and Library Services,* edited by Karen Venturella, 1–14. Jefferson, N.C.: McFarland, 1998.

———. "Libraries, Class, and the 'Poor People's Policy'." *American Libraries,* March 1998, 38.

Berman, Sanford, Carol Reid, and Charles Willett. "The American Library Association, Intellectual Freedom, the Alternative Press, and 'Libraries: An American Value'." *Counterpoise* 2, no. 4 (1998): 26–29.

Bernstein, Barton, ed. *Towards a New Past: Dissenting Essays in American History.* New York: Vintage, 1967.

Bertot, John, Charles McClure, and Joe Ryan. "Study Shows New Funding Sources Crucial to Technology Services." *American Libraries,* March 2002, 57–59.

Beyer, Landon, and Michael Apple, eds. *The Curriculum: Problems, Politics, and Possibilities.* Albany: State University of New York Press, 1988.

Biddiscombe, Richard. "The Changing Role of the Information Professional in Support of Learning and Research." *Advances in Librarianship* 23 (2000): 63–92.

Birdsall, William. "A 'New Deal' for Libraries in the Digital Age?" *Library Trends* 46, no. 1 (1997): 52–67.

Birkerts, Sven. *Gutenberg Elegies: The Fate of Reading in an Electronic Age.* New York: Fawcett/Columbine, 1994.

———. "Into the Electronic Millennium." *Boston Review,* October 1991, 15–19.

Blanke, Henry. "Librarianship and Public Culture in the Age of Information Capitalism." *Journal of Information Ethics* 5 (Fall 1996): 54–69.

———. "Libraries and the Commercialization of Information: Towards a Critical Discourse of Librarianship." *Progressive Librarian* 2 (1990/1991): 9–14.

———. "The Mass Culture Debate: Left Perspectives." *Progressive Librarian* 6/7 (1993): 15–29.

Bloom, Allan. *The Closing of the American Mind.* New York: Simon & Schuster, 1987.

Boggs, Carl. *The End of Politics: Corporate Power and the Decline of the Public Sphere.* New York: Guilford Press, 2000.

———. "The Great Retreat: Decline of the Public Sphere in Late Twentieth-Century America." *Theory and Society* 26 (1997): 741–80.

———. "The Myth of Electronic Populism: Talk Radio and the Decline of the Public Sphere." *Democracy & Nature* 5, no. 1 (1999): 65–94.

———. "Social Crisis and Political Decay: The Contemporary American Malaise." *New Political Science* 20, no. 3 (1998): 301–22.

Bowers, C. A. *The Cultural Dimensions of Educational Computing.* New York: Teachers College Press, 1988.

———. "Curriculum and Our Technocracy Culture: The Problem of Reform." *Teachers College Record* 78, no. 1 (1976): 53–67.

———. *Let Them Eat Data: How Computers Affect Education. Cultural Diversity, and the Prospects of Ecological Sustainability.* Athens: University of Georgia Press, 2000.

———. "The Reproduction of Technological Consciousness: Locating the Ideological Foundations of a Radical Pedagogy." *Teachers College Record* 83 (1982): 529–88.

Braman, Sandra. "Alternative Conceptualizations of the Information Economy." *Advances in Librarianship* 19 (1995): 99–116.

Braverman, Miriam. "From Adam Smith to Ronald Reagan: Public Libraries as a Public Good." *Library Journal,* 15 February 1982, 397–401.

Bremner, Robert. *American Philanthropy.* Chicago: University of Chicago Press, 1960.

Brin, David. "The Internet as Commons." *Information Technology and Libraries,* December 1995, 240–42.

Brooke, John. "Reason and Passion in the Public Sphere: Habermas and the Cultural Historians." *Journal of Interdisciplinary History* 29, no. 1 (1998): 43–67.

Brosio, Richard. *Philosophical Scaffolding for the Construction of Critical Democratic Education.* New York: Peter Lang, 2000.

———. *A Radical Democratic Critique of Capitalist Education.* New York: Peter Lang, 1994.

———. Review of *Boxed In: The Culture of TV,* by Mark Crispin Miller. *Educational Studies* 21, no. 1 (1990): 52–57.

Buchbinder, Howard, and Janice Newson. "The Service University and Market Forces." *Academe,* July–August 1992, 13–15.

Budd, John. "A Critique of Customer and Commodity." *College & Research Libraries,* July 1997, 310–21.

———. "An Epistemological Foundation for Library and Information Science." *Library Quarterly* 65, no. 3 (1995): 295–318.

Burnett, Kathleen. "Multimedia and the Library and Information Studies Curriculum." In *Sociomedia: Multimedia, Hypermedia, and the Social Construction of Knowledge,* edited by Edward Barrett, 125–39. Cambridge, Mass.: MIT Press, 1992.

Buschman, John. "Asking the Right Questions About Information Technology." *American Libraries,* December 1990, 1026–30.

———. "Conclusion: Context, Analogies, and Entrepreneurial Directions in Librarianship." In *Critical Approaches to Information Technology in Librarianship: Foundations and Applications,* edited by John Buschman, 211–20. Westport, Conn.: Greenwood, 1993.

———. "Editorial: Core Wars." *Progressive Librarian* 17 (2000): 1–2.

———. "Historical Notes on Reading and the Public: A Skeptical View from Librarianship." Society for the History of Authorship, Reading, and Publishing 2001 Conference, College of William and Mary, Williamsburg, Virginia, 21 July 2001.

———. "History and Theory of Information Poverty." In *Poor People and Library Services,* edited by Karen Venturella, 16–28. Jefferson, N.C.: McFarland. 1998.

———. "A House Divided Against Itself: ACRL Leadership, Academic Freedom & Electronic Resources." *Progressive Librarian* 12/13 (1997): 7–17.

———. "Information Technology, Power Structures, and the Fate of Librarianship." *Progressive Librarian* 6/7 (1993): 15–29.

———. "Issues in Censorship and Information Technology." In *Critical Approaches to Information Technology in Librarianship: Foundations and Applications,* edited by John Buschman, 125–49. Westport, Conn.: Greenwood Press, 1993.

———. "Libraries and the Underside of the Information Age." *Libri* 45 (1995): 209–15.

———. "Myths of the Information Society: A Guide for Librarians." *Urban Academic Librarian* 9, no. 1 (1994): 4–17.

———. "Taking a Hard Look at Technology and Librarianship: Compliance, Complicity, and the Intellectual Independence of the Profession." *Argus* 23, no. 2 (1994): 13–20.

———, ed. *Critical Approaches to Information Technology in Librarianship: Foundations and Applications.* Westport, Conn.: Greenwood, 1993.

Buschman, John, and Michael Carbone. "A Critical Inquiry into Librarianship: Applications of the 'New Sociology of Education'." *Library Quarterly* 61, no. 1 (1991): 15–40.

———. "De-Politicized Technology and Intellectual/Economic Problems of Information Technology: Notes on a U.S. Higher Education Case History." In *Managing Learning Innovation: The Challenges of the Changing Curriculum,* edited by Geoff Windle, 22–28. Lincoln, England: University of Lincolnshire and Humberside, 1999.

———. "Technocracy, Educational Structures and Libraries: Historical Notes from the United States." *Journal of Education Policy* 11, no. 5 (1996): 561–78.

Buschman, John, and Mark Rosenzweig. "Intellectual Freedom Within the Library Workplace: An Exploratory Study in the U.S." *Journal of Information Ethics* 8, no. 2 (1999): 36–45.

Buschman, John, Mark Rosenzweig, and Elaine Harger. "The Clear Imperative for Involvement: Librarians Must Address Social Issues." *American Libraries,* June 1994, 575–76.

Buschman, John, and Dorothy Warner. "A Slip Between the Cup and the Lip: Practical and Intellectual Problems of Marketing U.S. Academic Libraries." In *Education and Research for Marketing and Quality Management in Libraries,* edited by Rejean Savard, 269–78. Munich: K. G. Saur, 2002.

———. "Wider Access to Higher Education in the United States: An Evaluative Case Study of the Library." In *Researching Widening Access: International Perspective,* edited by Mike Osborne and Jim Gallacher, 60–65. Glasgow, Scotland:

Center for Research in Lifelong Learning, Glasgow Caledonian University, 2001.

Buss, Dennis. "The Ford Foundation in Public Education: Emergent Patterns." In *Philanthropy and Cultural Imperialism: The Foundations at Home and Abroad,* edited by Robert Arnove, 331–62. Boston: G. K. Hall, 1980.

Button, H. W., and Eugene Provenzo. *History of Education and Culture in America.* 2nd ed. Englewood Cliffs, N.J.: Prentice Hall, 1989.

Calhoun, Craig. "Introduction: Habermas and the Public Sphere." In *Habermas and the Public Sphere,* edited by Craig Calhoun, 1–48. Cambridge, Mass.: MIT Press, 1992.

———, ed. *Habermas and the Public Sphere.* Cambridge, Mass.: MIT Press, 1992.

Cambell, Leslie. "Keeping Watch on the Waterfront: Social Responsibility in Legal and Library Professional Organizations." *Law Library Journal* 92, no. 3 (2000): 263–86.

Carbone, Michael. "Are Educational Technology and School Restructuring Appropriate Partners?" *Teacher Education Quarterly* 22 (Spring 1995): 4–17.

———. "Critical Scholarship on Computers in Education: A Summary Review." In *Critical Approaches to Information Technology in Librarianship: Foundations and Applications,* edited by John Buschman, 41–57. Westport, Conn.: Greenwood, 1993.

Carbone, Michael, and Ann Wonsiewicz, eds. *Excellence in Teacher Education Through the Liberal Arts: Proceedings of the Conference.* Allentown, Penn.: Education Department, Muhlenberg College, 1986.

Carlson, Scott. "The Deserted Library: As Students Work Online, Reading Rooms Empty Out—Leading Some Campuses to Add Starbucks." *Chronicle of Higher Education,* 16 November 2001, A35.

Charles, John, and Shelley Mosley. "Keeping Selection In-house." *Library Journal,* 15 March 1997, 30–31.

Christian, Barbara. "The Race for Theory." *Feminist Studies* 14, no. 1 (1988): 67–79.

Clawson, Dan, and Mary Clawson. "Reagan or Business? Foundations of the New Conservatism." In *The Structure of Power in America: The Corporate Elite as a Ruling Class,* edited by Michael Schwarz, 201–17. New York: Holmes & Meier, 1987.

Clay, Edwin, and Patricia Bangs. "Entrepreneurs in the Public Library: Reinventing an Institution." *Library Trends* 48, no. 3 (2000): 606–18.

Clayton, Mark. "Food for Thought." *Christian Science Monitor,* 22 January 2002, 12.

Coffman, Steve. "What if You Ran Your Library Like a Bookstore?" *American Libraries,* March 1998, 40–46.

Cohen, David, and Marvin Lazerson. "Education and the Corporate Order." In *Education in American History: Readings on the Social Issues,* edited by Michael B. Katz, 318–33. New York: Praeger, 1973.

"Concerns Arise Over Corporate Branding." *SRRT Newsletter,* Spring 2001, 4–5.

Cordes, Colleen. "Technology as Religion?" *Chronicle of Higher Education,* 27 April 1994, A10, A15.

Corn, David. "Anatomy of a Netscam." *Washington Post,* 7 July 1996, C5.

Cronin, Blaise. "Shibboleth and Substance in North American Library and Information Science Education." *Libri* 45 (1995): 45–63.

Dahlgren, Peter. "Ideology and Information in the Public Sphere." In *The Ideology of the Information Age,* edited by Jennifer Daryl Slack and Fred Fejes, 24–46. Norwood, N.J.: Ablex, 1987.

Dalton, Margaret. "Old Values for the New Information Age." *Library Journal,* 1 November 2000, 43–46.

Danton, J. Periam. "Plea for a Philosophy of Librarianship." In *American Library Philosophy: An Anthology,* edited by Barbara McCrimmon, 63–85. Hamden, Conn.: Shoe String Press, 1975.

Darknell, Frank. "The Carnegie Philanthropy and Private Corporate Influence on Higher Education." In *Philanthropy and Cultural Imperialism: The Foundations at Home and Abroad,* edited by Robert Arnove, 385–411. Boston: G. K. Hall, 1980.

Davis, William, John Swan, and Sanford Berman. "Three Statements on Fees." In *Alternative Library Literature1990/1991,* edited by James Danky and Sanford Berman, 127–30. Jefferson, N.C.: McFarland, 1992.

Day, Mark. "Challenges to the Professional Control of Knowledge Work in Academic Libraries: A Proposed Agenda for Organizational Research and Action." *Choosing Our Futures: Proceedings of the 8th National Conference of the Association of College and Research Libraries.* 1997. <http://www.ala.org/acrl/papers.html#C24>.

———. "Discourse Fashions in Library Administration and Information Management: A Critical History and Bibliometric Analysis." *Advances in Librarianship* 26 (2002): 231–98.

———. "Transformational Discourse: Ideologies of Organizational Change in the Academic Library." *Library Trends* 46, no. 4 (1998): 635–67.

De Gennaro, Richard. *Libraries, Technology, and the Information Marketplace: Selected Papers.* Boston: G. K. Hall, 1987.

———. "Technology and Access in an Enterprise Society." *Library Journal,* 1 October 1988, 40–43.

de la Pena McCook, Kathleen. "Poverty, Democracy and Public Libraries." In *Libraries & Democracy: The Cornerstones of Liberty,* edited by Nancy Kranich, 28–46. Chicago: American Library Association, 2001.

Demac, Donna. "Hearts and Minds Revisited: The Information Policies of the Reagan Administration." In *The Political Economy of Information,* edited by Vincent Mosco and Janet Wasko, 125–45. Madison: University of Wisconsin Press, 1988.

Dervin, Brenda. "Information—Democracy: An Examination of Underlying Assumptions." *Journal of the American Society for Information Science* 45, no. 6 (1994): 369–85.

Dick, Archie. "Epistemological Positions and Library and Information Science." *Library Quarterly* 69, no. 3 (1999): 305–20.

Dilevko, Juris. "Why Sally Tisdale is *Really* Upset About the State of Libraries: Socio-Political Implications of Internet Information Sources." *Journal of Information Ethics*, Spring 1999, 37–62.

Dilevko, Juris, and Roma Harris. "Information Technology and Social Relations: Portrayals of Gender Roles in High Tech Product Advertisements." *Journal of the American Society for Information Science* 48, no. 8 (1997): 718–27.

Dole, Wanda, and Jitka Hurych. "Values for Librarians in the Information Age." *Journal of Information Ethics* 10, no. 2 (2001): 38–50.

Douglas, Sarah, and Thomas Guback. "Production and Technology in the Communication/Information Revolution." *Media, Culture and Society* 6 (1984): 233–45.

Downs, Robert. *Books That Changed the World*. New York: New American Library, 1956.

Dryzek, John. "Critical Theory as a Research Paradigm." In *The Cambridge Companion to Habermas*, edited by Stephen White, 97–119. Cambridge: Cambridge University Press, 1995.

Duberman, Martin. "Reclaiming the Gay Past." *Reviews in American History* 16, no. 4 (1988): 515–25.

———. *Stonewall*. New York: Plume, 1994.

Dunn, Christina. "Assessment of the Role of School and Public Libraries in Support of Educational Reform: Final Report on the Study." In *The Bowker Annual*. 45th ed., edited by Dave Bogart, 385–406. New Providence, N.J.: R. R. Bowker, 2000.

———. "Assessment of the Role of School and Public Libraries in Support of Educational Reform: A Status Report on the Study." In *The Bowker Annual*. 44th ed., edited by Dave Bogart, 440–43. New Providence, N.J.: R. R. Bowker, 1999.

Egelko, Bob. "FBI Checking Out Americans' Reading Habits: Bookstores. Libraries Can't Do Much to Fend Off Search Warrants." *San Francisco Chronicle*, 23 June 2002, A5.

Estabrook, Leigh. *Public Libraries' Responses to September 11, 2001*. Champaign: Library Research Center, University of Illinois, 2002.

———. "Sacred Trust or Competitive Opportunity: Using Patron Records." *Library Journal*, 1 February 1996, 48–49.

———, ed. *Libraries in Post-Industrial Society*. Phoenix: Oryx Press, 1977.

Everhart, Robert, ed. *The Public School Monopoly: A Critical Analysis of Education and the State in American Society*. Cambridge, Mass.: Ballinger, 1982.

"The Fate of the Undergraduate Library." *Library Journal*, 1 November 2000, 38–41.

Feenberg, Andrew. *Critical Theory of Technology*. New York: Oxford University Press, 1991.

Fialkoff, Francine. "Inside Track: The Hidden Costs of Online." *Library Journal*, 15 December 2001, 97.

Fischer, Michael. "Deconstruction: The Revolt Against Gentility." *Democracy* 1, no. 4 (1981): 77–86.

Fisher, Donald. "American Philanthropy and the Social Sciences: The Reproduction of a Conservative Ideology." In *Philanthropy and Cultural Imperialism: The Foundations at Home and Abroad,* edited by Robert Arnove, 233–68. Boston: G. K. Hall, 1980.

Fisher, William. "Library Management: The Latest Fad, a Dismal Science, or Just Plain Work?" *Library Acquisitions: Practice & Theory* 20, no. 1 (1996): 49–56.

Fister, Barbara. "Trade Publishing: A Report from the Front." *Portal: Libraries and the Academy* 1, no. 4 (2001): 509–23.

Flanagan, Richard. "The Wonder & Glory of Books." *Waterstone's Books Quarterly* 5 (2002): 32–35.

Flanders, Laura. "Librarians Under Siege." *Nation,* 5–12 August 2002, 42–44.

Fraser, Nancy. "Rethinking the Public Sphere: A Contribution to the Critique of Actually Existing Democracy." In *Habermas and the Public Sphere,* edited by Craig Calhoun, 109–43. Cambridge, Mass.: MIT Press, 1992.

Frazier, Kenneth. "The Librarians' Dilemma: Contemplating the Costs of the 'Big Deal'." *D-Lib Magazine* 7, no. 3 (March 2001). <www.dlib.org/dlib/march01/frazier/03frazier.html>.

Fricke, Martin, Kay Matheisen, and Don Fallis. "The Ethical Presuppositions Behind the Library Bill of Rights." *Library Quarterly* 70, no. 4 (2000): 468–91.

Frohmann, Bernd. "Communication Technologies and Human Subjectivity: The Politics of Postmodern Information Science." *Canadian Journal of Information and Library Science* 19, no. 2 (1993): 1–22.

———. "The Ethics of Information Science Theory." Information Democracy Session, 55th Annual American Society for Information Science Meeting, Pittsburgh, 27 October 1992.

———. "The Social and Discursive Construction of New Information Technologies." Internationales Symposium fur Informationswissenschaft, Graz, Austria, 2–4 November 1994.

Fukuyama, Francis. *The End of History and the Last Man.* New York: Free Press, 1992.

———. *The Great Disruption: Human Nature and the Reconstitution of Social Order.* New York: Free Press, 1999.

Fuller, Steve. "A Critical Guide to Knowledge Society Newspeak: Or, How Not to Take the Great Leap Backward." *Current Sociology* 49, no. 4 (2001): 177–201.

———. "Why Post-Industrial Society Never Came." *Academe,* November–December 1994, 22–28.

Galbraith, John Kenneth. "Are Public Libraries Against Liberty?" *American Libraries,* September 1979, 482–85.

Garnham, Nicholas. "The Media and the Public Sphere." In *Habermas and the Public Sphere,* edited by Craig Calhoun, 359–76. Cambridge, Mass.: MIT Press, 1992.

Garoogian, Rhoda. "Librarian/Patron Confidentiality: An Ethical Challenge." *Library Trends* 40, no. 2 (1991): 216–33.

Gates, Jean Key. *Introduction to Librarianship.* 2nd ed. New York: McGraw-Hill. 1976.

Gates, William. "Multimedia Technology and Education: Progressive Products and Powerful Promises." *Booklist,* 15 May 1994, 1705.

Gersh, David. "The Corporate Elite and the Introduction of IQ Testing in American Public Schools." In *The Structure of Power in America: The Corporate Elite as a Ruling Class,* edited by Michael Schwarz, 163–84. New York: Holmes & Meier, 1987.

"Gifts That Can Warp a Museum." *New York Times,* 31 May 2001, A26.

Giroux, Henry. "Citizenship, Public Philosophy, and the Struggle for Democracy." *Educational Theory* 37, no. 2 (1987): 103–20.

———. *Corporate Culture and the Attack on Higher Education and Public Schooling.* Bloomington, Ind.: Phi Delta Kappa, 1999.

———. "Education Incorporated?" *Educational Leadership,* October 1998, 12–17.

———. "Liberal Arts Education and the Struggle for Public Life: Dreaming About Democracy." *South Atlantic Quarterly* 89, no. 1 (1990): 113–38.

———. "Pedagogy of the Depressed: Beyond the Politics of Cynicism." *College Literature* 28, no. 3 (2001): 1–31.

———. "Public Philosophy and the Crisis in Education." *Harvard Educational Review* 54, no. 2 (1984): 186–94.

———. "Schooling and the Culture of Positivism: Notes on the Death of History." *Educational Theory* 29, no. 4 (1979): 263–84.

———. "Schools for Sale: Public Education, Corporate Culture, and the Citizen-Consumer." *Educational Forum* 63 (Winter 1999): 140–49.

———. "Theories of Reproduction and Resistance in the New Sociology of Education: A Critical Analysis." *Harvard Educational Review* 53, no. 3 (1983): 257–93.

———. *Theory & Resistance in Education: A Pedagogy for the Opposition.* South Hadley, Mass.: Bergin & Garvey, 1983.

———. "Vocationalizing Higher Education: Schooling and the Politics of Corporate Culture." *College Literature* 26, no. 3 (1999): 147–61.

———. "When You Wish Upon a Star It Makes a Difference Who You Are: Children's Culture and the Wonderful World of Disney." *International Journal of Educational Reform* 4, no. 1 (1995): 79–83.

Giroux, Henry, and Peter McLaren. "Teacher Education and the Politics of Engagement: The Case for Democratic Schooling." *Harvard Educational Review* 56, no. 6 (1986): 213–38.

Gorman, Michael. "The Corruption of Cataloging." *Library Journal,* 15 September 1995, 32–34.

———. "Human Values in a Technological Age." *Information Technology and Libraries,* March 2001, 4–11.

———. "Living and Dying with 'Information': Comments on the Report *Buildings, Books, and Bytes.*" *Library Trends* 46, no. 1 (1997): 28–35.

Govan, James. "The Creeping Invisible Hand: Entrepreneurial Librarianship." *American Libraries,* January 1988, 35–38.

Gray, Carolyn. "The Civic Role of Libraries." In *Critical Approaches to Information*

*Technology in Librarianship: Foundations and Applications,* edited by John Buschman, 156–57. Westport, Conn.: Greenwood, 1993.

Greene, Maxine. Foreword to *The New Servants of Power: A Critique of the 1980s School Reform Movement,* edited by Christine Shea, Ernest Kahane, and Peter Sola, i–x. New York: Greenwood Press, 1989.

———. "Imagining Futures: The Public School and Possibility." *Journal of Curriculum Studies* 32, no. 2 (2000): 267–80.

———. "Liberal Learning and Teacher Education." In *Excellence in Teacher Education Through the Liberal Arts: Proceedings of the Conference,* edited by Michael Carbone and Ann Wonsiewicz, 23–27. Allentown, Penn.: Education Department, Muhlenberg College, 1986.

———. "Microcomputers: A View from Philosophy and the Arts." *Computers in the Schools* 1, no. 3 (1985): 7–17.

———. *The Public School & the Private Vision: A Search for America in Education and Literature.* New York: Random House, 1965.

Greer, Colin. "Immigrants, Negroes, and the Public Schools." In *Education in American History: Readings on the Social Issues,* edited by Michael Katz, 284–90. New York: Praeger, 1973.

Griffiths, Jose-Marie. "Deconstructing Earth's Largest Library." *Library Journal,* August 2000, 44–47.

Guernsey, Lisa. "Corporate Largesse: Philanthropy or Self-Interest?" *Chronicle of Higher Education,* 24 April 1998, A28–29.

Gutmann, Amy. *Democratic Education.* Princeton, N.J.: Princeton University Press, 1987.

Haar, John. "The Politics of Electronic Information: A Reassessment." In *Critical Approaches to Information Technology in Librarianship: Foundations and Applications,* edited by John Buschman, 197–210. Westport, Conn.: Greenwood Press, 1993.

Habermas, Jürgen. "Further Reflections on the Public Sphere." In *Habermas and the Public Sphere,* edited by Craig Calhoun, 421–61. Cambridge, Mass.: MIT Press, 1992.

———. "Modernity Versus Postmodernity." *New German Critique* 22 (1981): 3–14.

———. *The Philosophical Discourse of Modernity.* Cambridge, Mass.: MIT Press, 1987.

———. "Problems of Legitimation in Late Capitalism." In *Critical Sociology: Selected Readings,* edited by Paul Connerton, 363–87. New York: Penguin, 1976.

———. "The Public Sphere: An Encyclopedia Article (1964)." *New German Critique* 3 (Fall 1974): 49–55.

———. "A Reply to My Critics." In *Habermas: Critical Debates,* edited by John Thompson and David Held, 219–83. London: MacMillan, 1982.

———. *The Structural Transformation of the Public Sphere.* Cambridge, Mass.: MIT Press, 1989.

———. "Systematically Distorted Communication." In *Critical Sociology: Selected Readings,* edited by Paul Connerton, 348–62. New York: Penguin, 1976.

———. "Theory and Practice in a Scientific Civilization." In *Critical Sociology: Selected Readings*, edited by Paul Connerton, 330–47. New York: Penguin, 1976.

———. *The Theory of Communicative Action*. Vol. I. Boston: Beacon Press, 1984.

———. *The Theory of Communicative Action*. Vol. II. Boston: Beacon Press, 1987.

———. *Toward a Rational Society: Student Protest, Science, and Politics*. Boston: Beacon Press, 1970.

Habermas, Jürgen, et. al. "Concluding Remarks." In *Habermas and the Public Sphere*, edited by Craig Calhoun, 462–79. Cambridge, Mass.: MIT Press, 1992.

Hadden, R. Lee. "Outsourcing Federal Libraries." *Progressive Librarian* 14 (1998): 44–46.

Hafner, Katie. "Gates's Library Gifts Arrive, but with Windows Attached." *New York Times*, 21 February 1999, A1.

Hage, Christine. "Books, Bytes, Buildings, and Bodies: Public Libraries in the 21st Century." *American Libraries*, January 1999, 79–81.

Hall, Stuart. "On Postmodernism and Articulation." *Journal of Communication Inquiry* 10 (1986): 45–60.

Harger, Elaine. "Editorial: Institutionalizing Silence Within ALA?" *Progressive Librarian* 14 (1998): 1–4.

———. "The 'Enola Gay' Controversy as a Library Issue." *Progressive Librarian* 10/11 (Winter 1995/96): 60–78.

Harrington, Michael. *The Politics at God's Funeral: The Spiritual Crisis of Western Civilization*. New York: Holt, Rinehart and Winston, 1983.

———. "Post-Industrial Society and the Welfare State." In *Libraries in Post-Industrial Society*, edited by Leigh Estabrook, 19–29. Phoenix, Ariz.: Oryx. 1977.

Harris, Michael. "The Dialectic of Defeat: Antimonies in Research in Library and Information Science." *Library Trends* 34, no. 3 (1986): 515–31.

———. "The Fall of the Grand Hotel: Class, Canon, and the Coming Crisis of Western Librarianship." *Libri* 45 (1995): 231–35.

———. "Portrait in Paradox: Commitment and Ambivalence in American Librarianship, 1876–1976." *Libri* 26, no. 4 (1976): 281–301.

———. "Public Libraries and the Decline of the Democratic Dogma." *Library Journal*, 1 November 1976, 2225–30.

———. "The Purpose of the American Public Library." *Library Journal*, 15 September 1973, 2509–14.

———. "State, Class, and Cultural Reproduction: Toward A Theory of Library Service in the United States." *Advances in Librarianship* 14 (1986): 211–53.

Harris, Michael, and Stan Hannah. *Into the Future: the Foundations of Library and Information Services in the Post-Industrial Era*. Norwood, N.J.: Ablex, 1993.

Harris, Michael, Stan Hannah, and Pamela Harris. *Into the Future: The Foundations of Library and Information Services in the Post-Industrial Era*. 2nd ed. Greenwich, Conn.: Ablex, 1998.

Harris, Michael, and Masaru Itoga. "Becoming Critical: For a Theory of Purpose and Necessity in American Librarianship." In *Library and Information Science Re-*

*search: Perspectives and Strategies for Improvement,* 347–57. Information Management, Policy, and Services Series. Norwood, N.J.: Ablex, 1991.

Harris, Roma. "Gender, Power, and the Dangerous Pursuit of Professionalism." *American Libraries,* October 1993, 874–76.

———. "Leadership, Professionalism, and Librarianship." 25th Annual Conference of the Corporation of Professional Librarians of Quebec, InterContinental Hotel, Montreal, 26 May 1994.

———. *Librarianship: The Erosion of a Woman's Profession.* Norwood, N.J.: Ablex, 1992.

———. "Service Undermined by Technology: An Examination of Gender Relations, Economics and Ideology." *Progressive Librarian* 10/11 (1995/1996): 5–22.

Hauben, Rhonda. "Privatizing the Internet? A Call to Arms!" *Counterpoise* 2, no. 4 (1998): 5–19.

Heckart, Ronald. "The Library as a Marketplace of Ideas." *College & Research Libraries,* November 1991, 491–505.

Heilbroner, Robert. "Technology and Capitalism." *Social Research* 64, no. 3 (1997): 1321–25.

———. *The Worldly Philosophers.* New York: Time, 1953.

Held, David. *Introduction to Critical Theory: Horkheimer to Habermas.* Berkeley: University of California Press, 1980.

Henderson, Albert. "The Devil and Max Weber in the Research University." *Journal of Information Ethics,* Spring 1999, 20–36.

Hernon, Peter, and Charles McClure. *Evaluation and Library Decision Making.* Norwood, N.J.: Ablex, 1990.

Herring, Mark. "10 Reasons Why the Internet is No Substitute for a Library." *American Libraries,* April 2001, 76–78.

Higonnet, Patrice. "Scandal on the Seine" *New York Review of Books,* 15 August 1991, 32–33.

Hill, Janet Swan. "Outsourcing: Understanding the Fuss." *The Bowker Annual.* 46th ed., edited by Dave Bogart, 218–32. New Providence, N.J.: R. R. Bowker, 2001.

Himmelfarb, Gertrude. "Revolution in the Library." *American Scholar,* Spring 1997, 197–204.

Hirshon, Arnold. "Running with the Red Queen: Breaking New Habits to Survive in the Virtual World." *Advances in Librarianship* 20 (1996): 1–26.

Hofstadter, Richard. *The American Political Tradition.* New York: Knopf, 1986.

Hohendahl, Peter. "Critical Theory, Public Sphere and Culture. Jürgen Habermas and His Critics." *New German Critique* 16 (Winter 1979): 89–118.

———. "Jürgen Habermas: 'The Public Sphere' (1964)." *New German Critique* 4 (Fall 1974): 45–48.

———. "The Public Sphere: Models and Boundaries." In *Habermas and the Public Sphere,* edited by Craig Calhoun, 99–109. Cambridge, Mass.: MIT Press, 1992.

Hollinger, David, and Charles Capper, eds. *The American Intellectual Tradition: Volume I 1630–1865.* 2nd ed. New York: Oxford University Press, 1993.

———. *The American Intellectual Tradition: Volume II 1865 to the Present.* 2nd ed. New York: Oxford University Press, 1993.

Hood, Joan. "Past, Present, and Future of Library Development (Fund-Raising)." *Advances in Librarianship* 22 (1998): 123–39.

Hughes, Robert. *Nothing if Not Critical: Selected Essays on Art and Artists.* New York: Penguin, 1992.

Huwe, Terence. "Libraries and the Idea of the Organization." *Advances in Librarianship* 21 (1997): 1–24.

Isaacson, David. "Instant Information Gratification." *American Libraries,* February 2002, 39.

Jansen, Sue Curry. "Censorship, Critical Theory, and New Information Technologies: Foundations of Critical Scholarship in Communications." In *Critical Approaches to Information Technology in Librarianship: Foundations and Applications,* edited by John Buschman, 59–81. Westport, Conn.: Greenwood Press, 1993.

Jefferson, Thomas. *The Life and Selected Writings of Thomas Jefferson.* Edited by Adrienne Koch and William Peden. New York: Modern Library, 1944.

Johnson, Pauline. "Habermas's Search for the Public Sphere." *European Journal of Social Theory* 4, no. 2 (2001): 315–36.

Joyce, Steven. "A Few Gates: An Examination of the Social Responsibilities Debate in the Early 1970s and 1990s." *Progressive Librarian* 15 (1998/1999): 1–13.

Kagan, Al. "IFLA and Human Rights." *Progressive Librarian* 10/11 (1995/1996): 79–82.

Karier, Clarence. "Liberalism and the Quest for Orderly Change." In *Education in American History: Readings on the Social Issues,* edited by Michael Katz, 303–18. New York: Praeger, 1973.

Kashatus, William. "Public Education in Private Hands." *New York Times,* 2 February 2002, A19.

Katz, Jonathon, ed. *Gay American History.* New York: Harper, 1985.

Katz, Michael B., ed. *Education in American History: Readings on the Social Issues.* New York: Praeger. 1973.

Katz, Michael S. "Critical Literacy: A Conception of Education as a Moral Right and a Social Ideal." In *The Public School Monopoly: A Critical Analysis of Education and the State in American Society,* edited by Robert Everhart, 193–223. Cambridge, Mass.: Ballinger, 1982.

Katz, Stanley. "In Information Technology, Don't Mistake a Tool for a Goal." *Chronicle of Higher Education,* 15 June 2001, B7.

Kaye, Harvey. "Marxian Questions, Working-Class Struggles, Socialist Aspirations." *Critical Sociology* 25, no. 1 (1999): 16–29.

Kellner, Douglas. "Habermas, the Public Sphere, and Democracy: A Critical Intervention." 12 October 2002. <http://www.gseis.ucla.edu/faculty/kellner/papers/habermas.htm>.

Kelly, George. "Who Needs a Theory of Citizenship?" *Daedalus* 108 (Fall 1979): 21–36.

Kessler, Jascha. "Epimetheus—or, A Reflection on the 'Box'." *Boston Review,* February 1992, 13–14.

Kinsella, William. "Communication and Information Technologies: A Dialectical Model of Technology and Human Agency." *New Jersey Journal of Communication* 1, no. 1 (1993): 2–18.

Kliebard, Herbert. "The Effort to Reconstruct the Modern American Curriculum." In *The Curriculum: Problems, Politics, and Possibilities,* edited by Landon Beyer and Michael Apple, 19–31. Albany: State University of New York Press, 1988.

———. *The Struggle for the American Curriculum.* Boston: Routledge & Kegan Paul, 1986.

Kozol, Jonathon. *Savage Inequalities: Children in America's Schools.* New York: Crown, 1991.

Kranich, Nancy. "Libraries as Civic Spaces." *American Libraries,* November 2000, 7.

———. "Libraries Create Social Capital." *Library Journal,* 15 November 2001, 40–41.

———. "Libraries Help to Build a Civil Society." *American Libraries,* June/July 2001, 7.

———. "Libraries: The Cornerstone of Democracy." *American Libraries,* August 2000, 5.

Laird, Ellen. "Internet Plagiarism: We All Pay the Price." *Chronicle of Higher Education,* 13 July 2001, B5.

Lakeland, Paul. "Preserving the Lifeworld, Restoring the Public Sphere, Renewing Higher Education." *Cross Currents* 43, no. 4 (1993): 488–502.

LAMA/LOMS Comparative Library Organization Committee (CLOC) and CLOC Bibliography Task Force. "Required Reading for Library Administrators: An Annotated Bibliography of Influential Authors and Their Works." *Library Administration & Management* 16, no. 3 (2002): 126–36.

———. "Required Reading for Library Administrators, Part Two: An Annotated Bibliography of Highly Cited Library and Information Science Authors and Their Works." *Library Administration & Management* 17, no. 1 (2002): 11–20.

Lasch, Christopher. "After the Foundations Have Crumbled." Review of *Crossing the Postmodern Divide,* by Albert Borgmann. *Commonweal,* 20 November 1992, 22–23.

———. "Mass Culture Reconsidered." *Democracy* 1, no. 4 (1981): 7–22.

———. *The Revolt of the Elites and the Betrayal of Democracy.* New York: W. W. Norton, 1995.

Lathrop, Ann, and Kathleen Foss. *Student Cheating and Plagiarism in the Internet Era: A Wake-Up Call.* Englewood, Colo.: Libraries Unlimited, 2000.

Latshaw, Patricia. "Beyond Censorship: Issues in Intellectual Freedom." *The Bowker Annual.* 36th ed., edited by Filomena Simora, 67–74. New Providence, N.J.: R. R. Bowker, 1991.

Lichtblau, Eric. "Rising Fears That What We Do Know Can Hurt Us." *Los Angeles Times,* 18 November 2001, A1.

Lievrouw, Leah. "Information Resources and Democracy: Understanding the Paradox." *Journal of the American Society for Information Science* 45, no. 6 (1994): 350–57.

Lievrouw, Leah, and Sonia Livingstone, eds. *Handbook of New Media: Social Shaping and Consequences of ICTs.* London: Sage, 2002.

Litwack, Leon. "Education: Separate and Unequal." In *Education in American History: Readings on the Social Issues,* edited by Michael Katz, 253–66. New York: Praeger, 1973.

Litwin, Rory. "Issues of Inside Censorship and the ALA." *Counterpoise,* January 1998, 11–13.

Long, Robert, ed. *The State of U.S. Education.* New York: H. W. Wilson, 1991.

Love, James. "A Primer on WIPO & Database Extraction Rights." *Progressive Librarian* 12/13 (1997): 18–31.

Lubans, John. "'I Borrowed the Shoes, But the Holes Are Mine': Management Fads, Trends, and What's Next." *Library Administration & Management* 14, no. 3 (2000): 131–34.

Luke, Timothy. *Screens of Power: Ideology, Domination, and Resistance in Informational Society.* Urbana: University of Illinois Press, 1989.

Lynch, Beverly, and Mark Rosenzweig. "What's the Matter With Membership Meetings?" *American Libraries,* December 1997, 41–44.

Lyon, David. "From 'Post-Industrialism' to 'Information Society': A New Social Transformation?" *Sociology* 20, no. 4 (1986): 577–88.

MacLeish, Archibald. "The Premise of Meaning." In *American Library Philosophy: An Anthology,* edited by Barbara McCrimmon, 229–35. Hamden, Conn.: Shoe String Press, 1975.

Mangan, Katharine. "In Revamped Library Schools, Information Trumps Books." *Chronicle of Higher Education,* 7 April 2000, A43–44.

Mann, Thomas. "Height Shelving Threat to the Nation's Libraries." In *Alternative Library Literature, 1998/1999: A Biennial Anthology,* edited by Sanford Berman and James Danky, 338–57. Jefferson, N.C.: McFarland, 2001.

———. "The Importance of Books, Free Access, and Libraries as Places—and the Dangerous Inadequacy of the Information Science Paradigm." *Journal of Academic Librarianship* 27, no. 4 (2001): 268–81.

———. *The Oxford Guide to Library Research.* New York: Oxford University Press, 1998.

Marchionini, Gary. *Information Seeking in Electronic Environments.* Cambridge: Cambridge University Press, 1995.

Margonis, Frank. "The Cooptation of 'At Risk': Paradoxes of Policy Criticism." *Teachers College Record* 94, no. 2 (1992): 343–64.

Marinko, Rita, and Kristin Gerhard. "Representations of the Alternative Press in Academic Library Collections." *College & Research Libraries,* July 1998, 363–76.

Marx, Leo. "The Idea of 'Technology' and Postmodern Pessimism." In *Does Technology Drive History? The Dilemma of Technological Determinism,* edited by Merritt Smith and Leo Marx, 237–57. Cambridge, Mass.: MIT Press, 1994.

———. "Technology: The Emergence of a Hazardous Concept." *Social Research* 64, no. 3 (1997): 965–88.

Mattern, Shannon. "A Receptacle for Irony and Data: Rem Koolhaas's Vision for Seattle Public Library." Society for the History of Authorship, Reading, and Publishing 2001 Conference, College of William and Mary, Williamsburg, Virginia, 21 July 2001.

McChesney, Robert. *Rich Media, Poor Democracy: Communication Politics in Dubious Times.* New York: New Press, 1999.

McChesney, Robert, and John Nichols. "The Making of a Movement: Getting Serious About Media Reform." *Nation,* 7–14 January 2002, 11, 13–15.

McChesney, Robert, Ellen Wood, and John Foster, eds. *Capitalism and the Information Age: The Political Economy of the Global Communication Revolution.* New York: Monthly Review Press, 1998.

McCrimmon, Barbara, ed. *American Library Philosophy: An Anthology.* Hamden, Conn.: Shoe String Press, 1975.

McDonald, Peter. "Corporate Inroads & Librarianship: The Fight for the Soul of the Profession in the New Millennium." *Progressive Librarian* 12/13 (1997): 32–44.

McLaughlin, Lisa. "Feminism, the Public Sphere, Media, and Democracy." *Media, Culture and Society* 15 (1993): 599–620.

Mech, Terrence. "Leadership and the Evolution of Academic Librarianship." *Journal of Academic Librarianship* 22, no. 5 (1996): 345–53.

Michelson, Stephan. "The Political Economy of Public School Finance." In *Schooling in a Corporate Economy,* edited by Martin Carnoy, 140–74. New York: David McKay, 1972.

Miller, Mark Crispin. "Reading in the Age of Global Media (with a response by John Buschman)." *Progressive Librarian* 18 (2001): 18–28.

———. "What's Wrong with This Picture?" *Nation,* 7–14 January 2002, 18–22.

Miller, William. "The Library as a Place: Tradition and Evolution." *Library Issues* 22, no. 3 (January 2002).

Mintzberg, Henry. "Managing Government, Governing Management." *Harvard Business Review,* May–June 1996, 75–83.

Mitchell, Alison. "Ingenuity's Blueprints, into History's Dustbin." *New York Times,* 30 December 2001, A1, A22.

Molnar, Alex, and Joseph Reaves. "Buy Me! Buy Me!" *Educational Leadership* 59, no. 2 (2001): 74–80.

Molz, Redmond Kathleen, and Phyllis Dain. *Civic Space/Cyberspace: The American Public Library in the Information Age.* Cambridge, Mass: MIT, 1999.

Moran, Robert, Jr. "The Campaign for America's Libraries: An Interview with Deborah Davis." *Library Administration & Management* 15, no. 2 (2001): 76–79.

Mosco, Vincent. "Introduction: Information in the Pay-per Society." In *The Political Economy of Information,* edited by Vincent Mosco and Janet Wasko, 3–26. Madison: University of Wisconsin Press, 1988.

————. "Myth-ing Links: Power and Community on the Information Highway." Davidson Dunton Lecture, Carleton University, Ottawa, November 1996.

————. *The Pay-Per Society: Computers and Communication in the Information Age.* Norwood, N.J.: Ablex, 1989.

Mosco, Vincent, and Janet Wasko, eds. *The Political Economy of Information.* Madison: University of Wisconsin Press, 1988.

Murdock, Graham, and Peter Golding. "Information Poverty and Political Inequality: Citizenship in the Age of Privatized Communication." *Journal of Communication* 39, no. 3 (1989): 180–95.

Nash, Gary. *Red, White, and Black: The Peoples of Early America.* Englewood Cliffs, N.J.: Prentice Hall, 1974.

National Commission on Libraries and Information Science. *Public Sector/Private Sector Interaction in Providing Information Services.* Washington, D.C.: U.S. Government Printing Office, 1982.

————. "The Role of Fees in Supporting Library and Information Services in Public and Academic Libraries (April 1985)." In *The Bowker Annual.* 31st ed., edited by Filomena Simora, 89–112. New York: R. R. Bowker, 1986.

Newhouse, Victoria. *Towards a New Museum.* New York: Monacelli Press, 1998.

Noble, David. "Digital Diploma Mills." Part I, 1998. Part II, 1998. Part III, November 1998 at <http://www.ucsd.edu/dl.htm>. Part IV, November 1999 distributed on e-mail by pagre@alpha.oac.ucla.edu on 26 November 1999. Part V, June 2001 at http://www.ucsd.edu/dl/ddm5.htm.

————. "Present Tense Technology, Part One." *Democracy* 3, no. 2 (1983): 8–24.

————. "Present Tense Technology, Part Two." *Democracy* 3, no. 3 (1983): 70–82.

————. "Present Tense Technology, Part Three." *Democracy* 3, no.4 (1983): 71–93.

Noble, Douglas. "The Underside of Computer Literacy." *Raritan* 3 (1984): 37–64.

Oder, Norman. "Outsourcing: Model—or Mistake?" *Library Journal,* 15 March 1997, 28–30.

O'Mahoney, Dennis. "Here Today. Gone Tomorrow: What Can Be Done to Assure Permanent Public Access to Electronic Information?" *Advances in Librarianship* 22 (1998): 107–21.

Omidsalar, Teresa, and Mohmoud Omidsalar. "Customer Service: A View from the Trenches." *American Libraries,* February 1999, 24–25.

Outhwaite, William. *Habermas: A Critical Introduction.* Cambridge: Polity Press, 1994.

Palatella, John. "Ivory Towers in the Marketplace." *Dissent,* Summer 2001, 70–73.

Parker, Ian. "Absolute Powerpoint." *New Yorker,* 28 May 2001, 76, 78–80, 85–87.

Perkinson, Henry. *The Imperfect Panacea: American Faith in Education, 1865–1965.* New York: Random House, 1968.

Perrolle, Judith. "Intellectual Assembly Lines: The Rationalization of Managerial, Professional, and Technical Work." In *Computerization and Controversy: Value Conflicts and Social Choice,* edited by C. Dunlop and R. Kling, 111–22. San Diego: Academic Press, 1991.

Peters, John Durham. "Distrust of Representation: Habermas on the Public Sphere." *Media, Culture and Society* 15 (1993): 541–71.

———. "Information: Notes Toward a Critical History." *Journal of Communication Inquiry* 12, no. 2 (1988): 9–23.

———. "Satan and Savior: Mass Communication in Progressive Thought." *Critical Studies in Mass Communication* 6 (1989): 247–63.

Poster, Mark. Introduction to *Jean Baudrillard: Selected Writings*, by Jean Baudrillard. Stanford, Calif.: Stanford University Press, 1988.

———. "Introduction: Culture and New Media." In *Handbook of New Media: Social Shaping and Consequences of ICTs*, edited by Leah Lievrouw and Sonia Livingstone, 479–84. London: Sage, 2002.

———. *What's the Matter with the Internet?* Minneapolis: University of Minnesota Press, 2001.

Postman, Neil. "The Contradictions of Freedom of Information." *WLA Journal*, June 1985, 4–19.

———. *Teaching as a Conserving Activity.* New York: Delta, 1979.

———. *Technopoly: The Surrender of Culture to Technology.* New York: Vintage, 1993.

Powers, Sally, David Halpin, and Geoff Whitty. "Managing the State and the Market: 'New' Education Management in Five Countries." *British Journal of Educational Studies* 45, no. 4 (1997): 342–62.

Powers, Sally, and Geoff Whitty. "Teaching New Subjects? The Hidden Curriculum of Marketized Education Systems." American Educational Research Association Annual Meeting, Chicago, March 1997 (distributed as ERIC document ED 406 757).

Pratt, Linda. "Liberal Education and the Idea of the Postmodern University." *Academe*, November–December 1994, 46–51.

Quinn, Brian. "The McDonaldization of Academic Libraries?" *College & Research Libraries*, May 2000, 248–61.

Radford, Gary. "Flaubert, Foucault, and the Biblioteque Fantastique: Toward a Postmodern Epistemology for Librarianship." *Library Trends* 46, no. 4 (1998): 616–34.

Radford, Gary, and Marie Radford. "Libraries, Librarians, and the Discourse of Fear." *Library Quarterly* 71, no. 3 (2001): 299–329.

Ratteray, Oswald. *A Survey of Librarians in the Middle States Region on the Role of the Library, Electronic Resources, and Information Literacy Training in Higher Education.* Philadelphia: Middle States Commission on Higher Education, November 1999.

Reynolds, Brian. "Public Library Funding: Issues, Trends, and Resources." *Advances in Librarianship* 18 (1994): 159–88.

Richardson, John. "Reference Is Better Than We Thought." *Library Journal*, 15 April 2002, 41–42.

Riggs, Donald. "What's in Store for Academic Libraries? Leadership and Management Issues." *Journal of Academic Librarianship* 23, no. 1 (1997): 3–8.

Riley, Melissa. "Notes from the Front Line at San Francisco Public Library." *Progressive Librarian* 12/13 (1997): 60–62.

Robins, Kevin. "Forces of Consumption: From the Symbolic to the Psychotic." *Media, Culture & Society* 16 (1994): 449–68.

Robins, Kevin, and Frank Webster. "Cybernetic Capitalism: Information, Technology, Everyday Life." In *The Political Economy of Information,* edited by Vincent Mosco and Janet Wasko, 44–75. Madison: University of Wisconsin Press, 1988.

———. "Information as Capital: A Critique of Daniel Bell." In *The Ideology of the Information Age,* edited by Jennifer Slack and Fred Fejes, 95–117. Norwood, N.J.: Ablex, 1987.

Rohmann, Gloria. "Media on Demand: Approaches to Web-Based Media Services in Libraries." *Advances in Librarianship* 23 (2000): 39–61.

Rosen, Jay. "Playing the Primary Chords." *Harper's,* March 1992, 22–26.

Rosenzweig, Mark. "Libraries at the End of History?" *Progressive Librarian* 2 (1990/91): 2–8.

———. "Many Voices, One Goal: Notes Towards a Critique of the 'One Voice' Policy for ALA." *SRRT Newsletter,* Spring 2001, 12–13.

Roszak, Theodore. *The Cult of Information: The Folklore of Computers and the True Art of Thinking.* New York: Pantheon, 1986.

———. "Politics of Information and the Fate of the Earth." *Progressive Librarian* 6/7 (1993): 3–14.

Rutstein, Joel, Anna DeMiller, and Elizabeth Fuseler. "Ownership Versus Access: Shifting Perspectives for Libraries." *Advances in Librarianship* 17 (1993): 33–60.

Sale, Kirkpatrick. "Lessons from the Luddites." *Ecologist,* August/September 1999, 314–17.

Sarup, Madan. *An Introductory Guide to Post-Structuralism and Postmodernism.* Athens: University of Georgia Press, 1989.

Savard, Rejean, ed. *Education and Research for Marketing and Quality Management in Libraries.* Munich: K. G. Saur, 2002.

Schama, Simon. "A Whiff of Dread for the Land of Hope." *New York Times,* 15 September 2002, sec. 4, 1, 6.

Schiffrin, Andre. *The Business of Books.* New York: Verso, 2000.

———. "Public-Interest Publishing in a World of Conglomerates." In *Alternative Library Literature, 1998/1999: A Biennial Anthology,* edited by Sanford Berman and James Danky, 236–38. Jefferson, N.C.: McFarland, 2001.

Schiller, Dan. "How to Think About Information." In *The Political Economy of Information,* edited by Vincent Mosco and Janet Wasko, 27–43. Madison: University of Wisconsin Press, 1988.

Schiller, Herbert. "Critical Research in the Information Age." *Journal of Communication* 33 (1983): 249–57.

———. *Culture Inc.: The Corporate Takeover of Public Expression.* New York: Oxford University Press, 1989.

———. "The Global Commercialization of Culture." *Progressive Librarian* 2 (1990/1991): 15–22.

———. "Public Information Goes Corporate." *Library Journal,* 1 October 1991, 42–45.

Schiller, Herbert, and Anita Schiller. "Libraries, Public Access to Information, and Commerce." In *The Political Economy of Information,* edited by Vincent Mosco and Janet Wasko, 146–66. Madison: University of Wisconsin Press, 1988.

Schneider, Karen. "The McLibrary Syndrome." *American Libraries,* January 1998, 68–70.

———. "The Patriot Act: Last Refuge of a Scoundrel." *American Libraries,* March 2002, 86.

Schuchard, Ronald. "Excavating the Imagination: Archival Research and the Digital Revolution." *Libraries & Culture* 37, no. 1 (2002): 57–63.

Schuman, Patricia. "Information Justice." *Library Journal,* 1 June 1982, 1060–66.

———. "Vanishing Act: The Collapse of America's Libraries." *USA Today,* July 1992, 10–12.

Schwarz, Michael, ed. *The Structure of Power in America: The Corporate Elite as a Ruling Class.* New York: Holmes & Meier, 1987.

Sciolino, Elaine. "Smithsonian Is Promised $38 Million, with Strings." *New York Times,* 10 May 2001, A16.

Sennett, Richard. "Cities Without Care or Connection." *New Statesman,* 5 June 2000, 25–27.

———. "How Work Destroys Social Inclusion." *New Statesman,* 31 May 1999, 25–27.

———. "The New Capitalism." *Social Research* 64, no. 2 (1997): 161–80.

Seybold, Peter. "The Ford Foundation and the Transformation of Political Science." In *The Structure of Power in America: The Corporate Elite as a Ruling Class,* edited by Michael Schwarz, 185–98. New York: Holmes & Meier, 1987.

Shattuck, Roger. "From the Swiss Family Robinson to Narratus Interruptus." *Boston Review,* May–July 1992, 22–24.

Shea, Christine, Ernest Kahane, and Peter Sola, eds. *The New Servants of Power: A Critique of the 1980s School Reform Movement.* New York: Greenwood Press, 1989.

Shera, Jesse. "Failure and Success: Assessing a Century." *Library Journal,* 1 January 1976, 281–87.

———. "What is Librarianship?" In *American Library Philosophy: An Anthology,* edited by Barbara McCrimmon, 165–71. Hamden, Conn.: Shoe String Press, 1975.

Shor, Ira. *Culture Wars: School and Society in the Conservative Restoration.* New York: Routledge & Kegan Paul, 1986.

Slack, Jennifer. "The Information Revolution as Ideology." *Media, Culture and Society* 6 (1984): 247–56.

Slack, Jennifer, and Fred Fejes, eds. *The Ideology of the Information Age.* Norwood, N.J.: Ablex, 1987.

Slater, Don, and Fran Tonkiss. *Market Society: Markets and Modern Social Theory.* Malden, Mass.: Blackwell. 2001.

———. "Social Relationships and Identity Online and Offline." In *Handbook of New Media: Social Shaping and Consequences of ICTs,* edited by Leah Lievrouw and Sonia Livingstone, 533–46. London: Sage, 2002.

Sloan, Douglas, ed. *The Computer in Education: A Critical Perspective.* New York: Teachers College Press, 1984.

Smith, Merritt, and Leo Marx, eds. *Does Technology Drive History? The Dilemma of Technological Determinism.* Cambridge, Mass.: MIT Press, 1994.

Smith, Tony. "Postmodernism: Theory and Politics." *Against the Current,* July/August 1993, 2–5.

Smithson, Marilyn. "By You, for You, or in Spite of You: Outsourcing and the Demise of the Public Library." *SRRT Newsletter,* March 1997, 16–19.

Smykla, Evelyn, comp. *Marketing and Public Relations Activities in ARL Libraries.* Washington, D.C.: Association of Research Libraries, 1999.

Sokal, Alan, and Jean Bricmont. *Fashionable Nonsense: Postmodern Intellectuals' Abuse of Science.* New York: Picador, 1998.

Southwick, Ron. "Scholars Fear Humanities Endowment Is Being Dumbed Down." *Chronicle of Higher Education,* 6 October 2000, A29–30.

Spring, Joel. *The American School: 1642–1985.* New York: Longman, 1986.

Staley, David. "Digital Technologies and the Mythologies of Globalization." *Bulletin of Science, Technology & Society* 18, no. 6 (1998): 421–25.

Stanley, Manfred. "The Mystery of the Commons: On the Indispensability of Civic Rhetoric." *Social Research* 50, no. 4 (1983): 851–83.

Starbuck, William. "Congealing Oil: Inventing Ideologies to Justify Acting Ideologies Out." *Journal of Management Studies* 19, no. 1 (1982): 3–27.

Stearns, Peter. "The Idea of Postindustrial Society: Some Problems." *Journal of Social History* 17 (1984): 685–93.

Steinberg, Jacques. "Buying In to the Company School." *New York Times,* 17 February 2002, A24.

Steinberg, Jacques, and Diana Henriques. "Complex Calculations on Academics." *New York Times,* 16 July 2002, A10.

Stevens, Norman. "The History of Information." *Advances in Librarianship* 14 (1986): 1–48.

———. "Research Libraries: Past, Present, and Future." *Advances in Librarianship* 17 (1993): 79–109.

Stille, Alexander. *The Future of the Past.* New York: Farrar, Straus and Giroux, 2002.

———. "Overload." *New Yorker,* 8 March 1999, 38–44.

Stoll, Clifford. *Silicon Snake Oil: Second Thoughts on the Information Highway.* New York: Doubleday, 1995.

Sussman, Barry. *What Americans Really Think and Why Our Politicians Pay No Attention.* New York: Pantheon, 1988.

Teich, Albert, ed. *Technology and Man's Future.* New York: St. Martin's Press, 1981.

Teitelbaum, Kenneth. "Contestation and Curriculum: The Efforts of American Socialists." In *The Curriculum: Problems, Politics, and Possibilities,* edited by Landon Beyer and Michael Apple, 32–55. Albany: State University of New York Press, 1988.

Thomas, Mary. "Redefining Library Space: Managing the Coexistence of Books, Computers, and Readers." *Journal of Academic Librarianship* 26, no. 6 (2000): 408–15.

Tisdale, Sallie. "Silence, Please." *Harper's,* March 1997, 65–74.

Tittenbrun, Jacek. "Ownership of Philanthropic Foundations." *Science & Society* 55, no. 1 (1991): 91–102.

Traub, James. "Drive-Thru U." *New Yorker,* 20 & 27 October 1997, 114, 116–18, 120–22.

United States Department of Education, Center for Libraries and Education Improvement. *Alliance for Excellence: Librarians Respond to A Nation at Risk.* Washington, D.C.: U.S. Government Printing Office. 1984.

United States Department of Education, National Commission on Excellence in Education. *A Nation at Risk: The Imperative for Educational Reform* Washington, D.C.: U.S. Government Printing Office, 1983.

Vaidhyanathan, Siva. "The Content-Provider Paradox: Universities in the Information Ecosystem." *Academe,* September–October 2002, 34–37.

Van House, Nancy, Beth Weil, and Charles McClure. *Measuring Academic Library Performance.* Chicago: American Library Association, 1990.

Venturella, Karen, ed. *Poor People and Library Services.* Jefferson, N.C.: McFarland, 1998.

Veysey, Laurence. "A Postmortem on Daniel Bell's Postindustrialism." *American Quarterly* 34, no. 1 (1982): 49–87.

Wallace, Patricia. "Outsourcing Book Selection in Public and School Libraries." *Collection Building* 16, no. 4 (1997): 160–66.

Walzer, Michael. "Civility and Civic Virtue in Contemporary America." *Social Research* 41, no. 4 (1974): 593–611.

———. *The Company of Critics: Social Criticism and Political Commitment in the Twentieth Century.* New York: Basic Books, 1988.

———. "The Idea of Civil Society." *Dissent* 38 (1991): 293–304.

Warner, Dorothy. "'Why Do We Need to Keep This in Print? It's on the Web . . .': A Review of Electronic Archiving Issues and Problems." *Progressive Librarian* 19/20 (Spring 2002): 47–64.

Warner, Dorothy, and John Buschman. "The Internet and Social Activism: *Savage Inequalities* Revisited." *Progressive Librarian* 17 (2002): 44–53.

———. "Studying the Reader/Researcher Without the Artifact: Digital Problems in the Future History of Books." Society for the History of Authorship, Reading and Publishing 2002 Conference, University of London, 11 July 2002.

Weaver, Barbara. "Federal Funding for Libraries: A State Library Perspective." In *The Bowker Annual.* 41st ed., edited by Dave Bogart, 213–20. New Providence, N.J.: R. R. Bowker, 1996.

Webster, Frank. "Information: A Sceptical Account." *Advances in Librarianship* 24 (2000): 1–23.

———. "Information, Capitalism, and Uncertainty." *Information, Communication & Society* 3, no. 1 (2000): 69–90.

———. "The Information Society Revisited." In *Handbook of New Media: Social Shaping and Consequences of ICTs,* edited by Leah Lievrouw and Sonia Livingstone, 22–33. London: Sage, 2002.

———. "Knowledgeability and Democracy in an Information Age." *Library Review* 48, no. 8 (1999): 373–83.

Webster, Frank, and Kevin Robins. "Plan and Control: Towards a Cultural History of the Information Society." *Theory and Society* 18 (1989): 338–44.

Wedgeworth, Robert. "Donor Relations as Public Relations: Toward a Philosophy of Fund-Raising." *Library Trends* 48, no. 3 (2000): 530–39.

Weischadle, David. "The Carnegie Corporation and the Shaping of American Educational Policy." In *Philanthropy and Cultural Imperialism: The Foundations at Home and Abroad,* edited by Robert Arnove, 363–84. Boston: G. K. Hall, 1980.

Weizenbaum, Joseph. *Computer Power and Human Reason: From Judgment to Calculation.* San Francisco: W. H. Freeman, 1976.

Welton, Michael. "Civil Society and the Public Sphere: Habermas's Recent Learning Theory." *Studies in the Education of Adults* 33, no. 1 (2001): 20–34.

White, Stephen, ed. *The Cambridge Companion to Habermas.* Cambridge: Cambridge University Press, 1995.

———. "Reason, Modernity, and Democracy." In *The Cambridge Companion to Habermas,* edited by Stephen White, 3–16. Cambridge: Cambridge University Press, 1995.

Whitty, Geoff. "The 'Privatization' of Education." *Educational Leadership* 41, no. 7 (1984): 51–54.

Whitty, Geoff, and Tony Edwards. "School Choice Policies in England and the United States: An Exploration of Their Origins and Significance." *Comparative Education* 34, no. 2 (1998): 211–27.

Wiegand, Wayne. "The Development of Librarianship in the United States." *Libraries and Culture* 24, no. 1 (1989): 99–109.

———. "Main Street Public Library: The Availability of Controversial Materials in the Rural Heartland, 1890–1956." *Libraries and Culture* 33, no. 1 (1998): 127–33.

———. "MisReading LIS Education." *American Libraries,* 15 June 1997, 36–38.

———. "The Politics of Cultural Authority." *American Libraries,* January 1998, 80–82.

———. "Research Libraries, the Ideology of Reading, and Scholarly Communication, 1876–1900." In *Libraries and Scholarly Communication in the United States: The Historical Dimension,* 71–87. Beta Phi Mu monograph series. New York: Greenwood Press, 1990.

———. "The Role of the Library in American History." In *The Bowker Annual.* 33rd ed., edited by Filomena Simora, 69–76. New York: R. R. Bowker, 1988.

———. "The Socialization of Library and Information Science Students: Reflections on a Century of Formal Education for Librarianship." *Library Trends* 34, no. 3 (1986): 383–99.

———. "The Structure of Librarianship: Essay on an Information Profession." *Canadian Journal of Information and Library Science* 24, no. 1 (1997): 17–37.

———. "Tunnel Vision and Blind Spots: What the Past Tells Us About the Present: Reflections on the Twentieth-Century History of American Librarianship." *Library Quarterly* 69, no. 1 (1999): 1–32.

Willett, Charles. "Consider the Source: A Case Against Outsourcing Materials Selection in Academic Libraries." *Collection Building* 17, no. 2 (1998): 91–95.

Wingo, G. Max. *Philosophies of Education: An Introduction.* Lexington, Mass.: D. C. Heath, 1974.

Winner, Langdon. *The Whale and the Reactor: A Search for Limits in an Age of High Technology.* Chicago: University of Chicago Press, 1986.

Wolin, Sheldon. "The New Public Philosophy." *Democracy* 1, no. 4 (1981): 23–36.

Yergin, Daniel, and Joseph Stanislaw. *The Commanding Heights: The Battle Between Government and the Marketplace That Is Remaking the Modern World.* New York: Simon & Schuster, 1999.

Young, Jeffrey. "The Cat-and-Mouse Game of Plagiarism Detections." *Chronicle of Higher Education,* 6 July 2001, A26.

———. "David Noble's Battle to Defend the 'Sacred Space' of the Classroom." *Chronicle of Higher Education,* 21 March 2000, A47–48.

Young, Peter. "Changing Information Access Economics: New Roles for Libraries And Librarians." *Information Technology and Libraries,* June 1994, 103–14.

Zerzan, John, and Alice Carnes, eds. *Questioning Technology: Tool, Toy, or Tyrant?* Philadelphia: New Society Publishers, 1991.

Zinn, Howard. *A People's History of the United States.* New York: Harper & Row, 1980.

Zweizig, Douglas. "How Firm a Foundation?" *Library Trends* 46, no. 1 (1997): 19–27.

# INDEX

# ABOUT THE AUTHOR

JOHN E. BUSCHMAN is department chair, collection development librarian, and professor-librarian, at Rider University Library, Lawrenceville, New Jersey. His previous book, *Critical Approaches to Information Technology in Librarianship*, was published by Greenwood Press. He has published many articles and is co-editor of the journal *Progressive Librarian* and is on the Coordinating Committee of the Progressive Librarians Guild. Prior to his current administrative appointment, he served on the National Council of the American Association of University Professors.